P9-DNH-996

My Time with GOD

JOYCE MEYER

NEW YORK NASHVILLE

FaithWords
Hachette Book Group
1290 Avenue of the Americas, New York, NY 10104
faithwords.com
twitter.com/faithwords

First Edition: October 2017

FaithWords is a division of Hachette Book Group, Inc. The FaithWords name and logo are trademarks of Hachette Book Group, Inc.

ISBNs: 978-1-4555-6014-1 (hardcover), 978-1-4555-6013-4 (ebook), 978-1-4555-6012-7 (large print)

Printed in the United States of America

LSC-C

10 9 8 7 6 5 4 3 2 1

Introduction

I wrote this devotional over a period of three years, and it is a collection of encouragements that I sensed God speaking to my heart in my time with Him. I want to share them with you, and I pray they will encourage you in your own personal devotion time with God. Some of them are longer than others; some include quotes and confessions, while others include a prayer you may want to pray.

This devotional is close to my heart simply because it is taken from my own life. The daily devotions consist of things God has taught me at various times, as well as specific things He was dealing with me about during the time I wrote them. I believe you will sense the presence of God as you take time to let Him speak to you through His Word.

In fact, this is one of my prayers for you as you jump into this devotional: that you will fully understand that God loves you completely, and He wants to have a close personal relationship with you. So although these various entries are insights into my time with God, my intention is that they would be a starting point for you as you go deeper in your relationship with Him.

God's Word is extremely powerful and it contains the power to renew our minds and change us into the image of Jesus Christ. I trust that as you read and study this devotional you will experience a new intimacy with our Lord.

God Is Your Vindicator

For we know Him who said, "Vengeance is Mine, I will repay," says the Lord. And again, "The Lord will judge His people."

HEBREWS 10:30 (NKJV)

In order to begin this new year properly, it is important not to enter it with any kind of bitterness or unforgiveness in our heart. It is unlikely that any one of us has made it through an entire year without being hurt by someone, but we only continue letting what they have done hurt us if we don't forgive them.

Ask yourself if you are angry with anyone for anything, and if you are, ask God to help you forgive, forget, and let it go. God is our Vindicator and if we will allow Him to, He will repay us for every injustice that has been done to us. In my life, I have learned that anger is something we should never carry around with us. God's Word says that we should not let the sun set on our anger, and if we do, then we give the devil a foothold in our lives (see Ephesians 4:26–27).

Do yourself a favor right now as you enter this new year and refuse to remain angry or bitter. God has good things planned for us, and we don't want to miss them by refusing to let go of things in the past. Start the new year with a peaceful heart and be determined to enjoy each day.

Prayer: Father, help me forgive everyone who has hurt me in the past year, and if I have hurt anyone, please help them forgive me.

⁕ Trust God at All Times ⁕

Trust in, lean on, rely on, and have confidence in Him at all times, you people; pour out your hearts before Him. God is a refuge for us (a fortress and a high tower). PSALM 62:8

It is important to live with an abiding trust in God. That means we form a spiritual habit of trusting Him at all times, rather than just when we have a need or when a problem arises in our lives. As a parent, I would not be happy with my children if they only called or visited me when they needed something.

God is merciful and there are many times when He helps us although we have ignored Him, but it isn't the way He wants our relationship with Him to be. God has been urging me to make this year a year when I come up higher in trusting Him at all times.

We all hope that each day contains nothing but good and exciting things and that it goes exactly as we had planned, but we know from experience that it rarely turns out that way—we may get stuck in traffic that makes us late for an important appointment, or someone may disappoint us or hurt us in some way. Making a decision to trust God totally, even before we have a challenge, is very helpful.

Prayer: Father, I trust You today for whatever this day brings. If this day contains difficulty that I did not expect, I put my trust in You now to take care of me and enable me to do what I need to do.

✱ You Are Loved ✱

But God demonstrates his own love for us in this: While we were still sinners, Christ died for us. ROMANS 5:8 (NIV)

God reminded me today of His unconditional love!

It is very important to begin each day knowing that *you are loved*! God loves you unconditionally, and His love is more valuable and important than anyone else's. He doesn't love us because we deserve it, but simply because He wants to.

As you receive God's love freely, it will give you confidence and enable you to live life without fear. God's perfect love casts out all fear and dread (see 1 John 4:18).

Perhaps you have known the pain of not being chosen. You were not picked for class president or asked to attend the party that *everyone* was going to. When we are left out it hurts, but the good news for you today is that God has chosen you! You are special to Him and His love for you will never end.

Prayer: Thank You, Father, for loving me. I receive Your love by faith today and ask that it will strengthen me.

✷ Seeking God ✷

One thing I have desired of the Lord, that will I seek: that I may dwell in the house of the Lord all the days of my life, to behold the beauty of the Lord, and to inquire in His temple. PSALM 27:4 (NKJV)

My life changed when I learned to seek God and His presence as my primary need. To seek is to pursue, crave, and go after with all of your might. Always set aside time to be with God, to study His Word and simply rest in His presence. Learn to be conscious and aware of Him at all times.

> We take time to seek what is truly important to us!

Speak this: I always spend time seeking God because His presence is my greatest need in life.

✷ The Power of Simplicity ✷

Truly I say to you, whoever does not accept and receive and welcome the kingdom of God like a little child [does] shall not in any way enter it [at all]. LUKE 18:17

I wrote in my journal this morning, "Keep it simple."

Life is certainly complicated and tends to be very stressful. I spent years praying that my circumstances would change so I could enjoy life, but finally realized I needed to change my approach to life. How about you? Do you feel the effects of stress and have a desire for simpler days? We often talk of the "good old days," when life was simpler, but that doesn't help us much today.

What we need is a change in our attitude and approach to life. Only foolish people think they can keep doing the same thing and get a different result. Learn how to think more simply. Don't think about too many things at once, or allow your schedule to get overcrowded. Saying no when you need to will help you keep your schedule manageable. Lots of people want lots of things from us, but we don't have to ruin our life and forfeit our joy to keep them happy. Take some time today to inventory your life. Ask yourself if you are enjoying it. If not, I urge you to make whatever adjustments are necessary in order to do so.

Prayer: Father, I love You very much, and I am grateful for the life You have given me. I want to enjoy life and use my time wisely, and I ask for Your help in making any changes that are necessary for me to live simply and powerfully.

⁕ The Beauty of Faith ⁕

Commit your way to the Lord, trust also in Him, and He shall bring it to pass. PSALM 37:5 (NKJV)

I see more clearly than ever before how simple and beautiful faith is and how self-effort complicates life and steals peace and joy. Man's mind plans his own way (see Proverbs 16:9), but God's ways are much higher than ours and they always work better (see Isaiah 55:9). I have finally learned that whenever I feel frustrated, it almost always indicates that I have trusted myself to do what only God can do. It is my signal to return to full faith in God and once again enjoy His peace.

Apart from faith we cannot please God (see Hebrews 11:6), and apart from Him, we can do nothing (see John 15:5). If you are worried or feel burdened by anything, I urge you to let it go and return to simple faith in God without delay. "Commit *your way* to the Lord" and "He shall bring it to pass" (Psalm 37:5). God already has a perfect plan for your situation, and as you rest in Him, He will work!

Prayer: Father, thank You that You are working in my life while I rest in You. I trust You to do the right thing at the right time. Help me walk in faith at all times.

✷ I Am Protected ✷

He who dwells in the secret place of the Most High shall remain stable and fixed under the shadow of the Almighty [Whose power no foe can withstand]. PSALM 91:1

Spending time with God protects us from the attacks of our enemies. When I remember this, it helps me feel safe, and that is something we all desire. Take a moment several times a day to simply turn your attention toward the Lord and say, "I know You are with me and that You are my Protector." Then take a few moments to dwell in that thought and let it comfort you.

> There is never a moment in your life when God is not with you.

Speak this: God is with me at all times. He will never forsake me, and He protects me from those who would harm me.

⁕ Be Healed ⁕

. . . With the stripes [that wounded] Him we are healed and made whole. ISAIAH 53:5

Jesus can heal you anywhere you hurt, and He delights in doing so. Whether you are hurting spiritually, physically, mentally, emotionally, socially, or financially, Jesus cares, and He wants to help you. God's will is for you to be in a growing, intimate relationship with Him through Jesus. He wants you to be healthy and energetic, to have peace of mind, enjoy emotional stability, have plenty of good friends and family relationships, and have all your needs met abundantly, including being able to give generously to others in need.

If you are experiencing lack in any of these areas, God is reaching out to you today and asking you to trust Him for healing. He is our physician, and His Word is our medicine. Perhaps it has never occurred to you that Jesus wants to heal you, but He does, and I pray you will ask and receive that your joy might be full (see John 16:24). You have not because you ask not (see James 4:2), so ask boldly and stand firm on the promises of God. Take your pain to Jesus, and through faith and patience you will be made whole.

Prayer: Father, heal me everywhere I hurt. I ask in Jesus' name that I might experience Your wholeness in my life. I receive healing by faith, and I declare that Your healing power is working in me right now!

✷ Living Large ✷

And God is able to make all grace abound toward you, that you, always having all sufficiency in all things, may have an abundance for every good work. 2 CORINTHIANS 9:8 (NKJV)

When I feel like my "get up and go" has got up and gone, I purposely stir myself up through aggressive expectation!

God is the God of abundance, the one who wants us to live a large, free, and full life. Dare to have big faith, big plans, and big ideas, because God is able to do exceedingly, abundantly, above and beyond all that you can ever dare to hope, ask, or think (see Ephesians 3:20). It is time to start asking God to do greater things! Have great expectations!

Don't be afraid to ask God for big things. The truth is that you cannot ask for too much as long as your heart is right and you are willing to not only be blessed by God, but also be a blessing everywhere you go. The Bible says God is searching for those in whom He can show Himself strong (see 2 Chronicles 16:9), and it can be you if you are willing to believe. You don't need a perfect performance to qualify for God's best; just love Him with all your heart. Don't settle for less than the best life that you can have.

Prayer: Amazing Heavenly Father, I am humbled that You want to offer me an abundant life. I know that I don't deserve Your goodness, but I do ask in faith that You would do great things for and through me. Thank You!

✷ Be Wise ✷

Wisdom cries aloud in the street, she raises her voice in the markets. PROVERBS 1:20

Wisdom stands at the intersection of every decision crying out, "Follow me." Wisdom always does now what it will be satisfied with later. Don't live in regret due to following emotions, popular opinion, or your own will. Wisdom will promote you, prosper you, and give you peace and joy.

Are you at a point of needing to make a decision? Obviously, we make decisions all the time, and they are all important, but some are more important than others. I believe that if you are facing a major decision, you need to let your emotions subside before you decide! Make the wise choice. Wisdom is first of all pure and then it is peace-loving, and I urge you to wait on wisdom so you can live without regret.

Prayer: Father, I commit to follow wisdom in all my decisions. Please make the path that You want me to take very clear. Thank You!

✷ *Hidden from Harm* ✷

In the secret place of Your presence You hide them from the plots of men; You keep them secretly in Your pavilion from the strife of tongues. PSALM 31:20

Unkind words spoken to us hurt, but this Scripture promises that if we spend time in God's presence, we will be protected from their effect. Even though evil words may be spoken against us, God will shield us and comfort us as we spend time with Him.

God's words are the ones that really matter anyway, and He always says good things about us.

God's words are more powerful than anyone else's.

Speak this: God's words protect me from evil words spoken against me, and His words are louder to me than anyone else's.

✷ Friends ✷

The man of many friends [a friend of all the world] will prove himself a bad friend, but there is a friend who sticks closer than a brother. PROVERBS 18:24

Everyone wants friends, and God wants us to have them. He encourages relationship throughout His Word, but it is important to have healthy, safe, and godly relationships. Some relationships are not safe for us because we are being used, manipulated, and taken advantage of. God wants us to pray for and love everyone, even our enemies, but that doesn't mean we should let people take advantage of us. I personally am not interested in having what I call one-sided relationships in which I do all the giving and the other party does all the taking.

God does use us at times in the lives of selfish, self-centered people, and we do make sacrifices, but there is a point at which we are hurting people if we let them manipulate us for their own pleasure. Stand up for yourself and always be willing to confront unhealthy relationships. Speak the truth in love (see Ephesians 4:15). You are very valuable and entitled to have good friends who will respect and honor you properly.

Prayer: Father, help me always be a good friend. I ask You for safe, healthy relationships in which I can flourish and grow. Amen.

✷ Wait on God ✷

. . . For You [You only and altogether] do I wait [expectantly] all the day long. PSALM 25:5

I am a person of action, and when there is a problem, I am ready to take action, but sometimes I make the situation worse because I didn't wait to get God's plan. Being aggressive has many benefits, but it can also cause problems if we are acting independently of God.

I am reminded today of the importance of maintaining an attitude of waiting on God. I am not suggesting inactivity but rather the highest form of spiritual activity, that of trusting God in every area of life. Wait on Him for supplies, for strength, healing, wisdom, and opportunity. Wait on God to reveal Himself to you and to show you His amazing favor. God is waiting to be good to us, and He looks for those who are waiting on Him (Isaiah 30:18).

Waiting on God is mostly an attitude of the heart. One that is fully aware that God is everything and we are nothing without Him. We should pray and refuse to take action without assurance that God is leading. Go to Him as early as possible each day, which is the moment you wake up. He is always near, and you need no special preparation to begin fellowshipping with Him. Always remember that God loves you unconditionally and is with you at all times.

Prayer: Father God, I desire to form a habit of waiting on You all throughout the day. Help me not to rush ahead into activities and decisions without acknowledging You. Thank You for Your presence.

✷ Time Is Valuable ✷

So teach us to number our days, that we may get us a heart of wisdom. PSALM 90:12

Spending time with God regularly is the foundation of living the victorious life that Jesus died to give us. Very often, people say that they want to spend more time with God, but they simply don't have the time. We all have the same amount of time, but not everyone chooses to use it in the best way.

You can be as close to God as you want to be; it all depends on how much time you are willing to put into seeking Him and learning His ways.

Are you investing or wasting your time?

Speak this: I have as much time as anyone else, and I will make changes in how I use it so I can seek God regularly.

✻ Holiness ✻

Since all these things are thus in the process of being dissolved, what kind of person ought [each of] you to be [in the meanwhile] in consecrated and holy behavior and devout and godly qualities.

2 PETER 3:11

This is a special day because it is one in which we have an opportunity to grow in holy behavior. We grow in holiness as we fellowship with God and follow the leading of the Holy Spirit, not as we work hard to follow religious rules and regulations. Spiritual disciplines are important, but we should avoid letting them become laws. For example, it is good to read and study God's Word as often as possible, but there is no law that says if you miss a day that God is mad at you or disappointed in you.

The way to grow in holiness is simple—just be committed to following peace. If you have peace about your thoughts, words, and behaviors, then continue in them, but if you sense an uncomfortable feeling in your spirit, or a lack of peace, it may well be a nudge from the Holy Spirit that your action isn't what it should be. The more you follow God's lead, the happier you will be. When God gives us another day to live, it is a valuable gift, and one that should be used for His glory and honor.

Prayer: Father, thank You that today I can grow in holiness. I ask You to help me sense what You approve of and what You do not approve of, and to live accordingly.

Make Each Day Count

To everything there is a season, and a time for every matter or purpose under heaven. ECCLESIASTES 3:1 (AMPC)

We all have the same amount of time each day, but some people seem to do more with theirs than others do. You might say that we all "spend" our time. We spend it doing things that will bear good fruit, or we spend it on activities that are totally useless. I think it is wise to occasionally take an inventory of what we are spending our time on and to make adjustments if they are needed. Today would be a good day to spend some time thinking about how you are spending your time!

Time is a gift, and the older you get the more you realize that. I believe we could avoid most of the stress we experience if we simply use the time we have wisely. Don't waste time doing frivolous things that are not important and then be frustrated when you don't have enough time to do the things that must be done. Always remember that when your time is spent, you can never get it back, so spend it on something that is an investment and pays good dividends.

Prayer: Father, I thank You for time, and I repent for all of it I have wasted in my life. Grant me wisdom concerning what I choose to do with my days, and help me make each one really count for something good.

✷ God's Timing ✷

My times are in Your hands; deliver me from the hands of my foes and those who pursue me and persecute me. PSALM 31:15

God's timing in our lives is perfect, and we will enjoy life much more if we believe that. He knows the exact right time to do the things we have requested of Him. Don't waste your time being upset about something that only God can change. If He withholds your desire for the time being, thank Him that He knows best.

Time is a gift—don't waste it being upset!

Speak this: I trust God's timing in my life, and I will not frustrate myself by trying to do what only God can do.

✷ Laughter ✷

Then were our mouths filled with laughter, and our tongues with singing. Then they said among the nations, The Lord has done great things for them. PSALM 126:2

We need to laugh more. It is good for the soul and adds health to our body. One of the reasons we may not laugh more is because we think too much about things that have no ability to bring joy. Thinking of what I have lost in life is not a joy-bringer, but thinking about what God has done for me and His promise to do even more does bring joy. Thinking about the people who have hurt us in life is not a joy-bringing thought, but thinking about the grace God has given us to forgive and trust Him for vindication makes us want to laugh (at least it does me).

God often reminds me to laugh more. I don't know about you, but sometimes I get too serious and I need to have a "laugh break." There are lots of things to laugh at or about if we will just take the time to do it. I believe laughter is much more important than we may realize. We aren't too old or too busy, nor do we have too many problems to laugh! Start paying attention to how much you laugh and try to do it as often as possible.

Prayer: Father, I believe You gave me the ability to laugh for a reason, and I want to take advantage of all the benefits of laughter. Help me take every opportunity to laugh and to make others laugh too.

✷ Self-Acceptance ✷

I will praise You, for I am fearfully and wonderfully made; marvelous are Your works, and that my soul knows very well.

PSALM 139:14 (NKJV)

The psalmist David confessed that he was a work of God and that God's work is indeed wonderful. Most of us would cringe at the thought of confessing that we are wonderful, but we need to accept and love ourselves as God's creation and children. I finally realized after years of struggling with self-rejection that if God, who is perfect, could accept and love me, I could too. Today I needed to be reminded of this truth and thought it might also encourage you.

We are not truly free until we love and accept ourselves in a godly and balanced way. You might think that if you did so, it would be selfish, but it is actually the opposite. It sets you free from being self-centered or needing to be first in everything in order to feel valuable. Selfishness drives us to try and get more and more for the outer man (fleshly man), but a God-ordained love and acceptance fills us with such satisfaction in the inner man that we no longer need to compare ourselves or compete with others. We are content just to be loved!

Prayer: Father, thank You for loving me and accepting me as Your child. Help me learn how to love—and like—myself even while You're working in me, making me the person You created me to be!

January 20

⁕ *Hearing from God* ⁕

So faith comes from hearing, and hearing through the word of Christ.
ROMANS 10:17 (ESV)

We all want to hear from God, but not everyone listens. Let your mind and soul be quiet and simply wait on God. You may or may not hear anything at that moment, but if you honor God by waiting on Him, He will speak to you at just the right time when you need it most.

To get started, invest five minutes a day simply being quiet and listening! In addition to this, spend some time in God's Word and talk to Him (pray) about anything and everything.

> Develop the habit of listening or you will never truly hear.

Speak this: I talk to God and I listen!

⁕ See the Good in People ⁕

Love bears up under anything and everything that comes, is ever ready to believe the best of every person . . . 1 CORINTHIANS 13:7

God is reminding me today to look for the good in everyone I meet. I have no difficulty locating what is wrong with people, and in fact, I sometimes seem to be an expert at it! I don't like being that way and am thankful that in Christ, I can choose another way of living. If you struggle with this then you can too.

Jesus has given us a new nature (see 2 Corinthians 5:17), and we can purpose to live out of it and actually learn to treat people the way Jesus would. I am asking for the "gift of awareness." I want to be aware of what is right and good about people and not merely what is wrong with them. I don't want to try and take the speck out of my brother's eye when I have a log in my own (see Matthew 7:4).

Let's make this year one of believing the best of everyone we know. It will help us have more joy, and we will enjoy the people in our lives much more than ever before.

Prayer: Dear Jesus, I long to be like You and see people the way You do. Help me take the time to really get to know people and not merely judge them at first glance.

✷ Serve God Joyfully ✷

And whatever you do, do it heartily, as to the Lord and not to men.
COLOSSIANS 3:23 (NKJV)

Whatever God has given you to do in life, do it with simplicity, gratitude, and joy. Do everything you do today for Jesus. Our work can be an offering to Him no matter what it is. Whether you are a stay-at-home parent or a bank president, a factory worker or a famous singer, do what you do to serve the Lord.

For years I divided my life into sacred and secular compartments. I felt better about myself when doing something spiritual or sacred, and less so when doing common, ordinary tasks. But God taught me that everything we do is equally important when we do all of it with Him and unto Him. This knowledge not only brought me great relief but has enabled me to enjoy all of life instead of only portions of it.

If you are simply mopping a floor, whisper to Jesus that you are doing it for Him and it will take on new meaning.

Prayer: Father in Heaven, I choose to do all that I do for You. Please accept all of my activity as an offering of my love. Help me remember that You are with me at all times, offering to help me if I will only ask and receive.

⁕ Enjoying God's Presence ⁕

Draw near to God and He will draw near to you...

JAMES 4:8 (NKJV)

God is everywhere all the time, and we can enjoy His presence anywhere, at any time. It is not necessary to be engaged in a spiritual activity to enjoy God's presence. He is interested in everything we do, both spiritual and secular. You can enjoy God's presence in the grocery store as well as in Bible study. God is never more than a thought away.

One moment with God can release hours of joy.

Speak this: I take time throughout the day to remember God and enjoy His presence.

⁕ Start Your Day Right ⁕

He then goes on to say, And their sins and their lawbreaking I will remember no more. HEBREWS 10:17

I am often tempted by the devil to start my day feeling guilty about the things I did wrong yesterday, but that is not God's will for you or me. Thankfully, because of God's mercy and willingness to forgive and forget our sins, we can begin each day as if we had never done anything wrong in our entire lives.

God's forgiveness is complete, and we can completely receive it. The blood of Jesus cleanses us of even the stain of sin (see 1 John 1:7). In Christ we are fresh and new, and we have a wonderful day to look forward to. The way we start our day can affect the way it goes all day, so be sure to get started right each day. Start by asking for and receiving God's forgiveness and being empowered by His grace not to waste today worrying about yesterday's mistakes. God knew the mistakes you would make yesterday before the world began, and He loves you anyway.

Prayer: Father, thank You for Your mercy and willingness to completely forgive all my sins. Help me start each day fresh by letting go of what is behind and looking ahead to Your good plan for me.

✵ Our Greatest Privilege ✵

Keep on asking and it will be given you; keep on seeking and you will find; keep on knocking [reverently] and [the door] will be opened to you. MATTHEW 7:7

I have made a commitment to pray more than ever, and I hope you will join me. Prayer is the greatest privilege that we have. Prayer makes all things possible! God's Word teaches us that we have not because we ask not (see James 4:2). It is tragic indeed to miss out on the immense benefits that prayer provides simply because we fail to take the time to ask.

My desire is to "pray my way through the day." It is another way of saying what the apostle Paul said, which is "Pray without ceasing" (see 1 Thessalonians 5:17). This does not mean that I intend to stay on my knees all day or sit somewhere with folded hands praying all day. I simply desire to understand that all failure is a prayer failure and to be wise enough to invite the Lord to help me with each thing I do.

The Bible says in Ephesians 6:18 that we should "pray at all times (on every occasion, in every season) in the Spirit, with all [manner of] prayer." Forming the habit of doing so will open the door to more victory and breakthrough than we can imagine. I don't want to miss any more opportunities to see God's amazing power manifested in my life, and I am sure you don't either, so please join me in discovering the power of simple prayer!

Prayer: Dear Father, I commit to praying my way through the day, and as I begin, I ask for Your help. I am praying that You will help me pray! Teach me the vital importance of talking with You about everything.

✷ An Unselfish Attitude ✷

Let all men know and perceive and recognize your unselfishness (your considerateness, your forbearing spirit). The Lord is near [He is coming soon]. PHILIPPIANS 4:5

Disciples of Jesus are called upon to deny themselves and their own interests (see Mark 8:34). I am sure that doesn't sound too exciting, but it does provide a quality of life that we cannot have while being selfish and self-centered. True happiness is only found when we find something to live for other than ourselves. I spent the first half of my life being self-absorbed, and then I discovered that Jesus died so I might no longer have to live only for myself. At that point I embarked on a journey of learning to live for God and others. I want to say right away that I have not arrived, but I do press on toward the goal.

Living only for yourself and selfishly seeking only what pleases you is like living in prison and being in solitary confinement. Unless we are willing to die to self, we abide alone; we live isolated lonely lives (see John 12:24); very few people call us friend; and when we are gone, nobody really cares that much. We have traveled through life, and the world is no better because we were here.

I invite you to declare war on selfishness! As occasion and opportunity open up to you, do good to all people (see Galatians 6:10). Be kind and do what is for their welfare.

Make a decision to put a smile on at least three faces today. You may be surprised to find that their smile will make you smile too!

Prayer: Father, help me use all of my faculties and abilities to be a blessing to other people today and every day. Grant me the grace to live a life that is pleasing to You.

⁕ Abide in Christ ⁕

If you abide in Me, and My words abide in you, you will ask what you desire, and it shall be done for you. JOHN 15:7 (NKJV)

To abide is to live, dwell, and remain. I don't visit my home—I live there. Far too many people only seek God when they have a problem. They merely visit to get the help they need, but they live in the world. If we spend time with God all the time, always recognizing that He is present wherever we are, then our prayers will produce amazing answers.

Let the Word of God dwell in you richly and live accordingly. It will guide your path, and you will have fewer problems to deal with.

> If you are too busy to seek God, then you are too busy!

Speak this: I live in God and He lives in me. Christ is my home!

✷ How to Handle Disappointment ✷

Why are you cast down, O my inner self? And why should you moan over me and be disquieted within me? Hope in God and wait expectantly for Him . . . PSALM 42:11

Today something happened that left me disappointed. I felt sad and my mood was starting to sink, but thankfully, God reminded me that if I would decide to simply have a good attitude, I could avoid wasting the day. When life disappoints us, we can get "reappointed." We can disappoint the disappointment by deciding to make the best out of the situation.

A positive attitude is a valuable thing to have. Our attitude today is the prophet of our future. It determines the level of our joy and is our best friend or our worst enemy. Your attitude is your thought life turned inside out. It is the posture you decide to take toward life's circumstances. If we can only have a good attitude when everything is going our way, then we are seriously lacking in spiritual maturity. But when we develop the ability to remain stable in the storm, it glorifies God and witnesses to other people.

Your attitude belongs to you and nobody can force you to have a bad one if you don't want to. You have decision-making power and you can decide right now what your attitude will be today. Misery is an option that you don't have to take!

Prayer: Dear Lord, I want to be a stable person who can handle disappointment without getting discouraged and sad. I need Your help and I ask You to strengthen me. Help me not to depend on my circumstances for my joy, but to always look to You. Amen!

✷ Be Honest with God ✷

Trust in, lean on, rely on, and have confidence in Him at all times, you people; pour out your hearts before Him. God is a refuge for us...

PSALM 62:8

Recently God whispered in my heart, "You can talk to Me about anything." This is a good reminder for all of us from time to time, because we have a tendency to think that we need to approach God from a standpoint of total faith and strength, pretending we have it all together, sounding eloquent in our prayers. One of the things we enjoy about a good friend is that we can be honest with them; we can tell them anything and expect them to understand. Surely we should not expect anything less from our Heavenly Father. He invites us to pour out our hearts to Him!

Where sin is concerned, we should never attempt to hide it. God already knows everything we have done wrong and He has provided for our forgiveness, but He wants us to confess our mistakes so we can release the burden of them. David said, "When I kept silence [before I confessed], my bones wasted away through my groaning all the day long" (Psalm 32:3).

If we are having difficulty trusting God in a situation, there is no need to pretend otherwise. Pour your heart out before Him in total honesty, because it will give you relief and open a door for Him to help you. If we are angry, we can tell God all about it. If we are confused or disappointed or weary or struggling with doubt, we can be totally open with Him. I don't know about you, but that makes me feel really good. You can never shock God, so try the "totally honest" approach. I think you will be glad you did.

Prayer: Father, I love You very much and I want to have a great friendship with You. Help me have the courage to be totally honest with You, and to never try to hide anything!

✷ Strength ✷

Seek the Lord and His strength; yearn for and seek His face and to be in His presence continually! 1 CHRONICLES 16:11

We need strength for each day, and it is best to ask for it before you find you are without it. God is our strength, and He releases strength into us as we spend time with Him. We all have challenges, but all things are possible with God (see Matthew 19:26). Truly we can do all that we need to do through Him (see Philippians 4:13). Don't be frustrated by weakness and failure when God's strength is yours for the asking.

> We cannot do much by ourselves, but
> we can do anything through Christ.

Speak this: I am strong in the Lord and in the power of His might.

⁕ Guardian Angels ⁕

For He will give His angels [especial] charge over you to accompany and defend and preserve you in all your ways [of obedience and service]. PSALM 91:11

The other day I was going down some steps and I missed the last step and fell. Although I could have seriously hurt myself, I was able to balance myself so that I dropped to the floor on one knee while holding a laundry basket in one hand and carrying a jar in the other. Did I balance myself or did I have divine help? I thought right away after the fall, *I believe an angel caught me and prevented me from injury.* I felt that God reminded me of the divine helpers (angels) that are with us at all times.

I admit that I don't think about angels very often, but I believe I should be more aware of the biblical truth that they are with us all the time, defending and protecting us. We tend to not pay much attention to the things we can't see with the natural eye, but we can learn to see more with the eye of faith. God is with us at all times, and He gives His angels to us as a special blessing. Perhaps they could help us more if we truly believed in their presence.

Angels ministered to Jesus when He was being tempted by the devil in the wilderness. When Daniel was in the lions' den, angels were sent to shut their mouths so they could not harm him. Actually, God's Word is filled with many examples of angels giving assistance, so I encourage you to believe they are with you today and to let that thought comfort you.

Prayer: Father, thank You for giving me angels to assist and defend me at all times. I want to be more aware of their presence in my life and more thankful for how often they keep me safe.

✷ Mental Attack ✷

Casting the whole of your care [all your anxieties, all your worries, all your concerns, once and for all] on Him, for He cares for you affectionately and cares about you watchfully. 1 PETER 5:7

For a few weeks now, I have been dealing with a physical affliction that is quite annoying. Some days I have been full of faith, but there have been a few days when I have felt that my mind has been "kidnapped" by the enemy. My thoughts were on all the wrong things and I could not seem to get them back. I know that we are to cast down wrong thoughts and choose right ones (see 2 Corinthians 10:4–5), but what are we supposed to do on those days when we just can't seem to have success? I believe we should simply wait for the attack to pass, trusting that God understands and that He sees the desire of our hearts to do the right thing.

The devil attacks our minds with all kinds of wrong thinking, and we are to withstand him and be firm in faith. Sometimes that means waiting for God's help and being patient. We may not feel that we have total victory every day of our lives, but even during those times we can still trust God. He sees everything, knows everything, and loves us at all times. God doesn't love you any less when you are weak than He does when you are strong.

Prayer: Father, I want to be victorious every day and always keep my mind on You; however, I admit that at times I fail. I am sorry and I ask for Your help in keeping my mind on You.

⁕ Pray Often ⁕

Be earnest and unwearied and steadfast in your prayer [life], being [both] alert and intent in [your praying] with thanksgiving.

COLOSSIANS 4:2

Don't put off praying until a more convenient time. Pray at all times, in every season, with all kinds of prayer (see Ephesians 6:18). Prayer need not be long to be effective. It is the greatest privilege we have, and it releases the greatest power on earth. We all need God's help, and we get it by asking for it.

Pray your way through the day.

Speak this: I believe that God is always listening, and I am diligent to pray often throughout the day.

February 3

⁕ Finishing Well ⁕

I have fought the good (worthy, honorable, and noble) fight, I have finished the race, I have kept (firmly held) the faith.

2 TIMOTHY 4:7

It seems to me that I can sense the satisfaction Paul felt in knowing he had finished what he had set out to do. I know that feeling, and I enjoy it very much. I doubt that any of us feel good about ourselves when we give up on something and don't finish what we begin. I encourage you today to stand strong in faith knowing that God is with you and that He wants you to go all the way to the finish line.

Even when we are weary and think of giving up, let's remember the joy we will have when we complete what we have started. God's grace and power are with us to help us keep going when it is difficult. Paul said it didn't matter how hard it was or what it cost him, if only he could finish his course with joy (see Acts 20:24). It requires determination, but with God's help we can do it!

Prayer: Father, help me finish what I have started no matter how challenging it is.

✷ Run to God, Not from Him ✷

All whom My Father gives (entrusts) to Me will come to Me; and the one who comes to Me I will most certainly not cast out [I will never, no never, reject one of them who comes to Me]. JOHN 6:37

When Adam and Eve sinned in the Garden of Eden, they tried to hide from God, and they sewed some fig leaves together hoping to hide their nakedness (see Genesis 3:7). I seem to be very impacted lately by remembering that we never have to run from God, we never need to hide, and we can be totally honest with Him about everything. In fact, instead of running away, He invites us to do the opposite and run *to* Him! He promises to never reject anyone who comes to Him, no matter their condition.

If you feel guilty about something or have failed miserably, run to God as fast as you can and get a hug from Him. He will forgive, restore, and set you right again. God is the only one who can help us in our times of discouragement, failure, and fear, so it is foolish to run away from the only help we have. Even if you are a little angry with God because of disappointments in your life, run to Him anyway. Tell Him how you feel and ask for His help.

Jesus is able to understand us because He was tempted, tested, and tried. He shared the feeling of our weaknesses and infirmities, and yet He never sinned (see Hebrews 4:15). Jesus knows exactly how you and I feel, and we have an open invitation to come into His presence anytime. We can come just as we are!

Prayer: Father, I am so grateful for Your love and acceptance. It is wonderful to know that You will never reject me. I need You! Help me to always run to You and never to run away.

✷ You Are Valuable ✷

For the Lord shall be your confidence, firm and strong, and shall keep your foot from being caught [in a trap or some hidden danger]. PROVERBS 3:26

Everyone wants to believe that they are significant, and that they matter and have a purpose. We need to feel valuable, and we are! The devil is on a mission to make us feel insignificant, but God has assigned value to each of us by personally creating us and giving us abilities and gifts. God does nothing without purpose; therefore, we can know that we have a purpose. Everything He does is good; therefore, we can know that we are good. Everything we do may not be good, but the essence of who God made us to be is good.

You are alive because God wants to be in relationship with you, He has a plan for you, and nobody can take your place. You are special! If you will begin to believe that, then your life will improve in many ways. God wants us to be confident, but without confidence we will be tormented by fears and insecurities and we won't accomplish anything in life. I encourage you to live courageously! Be the amazing person that God intends for you to be. Live life to the fullest and enjoy every moment of it. Enjoying life begins with enjoying God and enjoying yourself. Why not start right this moment? There is no need to wait any longer!

Prayer: Father, thank You for making me significant! Help me live with confidence and boldness. Help me fulfill Your will for my life.

⁕ Watch and Wait ⁕

In the morning You hear my voice, O Lord; in the morning I prepare [a prayer, a sacrifice] for You and watch and wait [for You to speak to my heart]. PSALM 5:3

Don't be discouraged when you pray if you don't hear from the Lord or see an answer to your prayer right away. Once you pray in faith, God begins to work on your behalf. Watch and wait for His answer, and while you're waiting, believe that God is working. Keep expecting to see God do great things in your life. Today may be your day of breakthrough!

> Expect something good to happen to you and through You today!

Speak this: God is working on my behalf right now, and I will see my prayers answered.

✷ Keep God First ✷

But seek first the kingdom of God and his righteousness, and all these things will be added to you. MATTHEW 6:33 (ESV)

It is good for all of us to occasionally examine our heart and make sure that we haven't allowed anything or anyone to take the place that belongs only to God. We do not need to struggle for things, position, or power. All we need to do is seek God first, and He will add everything else that is right for us to have.

Ask yourself what most of your thoughts, conversation, time, and effort goes into, and if the answer is not God and His kingdom, then quickly make some adjustments. Possessions are enjoyable for all of us, but they have no life in them; therefore, they cannot give us life. Only God can do that. He is our life, and unless He stands first and has the preeminent position in our lives, we will eventually begin to sense deadness and have no lasting enjoyment in anything we do.

Always seek God's face and not just His hand. Want *Him* more than you want what He can do for you. Delight yourself in the Lord and He will give you the desires of your heart (see Psalm 37:4).

Prayer: Father, I am sorry if I have put anything else before You. Forgive me and help me make the adjustments I need to make. You are more important than anything else in my life and I want all of my choices to reflect that truth.

⁕ Set Your Mind ⁕

And set your minds and keep them set on what is above (the higher things), not on the things that are on the earth. COLOSSIANS 3:2

I have learned over the years the value of purposely setting my mind on things I want to happen throughout the day, instead of passively waiting to see what kind of thoughts I happen to have. Just as we choose our clothes and purposely put them on, we can and should choose our thoughts, because what we meditate on often becomes our reality (see Proverbs 23:7). "Where the mind goes, the man follows" is one of my favorite sayings!

Today I set my mind to be strong, energetic, and joyful. I have decided to enjoy this day and to be a blessing everywhere I go. The more I think positive things, the more excited and empowered I feel! God is waiting to bless His children, but we need to expect Him to do so. What are you expecting from God today? Nothing? A little? A lot?

I taught this in our office chapel this week, and an employee came to work the next day and said, "I have lots of problems at home, especially with my teenage son who argues with me constantly. After hearing Joyce speak on expecting good things, I decided to try it. Instead of driving home dreading the evening, I went home expecting something good. My son looked at me when I got home and told me that he loved me, something I hadn't heard in a long, long time."

Aggressive expectation is faith in action! Release your faith for God's best in your life and get ready for an upgrade in blessings.

Prayer: Father, I am sorry I have been so passive about my thoughts. Forgive me, and help me learn to think in a way that will release Your best in my life.

February 9

✷ *Make the Most of It* ✷

Walk in wisdom toward outsiders, making the best use of the time.
COLOSSIANS 4:5 (ESV)

I try to take advantage of every opportunity that comes my way, because some opportunities only come once in a lifetime. Each moment God gives us is special, and we should always value our time. Don't rush through your life so fast that you miss it.

If you make good choices about how to use today, you won't have regrets tomorrow.

Speak this: I use my time wisely, and I take advantage of every good opportunity that God gives me.

⁕ See with the Eyes of Faith ⁕

This is the day which the Lord has brought about; we will rejoice and be glad in it. PSALM 118:24

When I woke up this morning, I didn't feel well. I was tired and would have loved to crawl back in bed and stay there a long time, but I couldn't because I had a full day ahead of me. When we don't feel well, it is easy to feel overwhelmed and start thinking negatively. But we don't have to!

Because I understand the power of our thoughts, while I was washing my face, brushing my teeth, and making my coffee, I thought and said, "Today is going to be a great day. I am energetic and joyful. I am blessed, and I am a blessing to others."

Today I have to take my eighty-nine-year-old mother to the eye doctor. In the past, this has been very challenging. She is losing her eyesight, but insists that the doctors don't know what they are doing, and trying to convince her of anything else often ends up in an embarrassing scene. Instead of dreading the trip, I have set my mind to expect that the appointment is going to be a peaceful and pleasant experience. I will let you know tomorrow how things go!

Whatever you might be facing today, you can get a head start on things going well by partnering with God and believing that He is on your side and something good is waiting to happen to you.

Prayer: Father, You are good and I am expecting You to show up in my life today and manifest Your goodness. Thank You!

February 11

✷ Give the Good Report ✷

Enter into His gates with thanksgiving and a thank offering and into His courts with praise! Be thankful and say so to Him, bless and affectionately praise His name! PSALM 100:4

It is very important that we remember to voice our gratitude for everything that God does for us. We need to give the good report! It is good for us, it is good for those who hear it, and it is what God instructs us to do. Jesus healed ten lepers, but only one came back to give thanks (see Luke 17:11–19). Let's make sure we are the one and not the nine! Think of something that God has done for you and give the good report right now.

Here is my good report for the day: My trip to the eye doctor yesterday with my mom went absolutely fabulous. The doctor couldn't have been any more perfect for her, and although she has lost her vision in one eye, they were able to do a procedure that may help the other eye. I am so glad we went expecting something good instead of dreading the trip.

What a great way to live. *Expect something good to happen, and when it does, give the good report*. It is easy to complain about what we think God isn't doing, but it is much better to talk about what He has done, is doing right now, and what we expect Him to do in the future.

Prayer: Father, I am sorry for all the times I have complained instead of noticing all the good things You do for me. Help me be the most thankful person on the planet because You are truly very good to me.

⁕ All for God ⁕

And whatever you do, whether in word or deed, do it all in the name of the Lord Jesus, giving thanks to God the Father through him. COLOSSIANS 3:17 (NIV)

Whatever you are going to do today, I want to remind you to do it all for God. Too often we do things for people, when the one we are actually serving is Christ the Messiah. If we do all for God and expect our reward from Him, we will never be disappointed. It pleases God when we do even the tiniest little thing for Him. Do even the most mundane task thinking, *Lord, I am doing this for You*.

Don't make the mistake of thinking that God is only interested in your spiritual activity, like prayer, Bible study, church attendance, or good works. He is interested in everything you do and wants to help you with all of it.

I leave today for another ministry trip, something I have done thousands of times throughout my life. These trips include hundreds of little details that are not very exciting, but I remind myself that I am doing all for God. I trust that He will give me energy and creativity, and that He will reward me for the work (see Colossians 3:24). When I do my tasks with this type of attitude, my enthusiasm increases. God pours His Life into all we do when we do it for and with Him.

Prayer: Father, I offer everything I am going to do today as something done for You and Your glory. I love You very much, and I want to please You at all times. Thank You for helping me and being with me in each detail of my day.

February 13

✷ Think About All God Has Done ✷

I remember the days of old; I meditate on all Your doings; I ponder the work of Your hands. PSALM 143:5

Write down five things you can think of that God has done for you, and continue pondering them throughout the day. If you get an opportunity, share them with someone else and ask them what God has done for them. If we think more about what God has done than what we want Him to do, our faith will become stronger and our joy will increase.

> If God can do something good for anyone,
> He can do it for you!

Speak this: I will think about the goodness of God more than I think about my problems.

✷ Praise in Troubled Times ✷

Trust in, lean on, rely on, and have confidence in Him at all times . . . PSALM 62:8

It is important that we thank, praise, and love God just as much in troubled times as we do in good times. It may be even more important to do it then. Anyone can be thankful and joyful when things are going their way because they have lots of good emotions to support them, but when times are tough, we have to bypass how we feel and praise God in spirit.

I finished three teaching sessions at a church this past weekend, and the next day I woke up with the stomach flu—not what I had planned, that is for sure. I decided to give God extra praise and thanksgiving and tell Him I loved Him even more than usual on that day. Most of the day, at different intervals, I spoke my gratitude out loud. I wasn't grateful for the stomach flu, but I had plenty to be grateful for in the midst of it.

One benefit was that I stayed in bed all day, and that is something I almost *never* do! The rest was probably good for me. It also stirred up compassion in me for other people who are sick, including a few people I know who are currently taking chemotherapy. I feel that if we can continue to praise God when things in our circumstances are not good, we are giving the highest kind of praise.

No matter what is going on in your life, make a decision to praise God, be thankful, and shower words of affection on Him. It will strengthen you as you go through the difficulty.

Prayer: Father, You are good and I want to bless You at all times. Help me remember that I don't have to feel like being thankful in order to give thanks! Help me praise You even more in troubled times than in good ones.

✷ The Hurry Sickness ✷

Be still, and know that I am God... PSALM 46:10 (ASV)

We need to ruthlessly eliminate hurry from our lives because it is one of the great enemies of the spiritual life. I find myself hurrying for no reason at all. Jesus never hurried. He had plenty to do and accomplished a great deal in His life, but the Bible never mentions Him rushing from thing to thing.

Hurrying physically is bad enough, but I find that inner hurry is even worse. It prevents us from truly meditating on anything long enough to get any value from it. When we hurry, we skim the surface of life and never enter into the depth of anything. Jesus meant for life to be enjoyed, not endured as we rush from thing to thing, often going nowhere. Hurry not only hinders joy, but it is harmful to our health. It also damages relationships because we end up not taking time for people.

When we fast, we give up something that is important to us, so I have decided to fast hurrying, beginning with a one-day commitment. I think if I tackle it one day at a time, I might succeed. I am excited to see what kind of difference it makes in my life. If you feel you need to do this too, please join me, and we can journey together in living life as Jesus did.

Prayer: Father, I am sorry that I have missed so much in life by hurrying. Forgive me and help me slow down!

✷ A New Day ✷

Behold, the former things have come to pass, and new things I now declare; before they spring forth I tell you of them. ISAIAH 42:9

Do you need a new beginning? Jesus is offering you one today! He doesn't dwell on the past, and He doesn't want us to either. No matter how many mistakes you have made, the Lord can and will work them out for your good if you ask Him to. God has a great future planned for you, but you cannot drag your past into it. You must let go to go on!

Since you can't undo anything from yesterday, you might as well do something great with today!

Speak this: I let go of the past, and I am excited about today!

✷ Discipline ✷

For the time being no discipline brings joy, but seems grievous and painful; but afterwards it yields a peaceable fruit of righteousness to those who have been trained by it... HEBREWS 12:11

Discipline is our friend, not our enemy. It helps us be the people we say we would like to be but never will be without the assistance of discipline and self-control. It is a fruit of the Holy Spirit that is in us as believers in Jesus Christ, but like all other fruit of the Spirit, it must be developed and will grow through use.

Discipline is the ability to subject less important things to more important ones. For example, spending time with my friends is important, but it is not as important as spending time with God. God gives us free choice as His children. He tells us in His Word what will work the best and produce good results, but we have the responsibility of choosing what we will do. Free choice is wonderful and we all enjoy it, but we also need to realize that we will be left with the result of those choices, good or bad.

People who imagine that they can make undisciplined choices, following the desires of the flesh instead of the Spirit, and still have a great life, are deceived. I urge you to embrace discipline as your friend. Don't groan when you think of discipline. It may not seem joyous now, but after it has been applied, you will enjoy the fruit of it.

Prayer: Father, please give me Your grace to live a life of discipline and self-control—one that is guided by Your Holy Spirit instead of my own fleshly desires.

⁕ Value Your Time ⁕

O [earnestly] remember how short my time is and what a mere fleeting life mine is... PSALM 89:47

It makes me sad when I ask a person what they're doing and they respond, "Just killing time." What they mean is that they are doing nothing in particular except waiting for the time to pass. I also hear others, as well as myself, say, "That was a waste of time." Time is too valuable and precious to either kill or waste. It runs out sooner than we think. When we are twenty, we think we have forever, but as we approach fifty, sixty, or seventy, we realize we have used up more of our allotted time than what we have left.

I encourage you to use your time wisely so you don't end up with lots of regrets over the things you didn't do in life. Always take time to develop your personal relationship with God, take time for family and friends, and take time to rest, to laugh, and to celebrate and enjoy life. We put a lot of time into our work, so it is important to do what leaves us fulfilled and satisfied, not empty and drained.

If there is something that you know in your heart you should do or accomplish, I encourage you not to put it off. Spend time with your parents while you can. Make peace with the person you are angry with. Tell the people you love how much they mean to you. The time you have *now* is valuable, so appreciate it and be sure you don't waste it.

Prayer: Father, help me use all of my time wisely. The time You have given me is a gift and I don't want to waste it. Guide me in all of my decisions so I can bear good fruit for Your glory.

✷ *Peace of Mind* ✷

And the peace of God, which surpasses all understanding, will guard your hearts and minds through Christ Jesus.

PHILIPPIANS 4:7 (NKJV)

Did you know that when you have lost your peace of mind you have the power to regain it? Anytime you find that you are worrying, fretful, or anxious about anything, release the problem to God through a simple heartfelt prayer and purposely think about something in your life that is good! Worrying is completely useless. It wears you out mentally, emotionally, and physically and it doesn't make your problem any better at all.

Peace of mind is valuable, and it is quite impossible to enjoy life without it. Seek and pursue the peace that is yours through Jesus Christ. Don't be deceived into believing that you can't help what you think, because you absolutely can. You can change your mind about anything! Practice "on purpose" thinking instead of being passive and merely waiting to see what thoughts fall into your mind.

I can share with you that I experience the same mental battles that many people do, and I have to practice having peace on purpose. You are a child of God, and His peace is in you. I recommend that you start recognizing the things that are stealing your peace and deal with them so they can no longer torment you.

Prayer: Father, I love You very much, and I want to enjoy peace of mind. I know that worry is useless, but I often do it and I am sorry. Work with me and teach me how to trust You enough to enjoy Your peace at all times.

⁕ Laugh ⁕

Then were our mouths filled with laughter, and our tongues with singing. Then they said among the nations, The Lord has done great things for them. PSALM 126:2

Happy Christians are a great advertisement for Christianity. Be as happy as you can all the time—laugh and laugh and then laugh some more! Take every opportunity to laugh, because it can actually improve your health. Humans are the only part of God's creation who can laugh, so surely it is something He wants us to do.

> Laughter begins with a smile, and you can decide to do that anytime.

Speak this: I will laugh every chance I get!

✷ Serving Others ✷

Not so shall it be among you; but whoever wishes to be great among you must be your servant. MATTHEW 20:26

A proud person finds it almost impossible to serve others, especially in small and hidden ways. The main reason Jesus teaches us to serve is not because He is unable to meet the needs of people, but because it is imperative for us that we do so. We benefit more than anyone when we serve. God is the ultimate Servant! Jesus humbled Himself and became a Servant! (See Philippians 2:7.)

Serving is not natural to my nature, so I choose to do it on purpose. I have to think about things I can do for other people, and I pray regularly, asking God to make me aware of ways (large or small) that I can serve—things like turning the light out in Dave's closet, cleaning up a mess someone else made (with a good attitude), letting someone go before me in line if they are rushed, or providing an item that a family member or friend needs or wants.

Quietly serving others adds much joy and fulfillment to our lives. Focusing on serving others helps us defeat selfishness and self-centeredness. Purpose to look for ways you can serve others, and you're sure to experience a greater intimacy with God, as well as with those whom you are serving.

Prayer: Father, I renounce selfishness and pride and desire with all of my heart to serve others according to Your will. Make me aware of needs around me and let me find joy in serving.

✵ Double Blessing ✵

Return to the stronghold [of security and prosperity], you prisoners of hope; even today do I declare that I will restore double your former prosperity to you. ZECHARIAH 9:12

Hope is a powerful force that will bring you through any storm. Our hope is in God; therefore, we can hope without any natural reason to do so. Hope is a positive expectation of good. Practice saying, "Something good is going to happen to me today, and something good is going to happen through me today." God is good and He wants to shower His goodness on you.

There are times of difficulty, loss, illness, and disappointment in life, but if we will endure with hope in our hearts, we will be rewarded with a double blessing for our former trouble. Let me strongly encourage you to refuse to be hopeless. Put your hope in God and things will always come around to being right in due time. I can't guarantee how long it will take, and it may not be quick, but hope will strengthen you to face life with joy even in the midst of trouble.

Live daily thinking, *Today may be the day of my breakthrough. It could happen suddenly... at any moment.* Hope is the anchor of our souls. It keeps us from giving in to wild emotions that attempt to lead us to do things we will regret later on. The wise man puts His hope in God. He listens for God's voice and follows it, knowing that there is always a light at the end of the tunnel. God is that Light and He is urging you to be a prisoner of hope.

Prayer: Father, anytime I feel discouraged or weary, help me remember that there is always hope. Help me be filled with hope in You and positive expectation. You are good, and I believe You want to be good to me.

February 23

✷ Love God ✷

We love Him, because He first loved us. 1 JOHN 4:19

Tell the Lord often that you love Him! He created us because He wanted us, and He loves us unconditionally. God's love is continually flowing toward us, and we can experience that love by receiving it and then giving it back to Him in words that express our heart. "I love You, Lord" is usually one of the first things I say when I wake up each morning. If you don't already do that, you should consider trying it! I think the Lord loves to hear us say that to Him, just as we love to hear our children tell us that they love us.

Loving God is our number one priority in life!

Speak this: I love the Lord with all of my heart, soul, mind, and strength.

✷ Has Your Get-Up-and-Go Got Up and Gone? ✷

Never lag in zeal and in earnest endeavor; be aglow and burning with the Spirit, serving the Lord. ROMANS 12:11

I have times when I get tired of doing what I am doing. We all do. No matter what your position is in life, there will be days when you will not feel like doing it. You might even go through a longer season in which you feel listless and uninterested in almost everything. There may be underlying reasons that you will need to prayerfully search out, but often we just need to stir ourselves up and get going again. We need to do it purposely instead of waiting for a feeling to show up and motivate us to action again.

Gratitude helps me do that. When I recount all of my blessings, I am amazed at the goodness of God in my life. It makes me thankful, and that always stirs me up and makes life look brighter. Having great expectations also energizes and motivates me. We don't have to wait and see if something good happens in our lives; we can aggressively expect something good to happen. David indicated that if he failed to believe he would see the Lord's goodness, it would affect him in a detrimental way. He said, "[What, what would have become of me] had I not believed that I would see the Lord's goodness..." (Psalm 27:13).

The third thing that energizes me is getting my mind off how I feel and on something I can do to be a blessing to someone else. When I do, it works every time. Before long, I find myself enthusiastic about life and excited to resume my service to the Lord.

Prayer: Father, I want to live life to the fullest. I want to live with passion, zeal, and appreciation for every opportunity that You give me. Help me approach this day with enthusiasm and do everything as unto You.

February 25

✷ Be Content ✷

...I have learned how to be content (satisfied to the point where I am not disturbed or disquieted) in whatever state I am in.

PHILIPPIANS 4:11

I am returning home today after being gone for two weeks writing and doing a variety of ministry things. I will be glad when I get home, but I am also happy right now, sitting on the airplane writing this devotional. I am leaving again in five days to go somewhere else. I will also be happy there, because I have decided to be content no matter what state I am in (Florida, Missouri, Arizona).

Much of life can be spent thinking, *I will be happy when...* But the truth is that we can be happy now if we want to. Contentment should be based not on where I am or what I am doing, but on knowing that wherever I am, God is with me! He is our place in life, and *in Him*, we can find joy and contentment.

You might not *enjoy* being at work as much as you do being at home, but you can be just as *joyous* either place. What we *enjoy* is determined by what is happening around us, but our *joy* is determined by the attitude we decide to have in life. Make a decision to enjoy each thing you do and each place you are, because Christ is your life and He is everywhere, all the time.

Prayer: Father, I want to stop dividing my life into things I enjoy and things I don't enjoy. Help me find joy in being anywhere as long as I know that You are with me!

✵ Hearing God ✵

When he has brought his own sheep outside, he walks on before them, and the sheep follow him because they know his voice.

JOHN 10:4

Who can hear from God? Does He only speak to the spiritually elite among us, or can every believer have a conversational relationship with Him? I spent many years practicing Christianity without ever being taught that I could hear from God. I talked to Him, mostly when I needed something, but it never occurred to me that He might want to say something back.

Thankfully, I have since learned that we can and should hear from God. He has no desire to give us minute-by-minute instructions about every choice we make, but He speaks to us regularly and we need to expect to hear Him. Education is vital in any area, and especially so in this one. I have read several books on the subject and I have also written one, but I am reading another right now because of how important it is.

God, of course, speaks through His Word. The Bible is God speaking to us! He speaks through circumstances, people, peace, wisdom, and nature, just to mention a few of the ways we can learn to perceive what He is saying. We don't normally hear God with our natural ears; we hear Him in our spirit through the still, small voice. We may discern, perceive, or know with certainty what God is communicating to us and yet not hear a voice. Or, if we do hear words, they often sound like our own voice because our mind is interpreting what our spirit knows.

If this is a new thought for you, I encourage you to study diligently in this area. There are people who do ridiculous and even wicked things claiming that God has told them to do so, but we should not let their sinful behavior frighten us and keep us from a wonderful privilege that is available to us. Learning to listen is the first rule of hearing. When you talk to God today, take a little time and listen. Let Him comfort you, sense His peace, and hear Him tell you that He loves you greatly.

Prayer: Father, I am sorry that I have spent so little time listening to You. I want to hear from You, and I believe it is Your will for me to do so. Teach me in this area. I am eager to learn.

⁕ First Things First ⁕

But seek first the kingdom of God and his righteousness, and all these things shall be added to you. MATTHEW 6:33 (ESV)

Keeping our priorities in the right order opens the door for many blessings in our lives. Seeking God should always be our number one priority. Putting Him and His way of doing things above all others adds peace and joy to our lives, and then God adds all the other things that we need. Don't ever struggle trying to get "things," but instead let pleasing God be your first priority, and at the right time, you will receive from Him an abundance of good things.

> Desire God more than anything else and you will have everything else!

Speak this: I put God first in all things, and He meets all of my needs.

✷ Bear Good Fruit ✷

When you bear (produce) much fruit, My Father is honored and glorified, and you show and prove yourselves to be true followers of Mine. JOHN 15:8

Our lives are not given to us for us to waste them. God desires that we bear good fruit on a regular basis. Doing good, being creative, helping others, accomplishing goals, and other such things gives me a feeling of accomplishment, and I must admit that it feels really good. On the other hand, when I waste a day doing nothing, feeling sorry for myself, being angry or lazy, that doesn't feel good.

I am not suggesting that we need to spend all of our time working, but we should be productive on a regular basis. Praying for others as we go about our day is productive. Being friendly and encouraging others is a simple way to bear good fruit. Yesterday I went to the hospital to visit my mother, and when I got there a young woman was in her room administering a heart test. She had lovely skin and hair and a beautiful smile. She was also very kind. Instead of just thinking these things, I told her that she was really pretty. The look on her face let me know that she didn't hear it nearly often enough and that it made her feel really good.

It is easy to focus on people's flaws and totally miss the good things about them, but we don't have to be like that if we purpose to bear good fruit by making a big deal out of each good thing we notice about people. You and I have the power to make someone else's day awesome by being God's voice and letting them hear through us the good things He sees in them. Make today and every day a special day by bearing good fruit that will honor God.

Prayer: Father, I love You very much. I want to bear good fruit and I need Your help in this, as I do in everything else in my life. I lean and rely on You to help me see various ways that I can make this day and every day fruitful!

⁕ Wisdom ⁕

That people may know skillful and godly Wisdom and instruction, discern and comprehend the words of understanding and insight.

PROVERBS 1:2

I believe wise people choose to do now what they will be satisfied with later on in life. All of our decisions influence our future, so we should never live as if there were no tomorrow, because tomorrow always comes. There are many things that each of us wishes we would have done in the past, but now it is too late. Let's do what is right now, so we won't have regrets tomorrow!

If you invest today, you will reap the benefits tomorrow.

Speak this: I will choose to do today what will produce good fruit in my future.

⁕ No Condemnation ⁕

There is therefore now no condemnation to those who are in Christ Jesus, who do not walk according to the flesh, but according to the Spirit. ROMANS 8:1 (NKJV)

In the past couple of weeks, I have done a few things that I regret. I showed extreme impatience in a specific situation, and my behavior was not a good example to my children. I also made a decision and started getting other people involved in my plan, only to realize I didn't have peace. I also realized I had not even prayed about it; I just acted on my own. Wow! I should have known better in both of these situations.

Do you ever do things and then think, *I cannot believe I did that*? Realizing our mistakes is the first step toward repentance. Thankfully, we can go to Jesus with all of our failures and weaknesses and be assured that He will never reject us. I am sorry for my foolishness, but I am also very glad that I don't have to waste several days feeling guilty.

Today, take all of your sins and failures to Jesus. Talk to Him about them openly and honestly, receive His forgiveness, and rejoice that you don't have to be condemned. I am sure that, like me, you want to change, and God will indeed change us into His image as we continue in His Word and place our trust in Him.

Prayer: Father, I am sorry for all my sins, and I ask You to strengthen me in every area where I am weak. I am excited about spiritual growth, and I trust You to change me to be more and more like You.

✷ *Take Your Life Back* ✷

If any of you is deficient in wisdom, let him ask of the giving God [Who gives] to everyone liberally and ungrudgingly, without reproaching or faultfinding, and it will be given him. JAMES 1:5

Sometimes we feel that our lives have gotten confusing or out of balance. They are not satisfying to us, and yet we don't quite know what to do. The first thing to do is ask God to grant you wisdom and be assured that He will. The second thing you can do is be prepared to take action. Knowing what we should do and doing it are two different things.

I recently felt that some things in my life had gotten out of balance and I was not even sure how it happened, but I knew something needed to be done. I heard myself complaining about dissatisfaction in some areas and finally realized that I was the only one who could do anything about it. It is quite common to want to blame circumstances or other people for our problems, but I have learned over the years that it is usually me who needs to take responsibility.

I needed to pray and get some direction from God and then take action. I determined to take my life back. I saw that I needed to be more organized, because disorganization causes confusion. Organizing my thoughts and following God's lead felt much better than floundering around aimlessly, murmuring about things that only I could change.

If you feel your life has gotten away from you and you're ready to take it back, God will help you. However, His directions do us no good if they are not followed. Set your mind and keep it set for victory!

Prayer: Father, I ask for Your wisdom in knowing how to make improvements in my life that will please You and enable me to be the person You want me to be. Thank You!

⁕ Fickle Feelings ⁕

So then those who are living the life of the flesh [catering to the appetites and impulses of their carnal nature] cannot please or satisfy God, or be acceptable to Him. ROMANS 8:8

When we follow the ever-changing impulses of our carnal nature, it is not pleasing or acceptable to God, because He has a much better life in mind for us. We all have times when emotions change without warning, and it is important that we learn how to handle ourselves in times like that. If we merely follow our feelings, we will surely end up making decisions and taking actions that we will regret later on.

Last Sunday, Dave and I had several people to our house for a party, and I was energetic and felt great. The next day, for no apparent reason, I woke up feeling dull-headed and a bit down emotionally. *Why? What is wrong with me?* Those are the first questions I asked myself. I didn't get an answer, so I had to make a choice. Should I continue to try to figure out my odd mood and get more and more confused, or should I pray, asking God to reveal anything He wants me to see and go on about the business of the day, asking God to help me live beyond my feelings?

I have learned over the years that being a stable, consistent person requires that I own my feelings instead of letting them own me. In other words, I may have them, but I cannot let them control me. Feelings are fickle. They change frequently and often without any notice. Sometimes we understand why, but much of the time we don't.

Our physical condition can affect emotions. Consider things like: *Did I get enough sleep?* or *Did I eat something that made me feel bad?* or *Is it allergy season?* Our spiritual condition can also cause mood fluctuation: *Have I spent enough time with God? Do I have hidden sin that needs to be dealt with? Is God chastising me about something?*

I recommend praying first to see if God reveals anything, and if He doesn't, then remain steady in the storm. Don't try excessively to figure out your feelings, because it will get you more and more focused on them. Trust God, use extra self-control, and very soon you will feel better.

Prayer: Father, I desire to be stable emotionally at all times. Help me stay steady when my emotions fluctuate. I want to live a life that is pleasing to You at all times, and I trust You to continue teaching me in this area.

⁕ *Life Is What You Make It* ⁕

And be constantly renewed in the spirit of your mind [having a fresh mental and spiritual attitude]. EPHESIANS 4:23

Two people may have the same problem, but one will be kind to others and joyful, while the other is harsh in his dealing with people and always discouraged. The difference is found in the attitude they choose to have toward their life and their problems. Our quality of life is not determined by our circumstances but rather by how we view those circumstances. Any life can be good if we choose to think and speak good things instead of finding fault and complaining.

> If you need a change, don't complain or you will remain where you are.

Speak this: Complaining is a waste of time—it never makes anything better.

✷ Confidence ✷

For the Lord shall be your confidence, firm and strong, and shall keep your foot from being caught [in a trap or some hidden danger].

PROVERBS 3:26

I am a fairly confident person, but lately I have been a bit double-minded in some of my decisions. God has reminded me of the importance of being confident at all times, because the double-minded person cannot receive the help that He wants to give them (see James 1:6–8). Perhaps you experience this lack of confidence at times. If you do, I am reminding you, as the Lord reminded me, to be firm in your decisions and not to waver back and forth.

Pray about all things and then follow the leading of the Holy Spirit as best as you can. Use wisdom and follow peace in your decision-making, but don't become afraid that you're doing the wrong thing when a decision needs to be made. If we don't know what to do in situations we face, we should ask God for wisdom and trust Him to give it, but we must ask in faith without wavering and hesitating (see James 1:6). The double-minded person does not receive what he asks for from the Lord. God wants us to come to Him with full confidence that He is always willing to help us, even in the midst of our imperfections.

I frequently say that we must "step out and find out." We may not always be right about everything we decide, but living in fear and making no decision is not the way to find out if we are right or not. Take a step of faith, and let God lead you. He is faithful and will guide you as you go forward.

Prayer: Father, I desire to do Your will. Lead and guide me in all of my decisions. Grant me wisdom, gracious Lord. Fill me with confidence so I will not be double-minded and unstable in my ways.

✻ Letting Go of Worry ✻

Casting the whole of your care [all your anxieties, all your worries, all your concerns, once and for all] on Him, for He cares for you affectionately and cares about you watchfully. 1 PETER 5:7

Don't worry about anything! Worry never changes our circumstances, but it can change us. It can turn into health problems, and it often makes us grouchy and difficult to get along with. Worry is completely useless. It keeps us busy, but it gets us nowhere. The Lord often reminds me not to worry about anything, and I am always glad to hear it again and again. There are endless things that we can worry about, but we don't have to because we have options. We can trust God and let Him take care of us.

Trusting God should not be the thing we do after we have done everything that we know how to do. It should be the first thing we do in every situation that can cause worry or concern. Casting our care on the Lord is what we are to do, and God's response is to take care of us. God can do more in a moment than we could in a lifetime.

When we worry, we rotate our minds endlessly around and around the same thing, trying to figure out what we can do to make the situation better. We should pray first, and trust that if God does want us to do something, He will show us what it is and give us the grace (ability) to do it without struggle. If He doesn't show us any alternative action to take, we can be assured that He has a plan and will execute it at the exact right time. God's rest is waiting for you, and you can enter it by trusting instead of worrying.

Prayer: Father, I choose to trust You instead of worrying about troublesome situations. Help me release all my worries and concerns and give them to You. I believe You love me and want to take care of me, and I am grateful.

March 8

✷ People Change ✷

Jesus Christ is the same yesterday, today, and forever.

HEBREWS 13:8 (NKJV)

Jesus is the only one whom we can depend on to always be the same. People and circumstances are subject to change, and we should not allow ourselves to expect that they will always be the same. People go through different seasons in their lives, and as they do, we see changes in them that we may or may not like. In order to not be devastated, keep your eyes on Jesus, because He is the Rock that never moves and always remains the same.

> Unrealistic expectations are the root cause of much of our unhappiness.

Speak this: I put my expectations in God because He is always faithful.

⁕ Count Your Blessings ⁕

Through Him, therefore, let us constantly and at all times offer up to God a sacrifice of praise, which is the fruit of lips that thankfully acknowledge and confess and glorify His name. HEBREWS 13:15

Recently I have been writing down ten things each day that I am thankful for, and each day I try to make them something different. I am literally counting my blessings, and it has been a fun project.

It is amazing how many things we can begin to take for granted unless we purpose to remember how blessed we are. By looking for ten different things each day, I have gone beyond the things I would normally think of and have been pleasantly surprised by all the things I have realized are blessings in my life that I certainly would not want to do without—even things like the smell of a good candle or hot and cold running water. Let's be aggressive in offering God the fruit of lips thankfully praising Him!

Prayer: Father, help me realize how much I have to be thankful for. Thank You for reminding me to be thankful!

March 10

✷ Refusing to Compromise ✷

And let us not lose heart and grow weary and faint in acting nobly and doing right, for in due time and at the appointed season we shall reap, if we do not loosen and relax our courage and faint.

GALATIANS 6:9

Always choosing to do what is right can be challenging at times, especially since we live in a world with a declining sense of excellence and morality. To compromise is to go a little bit below what you know to be right. Even though we live in the midst of many people who do compromise and have little or no godly standard for their lives, we can hold firm. As the Scripture above states, let us not grow weary in doing what is right.

God rewards those who make right choices, but sometimes we must continue making them over and over before we start getting a right result. Be committed to a standard of righteousness in your life and don't compromise. If you don't give up, you will reap a wonderful reward, and in the meantime, you will have the peace of a clear conscience.

Don't ever choose to do the wrong thing just because everyone else is doing it. Be an example for people to follow instead of someone that even you are ashamed to know! Live in such a way that your behavior puts a smile on God's face and your reputation is good in Heaven.

Prayer: Father, teach me Your ways and give me the strength to make right choices at all times. Forgive me for compromises I have made in the past, and help me hold firm to Your standard of excellence.

⁕ Hold On, Help Is on the Way! ⁕

O God, be not far from me! O my God, make haste to help me!

PSALM 71:12

When we pray and ask God to do something for us, receiving an answer requires faith and patience. The devil tries to make us think that God is not going to come through for us, but we should simply hold on because help is on the way.

I believe that the moment we pray in faith, God begins to work. I have developed a habit of saying, "God is working in my life right now!" Making that declaration reminds me to stay calm, and it releases words of faith in the atmosphere that God can work with.

The devil hates to hear a confession that is full of faith. He wants us to speak out words of doubt and fear. Paul taught the Romans that we serve a God who calls things that do not yet exist as if they already do (see Romans 4:17). We should do things the way God does them if we want to get a godly result.

Often, breakthroughs and answered prayers take longer than we would like them to, but just because we don't see anything doesn't mean that God isn't working. As long as we believe God and trust Him, He is working! When fear knocks on your door, or when doubt visits you, simply say out loud, "I'm holding on because help is on the way!"

Prayer: Father, please help me to be strong in faith until my breakthrough comes. I know You are faithful and I believe You are working in my life.

✷ Timing ✷

Whereupon Jesus said to them, My time (opportunity) has not come yet... JOHN 7:6

Jesus knew there was a right time for everything, and He disciplined His emotions to wait until that time came. We can all strive to do the same thing. We make a lot of messes in our lives by doing things in our timing instead of waiting on the right time, which is God's time. Impatience steals our joy and peace, but we can learn to enjoy today while we are waiting.

Make the most out of every day, because each new day is a gift from God.

Speak this: Today is a gift from God and I am not going to waste it.

✷ Relaxing with God ✷

Come to Me, all you who labor and are heavy-laden and overburdened, and I will cause you to rest. [I will ease and relieve and refresh your souls.] MATTHEW 11:28

I was thinking this morning about how wonderful it is to be relaxed with God. Spending time with Him should be enjoyable and comfortable, not rigid and filled with rules and lists of things we think we should do. We don't have to do a specified amount of reading and then pray for a certain length of time. We can come to Him and be ourselves. Our time with Him will include prayer (talking and listening to Him), and it should include reading and studying, because God's Word teaches and feeds us. It keeps us strong! But it is important to be led by the Holy Spirit and to follow your heart's desire rather than having a list of rules and checking them off one by one.

Even if we have not had perfect behavior, we don't have to shrink from His presence. We can come boldly to Him, loving Him and receiving His love and forgiveness. We can ask Him to meet our needs because He is good, not because we have been good.

Thankfully, we don't have to be afraid that God is mad at us because we have failed or been imperfect. He is filled with mercy and loving-kindness and is waiting to shower it on you!

Go to God and tell Him that you love Him, because that is what He desires more than anything. Picture God as smiling at you with arms open wide! Let His presence be the most comfortable and relaxing place that you know of. We are made acceptable to

God through our faith in Jesus, and He receives us as we are and helps us become what we should be.

Prayer: Father, I need to be refreshed and relieved of all burdens. I come to You today in faith, believing that You accept me as I am. Help me to always enjoy You and to be relaxed in Your presence.

✷ Receive Forgiveness ✷

. . . Open their eyes that they may turn from darkness to light and from the power of Satan to God, so that they may thus receive forgiveness and release from their sins and a place and portion among those who are consecrated and purified by faith in Me.

ACTS 26:18

God has provided forgiveness for our sins through Jesus, but we must learn to receive the amazing gift that He has given. If you are angry with yourself for past sins, then you have not received what God has provided for you. No matter how long you feel guilty, you can never pay for your sins. The only thing that any of us can do is admit our sins, be willing to turn from them, and then joyfully and thankfully receive the amazing free gift of total and complete forgiveness.

Imagine how you would feel if you sacrificed and paid a high price for a gift that you wanted to give to someone, but when you offered it, they refused to receive it. Perhaps they felt that they didn't deserve it, or that it was too expensive for them to take. Or maybe they had wronged you in the past in a similar way to how we have wronged God by our disobedience, and that made them feel they could not receive such an amazing free gift as you were offering.

All the effort you had made in providing the gift would be useless unless they received it. The same is true when we do not receive the gift of forgiveness God has provided for us. When you receive it, you will feel relieved of the burden you have been carrying; guilt and condemnation will no longer be present and your joy will return.

Prayer: Father, thank You for the amazing gift of forgiveness. I know that I don't deserve it, but by faith, I receive it now. I let go of my sins and the guilt and condemnation they have caused. I am grateful that I am forgiven!

⁕ Harmony with God ⁕

But all things are from God, Who through Jesus Christ reconciled us to Himself [received us into favor, brought us into harmony with Himself] and gave to us the ministry of reconciliation [that by word and deed we might aim to bring others into harmony with Him].

2 CORINTHIANS 5:18

As a teacher of God's Word, it is not my job to preach amazing sermons that will impress people, but rather to share God's Word in such a way that they might desire to be brought into harmony with Him. God has brought us into harmony with Himself, and His desire is to work through us to do the same thing for the multitudes that are separated from Him and living in darkness.

What a great privilege it is to bring people to God! Life lived out of harmony with God is a miserable life. It is one filled with sin, darkness, fear, anger, confusion, and never-ending disappointment. It is one lived without the awareness of God. I remember living a life like that, and I will be forever grateful for the new life that Jesus has provided and brought me into. Let us be thankful today that we are aware of God and that we can come to Him without fear of rejection.

Let us ask ourselves this question: Are people being brought to God by my words and deeds? I pray that they are! We have an amazing opportunity to partner with God in the reconciliation of the lost people in this world. We are ambassadors for God, and as such, we represent Him in the earth today. God is making His appeal to the world through us (see 2 Corinthians 5:20). Working with and for God is the greatest privilege that anyone could ever have. Let the people around you see Christ shining through you today!

Prayer: Father, I am excited to partner with You in the reconciliation of the human race. Grant me the grace to live my life in such a way that people would see You through me! Let my life today bear good fruit for Your kingdom.

March 16

✱ Consistency ✱

And we have confidence in the Lord concerning you, that you are doing and will continue to do the things which we suggest and with which we charge you. 2 THESSALONIANS 3:4

It is not what we do right one time that changes our life, but what we continue to do right over and over again. Consistency is the key to success in any area of life. Paul had confidence that those whom he taught would continue to do what he taught them to do, and we must do likewise if we want to see the fullness of God's promises come to pass in our lives.

Whether it is studying God's Word, prayer, obedience, giving, exercise, or anything else, I encourage you to be consistent!

> If you refuse to give up, you will succeed in reaching your goals.

Speak this: I will not quit! I will not give up! I will be consistent!

✷ Follow Your Heart ✷

The fear of man brings a snare, but whoever leans on, trusts in, and puts his confidence in the Lord is safe and set on high.

PROVERBS 29:25

The fear of man offends God (see Isaiah 8:13) because He wants us to follow Him and do all that He places in our hearts. God has a plan for you, and He will lead you to take steps of faith that will always keep you in the center of His good will, but you will need to be courageous. Satan uses fear, and in particular the fear of man, to prevent us from following God. I encourage you to make a firm decision today that you will put your confidence in God and never allow the fear of man to steal your destiny.

We can receive the fear that Satan offers us, or we can take courage, knowing that God is greater than anyone, and that He is always with us. Yes, God is on our side, so why should we fear man? Man may reject us, but God accepts us. Man may disapprove of us, but God approves of us. God has a wonderful destiny awaiting you. Don't let the devil steal it through fear of what man will say, think, or do.

If we follow our heart, we will be fulfilled and satisfied. We will respect ourselves because we have followed what we believe is God's direction for us. If you are allowing the fear of man to direct your life, make a decision today to follow God instead. Start taking steps of faith to do what you believe God wants you to do, and He will be with you and guide you at all times. You are safe with the Lord!

Prayer: Father, I am sorry for all the times that I have let the fear of man hinder me from obeying You. Forgive me, Lord, and give me a fresh start. Put Your will in my heart and grant me courage to always follow You!

March 18

✷ The Lord Is My Strength ✷

The Lord is my strength and my [impenetrable] Shield; my heart trusts in, relies on, and confidently leans on Him, and I am helped...
PSALM 28:7

I am continually amazed by, and thankful for, the enabling power of God in our lives. Through Him, we truly can do all things that He has given us to do. Throughout my journey with God, I can say without a doubt that God is faithful, and I want to assure you that He will enable you to do all that you need to do.

Keeping a good attitude and staying in faith opens the door for God to grant any strength, ability, and wisdom that you require. You may not always feel that you have it, but when you step out, you will find that God is in you, giving you the ability to do what you need to do.

I encourage you to believe that you "can" instead of being afraid that you "can't." God gives us grace (ability and strength) one day at a time, so it is unwise to look too far ahead in life. If we do, we may feel overwhelmed concerning all we have to do. Any one of us can take time to look back at what God has already enabled us to do and what He has brought us through, and we will be assured that through Christ, we can also do whatever we need to do now and in the future.

You are stronger than you think! God is in you; He is for you and He will never leave you or forsake you, so live courageously and always remember that *God is your strength*!

Prayer: Father, I appreciate my relationship with You, and I am grateful for Your strength and ability. At times, life seems overwhelming, but I trust that You will always enable me to do whatever I need to do. You are my strength!

✷ Appreciation ✷

Now also we beseech you, brethren, get to know those who labor among you [recognize them for what they are, acknowledge and appreciate and respect them all] . . . 1 THESSALONIANS 5:12

I urge you to appreciate the people in your life and those who work for and with you. Don't take people for granted, especially your family and close friends. Tell people how important they are to you and always thank them for all they do for you. We never know for sure how long someone will be in our life, so it is important not to wait until it is too late to say the things we should say.

The only way to live without regret tomorrow is to do the right thing today.

Speak this: I am blessed beyond measure, and I always show appreciation to all the people God has put in my life.

✷ From Disappointment to Reappointment ✷

O my God, I trust, lean on, rely on, and am confident in You. Let me not be put to shame or [my hope in You] be disappointed; let not my enemies triumph over me. PSALM 25:2

I was recently disappointed when one of my books didn't sell as well in the marketplace as I had hoped that it would, but I didn't stay that way very long. I have learned in life that we can either be disappointed or "reappointed." We can look at what didn't happen, or at what can happen in the future, through God's love and mercy. As long as we continue to hope, we always have something to look forward to.

When we see things from God's viewpoint, we realize that endings always provide new beginnings. One door closes and another one opens. We should not dwell on what didn't happen, but on what can happen. We can trade disappointment for reappointment. If one thing doesn't work out as planned, keep going forward with a good attitude, expecting the next thing to be amazingly wonderful.

We all have disappointments in life, but we don't have to live disappointed. Scripture says that all those who put their trust in Jesus will not be put to shame, or disappointed (see Romans 10:11). We may experience disappointments, but thankfully we won't live disappointed lives. When things don't work out the way you had hoped that they would, trust God and keep going forward with an expectant attitude. Good things are waiting for you in the future!

Prayer: Father, I ask You to help me live with an attitude of positive expectation. Even when I am disappointed due to circumstances, help me remember that in You, all things work together for good. Help me always look forward to the good things ahead, and not dwell on the things that didn't work out as I had planned.

✷ Learning to Receive ✷

And of His fullness we have all received, and grace for grace.
JOHN 1:16 (NKJV)

When I give someone a gift and they say something like, "You didn't have to do that," or "No, no, I can't take that," or "Oh, that is too much," I really don't like it. I much prefer that someone say, "Thank you so much. I really appreciate it." I think God is the same way! He is a giver, and givers need receivers or they are stifled in their desire to give.

God's Word says that we are to receive grace, favor, forgiveness, mercy, and many other wonderful gifts from God. Do you desire certain things but don't know how to ask? Or even worse, do you ask and then not receive? We are to ask and receive that our joy might be full (see John 16:24).

God's goodness certainly is amazing, and we don't deserve all the wonderful things He does for us, but He does want us to graciously receive them with an attitude of gratitude. Learn to be a good receiver!

Prayer: Thank You, Father, for all the wonderful things You do for me. Teach me to be a gracious receiver and to always appreciate Your goodness!

March 22

✷ Pure Motives ✷

... For the Lord sees not as man sees; for man looks on the outward appearance, but the Lord looks on the heart.

1 SAMUEL 16:7

Something God taught me early in my journey with Him, and reminds me of often, is that He is not nearly as interested or impressed with *what* we do as He is in *why* we do it. If we give to the poor in order to be seen by men, we lose our reward, because God is only pleased with good works done for right reasons. If we fast or pray in order to be noticed or admired, we lose our reward, because God does not admire good works done for wrong reasons.

Let us be sure that we do what we do for God and His glory because we love Him and want to be a blessing to other people—never to *get* anything! There have been times in my life when I have done the right thing but for wrong reasons. I have done things thinking I might earn a blessing from God. I have done things to please people with no thought of pleasing God in mind. I have done things to get attention or to gain acceptance. I often wondered why I wasn't really happy, even though I was doing good things, but eventually I learned that true joy only comes from serving God with a pure heart.

It is often difficult for a person to take a deeper, more honest look at the true motives behind the things they do, but I strongly encourage you to do so. You may learn a truth about yourself that will be life-changing and will set you free. We are not truly free until we have no need to impress anyone and our motives for all of our actions are pure. This is an ongoing, lifelong process, but it is one that pleases God. Everyone else will see our actions, but God sees our heart!

Prayer: Father, I ask You to forgive me for doing things with impure motives. I want to serve You with a pure heart and I ask for Your discernment as I go forward. Help me to be honest with myself about why I am doing things!

March 23

⁕ Expect Favor ⁕

For You, O Lord, will bless the righteous; with favor You will surround him as with a shield. PSALM 5:12 (NKJV)

We can expect God to do what He promises; therefore, we can go through our days expecting favor. When God gives favor, He opens doors for us and causes people to do things for us that they wouldn't ordinarily be inclined to do. As a simple example, recently I was at a clothing store I go to often, and when I paid my bill the owner decided to give me a 20 percent discount on my purchases that day. That is favor! Get excited and expect God's favor today!

> I would rather ask for a lot and get part of it than ask for nothing and get all of it!

Speak this: I am expecting favor today everywhere I go!

What Causes Strife?

What leads to strife (discord and feuds) and how do conflicts (quarrels and fightings) originate among you? Do they not arise from your sensual desires that are ever warring in your bodily members?

JAMES 4:1

We can ask God for anything, trusting that if it is His will, He will give it to us at the exact right time. If we delight ourselves in God, He will give us the desires of our heart (see Psalm 37:4). However, lusting after things is an unhealthy desire that causes strife.

God has called us to peace, and it is important that we do all that we can to always maintain peace in our hearts and in our daily lives.

There is nothing that the world offers that is worth losing our peace over in order to get it. Keep God first at all times, ask Him for what you want, and let Him add the things that are right for you.

Prayer: Father, I ask You to give me the things that are right for me and help me to stay peaceful while I wait on You.

March 25

✷ Grace and More Grace ✷

... God sets Himself against the proud and haughty, but gives grace [continually] to the lowly (those who are humble enough to receive it).

JAMES 4:6

Grace is not only God's undeserved favor that provides forgiveness and mercy when we sin, but it is also His power that enables us to do whatever we need to do in life. But He only gives it to those who are humble enough to admit that they need help. We all need help, but a prideful, independent attitude will cause us to keep trying to do things in our own strength, instead of admitting our inability and leaning entirely on God.

We should trade "trying" for "trusting." Instead of struggling and being frustrated because our efforts always fail to produce what we want, we can ask for God's help at the beginning of, and all the way through, each thing that we undertake in life. We can learn to lean on God, and as we do, it takes the pressure off of us. He can do more in one moment than we can do in a lifetime. Faith the size of a grain of mustard seed can do more than all the willpower and self-determination in the world (see Matthew 17:20).

Frustration always equals works of the flesh, which happen when we try to do in our own strength and effort what only God can do. We are partners with God, and as such, He will assign things for us to do, but we cannot complete what He asks us to do without leaning entirely on Him, let alone trying to do things He hasn't told us to do. For example, it is not our job to change our family and friends, but it is our responsibility to pray for them and represent Christ in all of our interaction with them. If you are ready for help, humble yourself, admit that you can do nothing without Jesus, and receive His wisdom, strength, and help!

Prayer: Apart from You, Jesus, I can do nothing. I will fail completely without You, so I ask for Your help, and I will give You the glory for any success that I achieve.

⁕ *Fullness of Joy* ⁕

You will show me the path of life; in Your presence is fullness of joy, at Your right hand there are pleasures forevermore. PSALM 16:11

We seek many things in life that we think will give us joy and enjoyment, but we often fail to seek the one thing that brings *fullness* of joy. If we seek God first as our vital need, His presence will enable us to enjoy other things, but without Him, they will always be lacking in some way. Include the Lord in all that you do and speak with Him throughout the day. He is your joy!

God is everything, and we are nothing without Him.

Speak this: I will seek God first as my vital need in life, and I will experience fullness of joy.

⁕ Answered Prayer ⁕

[Yes] I will grant [I Myself will do for you] whatever you shall ask in My Name [as presenting all that I Am]. JOHN 14:14

My experience with God has taught me that He cares about everything that concerns us and He loves to be involved in our lives if we will only invite and welcome Him. My twelve-year-old dog had to be put to sleep and I missed her a lot. I started wanting another one, but for me to have a dog with all the travel I do, it had to be almost the perfect dog—sweet, obedient, calm, intelligent, easy to train, and able to be in lots of places with lots of different people! I was told that would be very difficult to find, but difficult and even impossible things become easy when God is working in our behalf.

I did get the perfect dog, and I do mean "perfect." My story, however, is not really about the dog so much as about the fact that God cared enough about my need to get involved! He also cares about you and all your needs. Our needs don't have to be "spiritual" for God to be interested. This truth is one of the most exciting things about my walk with God. I thoroughly enjoy watching Him work in my life in everyday events, many of which are important only to me. I am still amazed that the God of the entire universe took time to find me the perfect dog.

I called about an ad on the Internet, and the breeder *happened* to be a partner with our ministry and was willing to keep the puppy four weeks until we came to her area to do a conference. She and her entire family came to the conference and her daughter ended up recommitting her life to Christ. God was blessing everyone, and it all got started over a dog. I recommend that you don't do anything without getting God involved. Then you will see amazing things!

Prayer: Thank You, Father, that You care about every area of my life and that I can ask You to help me with absolutely anything. Show Yourself strong, Lord, in my life and do things that will amaze me.

✷ Too Busy Not to Pray ✷

The Lord is my Strength and my [impenetrable] Shield; my heart trusts in, relies on, and confidently leans on Him, and I am helped; therefore my heart greatly rejoices, and with my song will I praise Him. PSALM 28:7

I am in a season of my life right now when I feel that I have too much to do. I am sure that I created it myself, and I plan to work toward not doing this again in the future, but for now I am committed to several deadlines that I have to meet. What can I do to get them all done and not get frustrated in the process?

Jesus said that if we are weary and overburdened we should come to Him (see Matthew 11:28). When we are busy, we often think we don't have time for prayer or studying God's Word, but that is exactly when we must make time. I heard one man say that he had more to do than ever so he was going to pray an extra hour a day. When asked how he could find time to do that with all he had to do, he replied, "That is the only way I will ever get it done. I am too busy not to pray!"

I have learned that if I lean on God and take things one day at a time, He will help me and teach me how to arrange my life better in the future. The grace we need is always there when we need it, not before we need it. You may look at all you are facing over the next few weeks and feel overwhelmed, but pray more, lean on God more, take it one day at a time, and everything will get done!

Prayer: Father, I need Your help in getting done everything I have committed to do. I want to do it without frustration. Help me use more wisdom in the future when I am making plans!

✷ Waiting on God ✷

For God alone my soul waits in silence; from Him comes my salvation. PSALM 62:1

This morning, I spent a long time reading, rereading, and pondering the subject of waiting on God. Isaiah promised that those who wait on God will renew their strength, and they will be able to run and not become weary (see Isaiah 40:31). In other words, they will be able to do all that they need to do no matter how difficult it is and still have strength remaining. This sounds really good to me, and I am sure that it also does to you.

We often wear ourselves out running in our own strength, but it is never sufficient, because God has created us in such a way that we need Him. God waits to be wanted, and when He is, He always comes to our aid and grants us the ability to do what needs to be done. We can live in the strength of God if we will take the time to let Him know that we need Him and refuse to take action without having first secured His presence and assistance by faith.

To wait on God is to look for, expect, and hope in Him. We look to Him to be our strength, our wisdom, our creativity, and anything else that we need. Everything we need is in Him; therefore, if we have sought Him, we have everything else we need. Jesus said, "Apart from me you can do nothing" (John 15:5 [NIV]). Take some time each morning, before beginning any activity, and sit quietly in God's presence, whispering to Him that you need Him, you want Him, and you desire Him more than any other person or thing. By faith, wait in His presence and trust that you are receiving the strength you need for whatever you have to do that day or for whatever may come up that you are currently unaware of.

Remember, God waits to be wanted! Seek Him, for He has promised that those who come to Him will never be rejected (see John 6:37).

Prayer: Father, I ask You to forgive me for all the times I have run in my own strength and ignored You. I wait on You to grant me strength to do all that I need to do and to be all that You want me to be.

March 30

✷ Godly Behavior ✷

These people draw near Me with their mouths and honor Me with their lips, but their hearts hold off and are far away from Me.

MATTHEW 15:8

We should not go to church on Sunday and sing songs and pray prayers, acknowledging faith in God, and then go spend our weekdays behaving like the world. Jesus told the people not to be hypocritical, and that means that we are not to say one thing and then do another. We are called to be worshippers who worship Jesus all the time, not just when we are in an environment where we won't be rejected for doing so.

> Don't try to be so relevant to the world that you become irrelevant to God!

Speak this: I will seek God with my whole heart and strive to be sure my actions agree with my words.

⁕ The Present Moment ⁕

...And, lo, I am with you always, even unto the end of the world.
MATTHEW 28:20 (KJV)

If someone were to ask you what the greatest moment of your life has been, you might think of some great or exciting event. You might think of the day you were married or the birth of a child or graduating from college or the day you became aware of God. I would like to suggest that although these were great moments, they were not the greatest, because the greatest moment of your life is the present moment. This moment is where God is. He is the great "I Am."

We often live in the past or the future in our thinking, but I have discovered over the years that I miss most of my life if I don't devote myself to the present. I may go through the motions of the day, but I don't truly live it if I don't devote myself to what I am currently doing.

God is with us always. There is never one moment in our lives that He is not present, and yet we often feel alone. Don't waste your life looking for something that you already have. God is with you right now! Believe it and start to enjoy each moment. The present moment may not be perfect—it may even be painful—but recognizing that God is present with you will comfort and encourage you. It will strengthen you to do what needs to be done and go through the day with courage.

Discovering God in the smallest details of your life is perhaps the greatest and most blessed thing you will ever do. It makes every moment that you live amazing and filled with wonder. You don't need to search for God any longer...He is in this moment!

March 31

Prayer: Father, I am sorry that I have missed so many moments with You, but I ask You to help me live every moment that I have left in Your presence. Let me make every moment a special one, and help me always remember that You are with me always and You will never leave me!

⁕ Divine Opportunities ⁕

A man's mind plans his way, but the Lord directs his steps and makes them sure. PROVERBS 16:9

When your day doesn't go as planned, do you get irritated because someone or something has interrupted you? I know I do at times. What if we would see these changes in our plans as divine opportunities rather than interruptions that irritate us? Could that last-minute request from a friend for help be an opportunity to serve Christ that would produce more good fruit in our lives than our original plan? Would a one- or two-hour delay perhaps end up putting us in the right place at the right time for an opportunity we would have missed had we refused to change our plan?

There is nothing wrong with having a plan—as a matter of fact, I think it is wise to do so—but we should be ready at any time to drop our plans and follow God. He often gives us opportunities to help someone or to follow Him in an adventure that will bring blessings into our lives, but we can easily miss out on His better plan if we are not willing to "let go and let God lead."

There are also times when what seems like an interruption is God's protection from some unseen danger we would encounter if we continued in the path we had planned. Can heavy traffic that disrupts our plan save us from being in an accident? Could the airport delay be a blessing in disguise? The answer to these examples is yes, and if we will trust God with things like this and believe that our times are in His hands (see Psalm 31:15), we will enjoy more peace and have less stress.

Prayer: Father, help me follow Your lead at all times. I want Your will to be done in my life, and I want to always be available for You anytime You need me. Help me to never miss a divine opportunity with You!

⁕ God's Power ⁕

But He gives us more and more grace (power of the Holy Spirit, to meet this evil tendency and all others fully)... JAMES 4:6

God revealed this Scripture to me at a time in my life when I was about ready to give up thinking I could ever change and be the person I knew God wanted me to be. I was trying to change myself instead of leaning on the Holy Spirit to do it. I want to encourage you to ask for grace, grace, and more grace every day, and watch God work on your behalf to do things that are impossible for you to do alone.

Grace is the power of the Holy Spirit to help you do with ease what you could never do on your own with any amount of struggle and effort.

Speak this: I cannot change myself, but God is changing me by His grace.

⁕ God Hears You ⁕

The Lord has heard my supplication; the Lord receives my prayer.
PSALM 6:9

Have you ever wondered whether or not God heard your prayer? It is easy to do if He seems to be taking a long time in answering. It is good to remember that a delay is not a denial. Be assured that God heard you when you prayed and that He will answer at the exact right time.

Some answers to prayer come very quickly, but for reasons we don't fully understand, others can take years for us to see answered. I prayed for my father to accept Christ for at least thirty years before he finally did.

Are you waiting on something right now? If you are, I encourage you to remember that God heard you when you prayed, and although He may take longer than you would like Him to, He will not be late!

Prayer: Father, thank You for always hearing my prayers. Help me remember that a delay is not always a denial.

April 4

✷ Choosing Not to Complain ✷

Do all things without grumbling and faultfinding and complaining... PHILIPPIANS 2:14

Last night I was lying in bed and suddenly I felt an overwhelming need to repent for any complaining I had ever done in my life. I was watching a movie in which the main character had experienced a great tragedy and endured tremendous difficulty and yet he was maintaining a good attitude. We often complain and murmur about minor inconveniences and difficulties that, in reality, are nothing compared to what some people endure.

I am leaving in a few days for a mission trip to Africa, and I already know that I will see unimaginable suffering and deprivation. It is always good for me to go on these trips just to remind me of how blessed I am and to renew my determination to live my life to help others.

Do you complain about things that are not that important in the larger scope of life? Are you, in reality, extremely blessed but have fallen into a trap of focusing on what you don't have instead of what you do have? I know I do at times, and I was grateful for the reminder from the Lord to be thankful in all things (see 1 Thessalonians 5:18) and realize that complaining is evil in His ears. Let us be committed to thank God throughout each day of our lives and voice that thankfulness to Him.

Prayer: Father, please forgive me for any, and all, complaining I have ever done in my life, and help me realize how good You are to me. I want to be extremely thankful for all the blessings You give me.

✷ Do unto Others ✷

So then, whatever you desire that others would do to and for you, even so do also to and for them... MATTHEW 7:12

I was awake for a couple of hours last night due to jet lag from traveling in Africa, and while I lay in the darkness, the words of Jesus—"Do unto others as you would have them do unto you"—came to my mind. I thought about it until I fell asleep, and then this morning I continued to ponder it. I opened my Bible, and as I studied this passage and the Scriptures surrounding it, I received some insight regarding this Scripture; it's in connection to answered prayer.

Prior to the statement about how we treat others, we find an invitation from our Lord Jesus to ask and keep on asking, seek and keep on seeking, and knock and keep on knocking. He also promises that we will receive favorable answers to each request. We will receive, we will find, and doors will be opened (see Matthew 7:7–8). He assures us of His goodness and willingness to help us and then makes this statement: "So then, whatever you desire that others would do to and for you, even so do also to and for them" (Matthew 7:12). The phrase "so then" means there is a connection between answered prayer and how we treat other people.

I think we would be astonished at the difference in our lives in every respect if we truly did treat others the way we want to be treated. It certainly would change many things in how we respond to people and how we live our lives. Actually, it would change the world! I have decided to purposely be more focused every day on doing so, and I pray you will join me. That Scripture is often called the Golden Rule, but I prefer to call it the "Golden Key" that will unlock and release God's best in our lives.

April 5

Prayer: Father, please help me treat other people the way I want to be treated. Forgive me for my failure in the past in this very important area and grant me a fresh start. Grant me Your grace because I know I will fail without Your help.

⁕ Helping Orphans ⁕

And whoever receives and accepts and welcomes one little child like this for My sake and in My name receives and accepts and welcomes Me. MATTHEW 18:5

As I write this, I am in Madagascar, ministering to children who live on the streets because they have no home. A few live with their parents, but most of them are orphans. They eat what they can scrape together each day, sleep where they can, are dirty beyond anything most of us could even imagine, and wear tattered, filthy clothes. In the city, it is reported that there are more than fifty thousand such children.

We were privileged to host an event that included over forty thousand of these children in which we shared the Gospel through drama, fed them, and gave them hygiene items. Each one received a jacket for warmth in the winter months. We also hosted a medical outreach especially for them, and our team washed over one thousand children's feet and gave them new shoes.

I must say that I have been many places in the world and have seen despicable things, but this is one of the worst ever. Today, our final day with them, by the grace and mercy of God, we dedicated an overnight shelter that will house fifty of these unfortunate children. They will receive showers, be able to use toilet facilities, eat two meals each day, and have clean clothing. At the dedication, many children actually had to be taught how to wash their hands before meals in the sinks we provided that lead into the food line.

We must respond to this desperate situation, which is not isolated in Madagascar but is repeated in many places around the world. Respond by praying, helping, and being more thankful than ever before for the amazingly wonderful life that you have.

April 6

Before we ever complain again, let's be grateful that we know how to wash our hands and are not sleeping on the side of a dirt road covered with plastic, paper, or cardboard.

Prayer: O God, please comfort and provide for children that are homeless, hungry, and alone. Show me what I can do to make a difference, and help me realize that when I do, I am ministering to You! Thank You for every tiny blessing in my life!

✷ Focus on Jesus ✷

Delight yourself also in the Lord, and He will give you the desires and secret petitions of your heart. PSALM 37:4

Ask God for what you want and then focus on loving and serving Him instead of on what you want Him to do for you. Seek God's presence, not His presents! Seek His face, not His hand! When you seek God's face (His presence), you will find that His hand is always open to you.

> Crave and pursue God as a hungry man who is starving craves and pursues food!

Speak this: I seek God with my whole heart and as my vital need, and He gives me the desires of my heart.

April 8

⁕ Set Free ⁕

... He has sent me ... to proclaim liberty to the [physical and spiritual] captives and the opening of the prison and of the eyes to those who are bound. ISAIAH 61:1

I am writing in Namibia, Africa, while preparing to go to a men's prison here. I intend to share with them that they can be in prison and still be free, and that many people in the world, although not in prison, are still prisoners.

I was a prisoner for much of my life because I was filled with fear, guilt, shame, bitterness, and hatred, including self-hatred. I didn't live behind iron bars, but I was definitely a prisoner to those tormenting emotions. If you or someone you know is bound by these things, you can be free. Jesus came to set us free and to help us see and enjoy the new life He offers—a life that is abundant and filled with great joy (see John 10:10).

I hope to encourage the men in prison today with the good news of the Gospel. I also hope to encourage you to know that as you continue in God's Word, you will know the truth and it will make you free (see John 8:31–32). No matter what your circumstances are, if you are free in your heart and mind, then you are free indeed! Examine what is going on inside you and ask God to help you with any tormenting emotion that is holding you captive. If you are brokenhearted due to painful things in your past, Jesus will heal you and set you free!

Prayer: Father, I thank You that Jesus came to make us free, and I do want to be free in every area of my life. Please reveal areas that You want to work in, and help me cooperate with the Holy Spirit as He brings healing and freedom in my life.

✷ Never Say, "No Way" ✷

Jesus said to him, I am the Way and the Truth and the Life; no one comes to the Father except by (through) Me. JOHN 14:6

I often hear people say, "There is no way that is going to work," or "There is no way I can do this," or "There is no way I will ever get out of debt." I have said similar things in my life, and those statements are inaccurate, because Jesus is the Way! With men, many things are impossible, but with God *all things* are possible (see Matthew 19:26).

Are you facing a seemingly impossible situation right now? If so, don't despair and don't say, "There is no way!" Isaiah said that God would even make a way in the wilderness and bring rivers in the desert (see Isaiah 43:19). There is always an answer to any problem when Jesus is working on our behalf. Our part is to believe, and when we do, God will go to work and we will be amazed as we witness the things that only He can do.

After being sexually abused for many years by my father and abandoned by my mother, I thought there was no way I could ever have a happy, normal life, but I was wrong. God heals the brokenhearted! He makes all things new and gives us a life worth living. Only believe, and you will see the glory of God! (See John 11:40.) Doubt your doubts, face your fears, and even when all human reason for hope seems gone, hope in faith that God will make a way!

Prayer: Thank You, Jesus, that You always make a way, even when there seems to be no way. You are the "Way-maker."

✷ Pursue Peace ✷

Depart from evil and do good; seek, inquire for, and crave peace and pursue (go after) it! PSALM 34:14

Peace is one of the most valuable things we can have, but if we want it, we must pursue and go after it. I spent a lot of my life wanting my circumstances and the people around me to change so I could have peace, and then I finally learned that I could greatly increase my peace by being willing to adapt myself to people and things.

What could you change that would give you more peace right away?

God wants to change *you* more than He wants to change your circumstances!

Speak this: I am willing to change anything God shows me to change because it means I can have more peace.

⁕ Strength ⁕

The Lord will give [unyielding and impenetrable] strength to His people; the Lord will bless His people with peace. PSALM 29:11

It is wonderful to have the confidence that no matter what we need to do in life, God will strengthen us and enable us to do it. We all have weaknesses, but God's strength is also available to all of us. I ask for God's strength every day first thing in the morning, and sometimes more than one time a day. It may be early in the morning and I don't know yet what all will occur in my life that day, but I do know that I need God's strength in order to handle it.

When we merely "try" to be strong, we will always ultimately fail, but if we trust God to be strong through us, we will never run out of strength. I don't know what you might be facing today, but I do know that God loves you and is waiting to help you. He wants to give you strength and bless you with peace! Take a few minutes several times a day and wait on God for strength, ability, and wisdom. They who wait on the Lord shall renew their strength (see Isaiah 40:31). And you can do all things through Christ who is your strength (see Philippians 4:13).

Prayer: Father, I am excited to know that I can always depend on You to give me the strength I need. Help me always remember that apart from You, I can do nothing!

⁕ Thoughts and Words ⁕

Let the words of my mouth and the meditation of my heart be acceptable in Your sight, O Lord, my [firm, impenetrable] Rock and my Redeemer. PSALM 19:14

The more our thoughts and words are in line with God's will, the better our day will be. The power of thoughts and words is truly amazing, and God urges us in many places in His Word to choose both carefully.

Think about it: How would it change your day if all your thoughts and words were pleasant, loving, and full of faith? What if we could make it through the day without uttering one word of complaint? What if we found no fault with anyone, but instead gave each person we encounter a compliment? I think life would be utterly amazing! I am sure we would enjoy the day more than we can imagine.

The power of life and death are in the tongue (see Proverbs 18:21), and as a man thinks in his heart, so does he become (see Proverbs 23:7). Wow! No wonder David prayed that the words of his mouth and the thoughts in his heart would be acceptable to God. I pray the same thing very often, and I encourage you to do the same. Two of the many ways we can glorify God is through our thoughts and words, and with His amazing grace we can do it!

Prayer: Father, I ask You to help me resist the temptation to think and say things that are filled with death. Let me instead think and speak life! I submit my mind and mouth to You and ask that You fill both with Your wisdom.

✷ God's Word ✷

For the Word that God speaks is alive and full of power [making it active, operative, energizing, and effective]... HEBREWS 4:12

I have been thinking about the power of God's Word this morning and all the changes I have seen in my life and thousands of other lives because of it. Jesus is the Word made flesh, so when we read, study, and meditate on the Word of God, we are fellowshipping with Jesus. As His Word becomes part of us, we are transformed into His image (see 2 Corinthians 3:18). His Word has inherent power in it, and it changes us!

We are instructed in the Bible to meditate on the Word of God, and that simply means to think about it, roll it over and over in our minds, speak it, and know that as we do, it is renewing our minds and teaching us to think as God thinks. Our thoughts are extremely important because they go before our words and all of our actions. God has a good plan for each of us and we will see it come to pass as we renew our minds (see Romans 12:2).

We seem to find it very easy to meditate on our problems. We call it worry! It is a bad habit that can easily be eliminated from our lives by learning to meditate on God's Word instead. Each time a worry or a fear comes to your mind, find a Scripture that teaches you that God will take care of the problem for you and meditate on it instead of worrying. For example, if you are having financial difficulty, you can worry all day and night about it, or you can think about what God's Word says concerning Him taking care of you:

> Casting the whole of your care [all your anxieties, all your worries, all your concerns, once and for all] on Him, for He

cares for you affectionately and cares about you watchfully (1 Peter 5:7).

God's Word has an answer for every need we have. I intend to spend a lot of time today just thinking about the power that is in God's Word, and I pray that you will join me. God's Word contains the power we need to be successful in all areas of our lives.

Prayer: Father, help me discipline myself to meditate on Your Word. Let it become a habit in my life. I ask You to continue teaching me Your Word and renewing my mind accordingly.

✷ Let God Help You ✷

Commit your way to the Lord [roll and repose each care of your load on Him]; trust (lean on, rely on, and be confident) also in Him and He will bring it to pass. PSALM 37:5

My first Bible was given to me by my mother-in-law forty-nine years ago, and she wrote out Psalm 37:5 inside the cover. I had no idea what it meant and went on to have at least twenty very frustrating years before learning that worry and care accomplish nothing except making us miserable. If you are worried about anything, don't waste your time. Give it to God and let Him care for you.

> Worry and hurry are the twins that can steal your health!

Speak this: By God's grace I will not worry, and I will not hurry!

✷ Grace and Peace ✷

Grace (favor and blessing) to you and [heart] peace from God our Father and the Lord Jesus Christ (the Messiah). PHILIPPIANS 1:2

As I began my prayer time this morning, I asked the Lord to speak something to my heart that would be important for my life. The thought that roared into my heart was, *Be at peace—always be at peace!*

Very often letters written to the church by Paul and other apostles begin with, "Grace and peace be multiplied to you through the knowledge of our Lord and Savior Jesus Christ." The words may vary, but the message is the same: Peace is always preceded by grace. God's grace gives us peace! Grace can be defined in many ways. It is God's undeserved favor and blessing. I often define it as God's power coming to us freely to help us do with ease what we could never do alone with any amount of struggle and effort. Grace manifests as forgiveness, mercy, strength for our weakness, and probably in thousands of other ways.

Because of His grace, God forgives our sins, and that leads us to peace with Him and freedom from guilt. Because of grace, we can face our weaknesses and still know that God loves us and that our weaknesses don't disqualify us for His kingdom. I would like to suggest that you ask yourself if you lack peace in any area of your life. If you do, then believe that God's grace (goodness, favor, and power) are enough to meet that need through your faith in Christ.

If you lack peace about your own spiritual maturity, you can turn your reconstruction project over to God's grace, because only He can truly change us. If you long to see change in your loved ones or your circumstances, those too must be turned over to God. Ask God for anything that you need and trust His timing. Thankfully, we don't have to be perfect in order to receive God's help. Another definition of grace is God's riches at Christ's expense, and that is exactly what we have available to us daily through our faith.

Prayer: Father, thank You for grace that leads to peace. Help me receive Your grace always instead of struggling in my own strength.

April 16

✷ God Is Working! ✷

And I am convinced and sure of this very thing, that He Who began a good work in you will continue until the day of Jesus Christ [right up to the time of His return], developing [that good work] and perfecting and bringing it to full completion in you.

PHILIPPIANS 1:6

Good news! You and I don't have to struggle to find perfection. We are perfected in Christ, and He is working in us daily, helping us manifest more and more of His character. God loves us right where we are on the way to where He knows we will be. He sees the end from the beginning and knows all things. God sees and knows things about us that even we have not realized, and He is committed fully to finishing the work in us that He began at the moment we placed our faith in Him and received Him as our Savior. You can rest in knowing that there is nothing about you that is a surprise to God. He knows everything and loves you anyway!

What blessed rest we find in knowing that even on our worst day God is still working and that He will never give up on us. Our part is to believe, and God's part is to work in us and through us. Whether you are looking at yourself and considering changes you desire or looking at others whom you have been praying for, God has promised to finish what He started!

Enjoy yourself today right where you are, or as I often say, "Enjoy where you are on the way to where you are going."

Prayer: Father, thank You for never giving up on me and for working in me daily to make me what You want me to be. Help me trust You and enjoy being at rest in You.

✷ God's Strength in You! ✷

May He grant you out of the rich treasury of His glory to be strengthened and reinforced with mighty power in the inner man by the [Holy] Spirit [Himself indwelling your innermost being and personality]. EPHESIANS 3:16

When we are strong inwardly—in our determination, thoughts, and attitudes—as well as strong in our faith, we can do whatever we need to do in life. This is a prayer that I pray almost daily for my family and me. Don't just "try" to be strong, but instead go to God for your strength, knowing that He can enable you to do all things through Him.

> When the Holy Spirit is on the inside, His strength will show up on the outside.

Speak this: I am daily filled with God's strength, and I can do whatever I need to do with joy!

⁕ Divine Comfort ⁕

In the multitude of my [anxious] thoughts within me, Your comforts cheer and delight my soul! PSALM 94:19

I am sad this morning. A friend of mine was given the news this week that she has cancer. It is quite severe, and at this time, the prognosis is uncertain. She and her husband have two young children and are both in their middle to late thirties. Tragic to say the least!

When we hear news like this, how should we respond? My first response was to call the husband, who has worked for us since he was seventeen years old. Then I started praying, and have been doing so several times a day. Anytime they come to my heart—and that is frequently—I pray! I pray for God's divine comfort and His grace to take over in this situation. I pray for healing (preferably a miracle), right doctors, accurate diagnosis, and wisdom for the family in making decisions. I offer to do anything I can to help, although I know that there is not much I can do except "be there."

I made a promise that we would be there for them all the way through the journey, and I think that means more to people than we may comprehend. We don't have to feel the pressure to give answers or advice that we don't have. We help people who are hurting immensely when we don't "forget" them in their pain, especially if what they are going through takes a while to get through.

God's Word teaches that we are more than conquerors (see Romans 8:37), and I believe that is true. To me, it means that we can know even before difficulty begins that in the end, we will have the victory, and God will comfort us all the way through it. He will enable us, strengthen us, and hold us every step of the way. Yes, we cry, we feel unimaginable pain, and we may get confused and ask questions that can't be answered at the time, but through it all, God is there, giving us assurance that we are loved!

Prayer: Father, please comfort all the people who are hurting today. You are the one who comforts us in our affliction, and we trust You to give us grace and more grace to stand firm, even in the midst of tragedy.

⁕ Something Is Missing ⁕

And not only the creation, but we ourselves too, who have and enjoy the firstfruits of the [Holy] Spirit [a foretaste of the blissful things to come] groan inwardly as we wait for the redemption of our bodies [from sensuality and the grave, which will reveal] our adoption (our manifestation as God's sons). ROMANS 8:23

I must admit that at times I feel that something is missing in my life and I don't quite know what it is. Then I feel frustrated with myself because I am amazingly blessed in many ways and think I should never feel that I need or want "more" of anything to be completely satisfied.

After a great deal of pondering and praying about what the problem is, I am happy to say that God has given me understanding and I now have rest! We are created for the garden (see Genesis 2:7–8), but we live in the world! We are longing for Heaven—our true home—and we will never feel 100 percent settled until we see Jesus and live in His presence. As long as we are in this world, it is like we are on a long trip, living in a motel and longing for home.

We are created for perfection and yet we are currently assigned to being in a place where nothing and nobody, including us, is perfect. Since we are created for perfection, anytime we are confronted with imperfection, we sense a disappointment that I have learned is not wrong to feel. The more deeply we understand this, the more we can enjoy what we do have and the more we will be able to love people, even with their imperfections. I have found rest in realizing that what I feel and deal with every day is quite normal—at least it is normal for someone who is longing for home!

Prayer: Father, thank You that someday we will be coming home, and until then, we have the presence of the Holy Spirit with us, reminding us of the perfection that is to come.

✵ Peacemakers ✵

Blessed are the peacemakers, for they shall be called sons of God.
MATTHEW 5:9 (NKJV)

A peacemaker is someone who works for and maintains peace. They realize how valuable peace is and they are aggressive in keeping it. If we are to live in peace, we cannot expect everyone to adapt to us; instead, we must be willing to adapt to them, especially in matters that are not really important when all things are considered. For example, is it worth it to prolong an argument just so you can have the last word or "be right" when there is a disagreement? It is best to humble yourself and remain peaceful, which is the will of God. He will consider you a mature son or daughter and it will open the door for greater blessing in your life.

"Peace = Power" and "No Peace = No Power."

Speak this: I will be a maker and maintainer of peace at all times!

✷ Living Truly ✷

Rather, let our lives lovingly express truth [in all things, speaking truly, dealing truly, living truly]. Enfolded in love, let us grow up in every way and in all things into Him Who is the Head, [even] Christ (the Messiah, the Anointed One). EPHESIANS 4:15

Satan is the deceiver, and his goal is to prevent us from walking in the truth. But Jesus came that we might know the Truth, and He said the Truth would make us free (see John 8:32).

When I began to seriously study God's Word, I found that I had a life built on deception and lies. I believed many things that simply were not true, yet they were true for me because I believed them. Lies become our reality if we believe them! For example, I believed I could never overcome my past, but God's Word taught me that I could let go of what was behind and learn to enjoy the good life God had planned for me (see 2 Corinthians 5:17).

It is important for us to know the truth and apply it to our lives. It is also important to tell the truth in all situations and to be truthful with ourselves about our motives and actions. Any person who makes a commitment to "live truly" will learn many things about him or herself, some of which may not be pleasant. Even though it is difficult to face truth at times, it is also wonderful to be free from lies and deception. I spent many years blaming my problems on other people, but the truth was that I had a bad attitude and a lot of bitterness from my past. It was painful to face, but that truth ultimately set me free and brought healing into my life.

I encourage you to join me in praying daily that God will reveal truth to us in every situation and give us the courage to face it. A few days ago, Dave and I had a heated conversation, and I was sure it was his fault until I asked God to show me truth in the situation.

When I did, God revealed to me that I had created the situation by saying several things that were totally useless and that put Dave on the defensive. That wasn't what I wanted to hear, but it will help me not to make the same mistake again! Truth is very valuable. Let's be committed to living truly!

Prayer: Father, I ask You to reveal truth to me in every situation in my life and to give me the courage to face it. Thank You!

✷ God in Our Thoughts ✷

. . . You shall love the Lord your God with all your heart and with all your soul and with all your mind (intellect). MATTHEW 22:37

While studying about being closer to God, I was reminded today that He is only one thought away at all times. We can be with God anytime by simply thinking about Him. God wants us to think about Him, and His thoughts toward us are more than the grains of sand on all the beaches in the world (see Psalm 139:17–18). Those are a lot of thoughts!

It is in our minds that we live in conscious interaction with God. We can bring Him close at any time by conversing with Him or thinking of Him. I sometimes stop what I am doing and simply think, *God is here right now!* Then I take a moment to realize what that means to me. God is with us, but if we never or rarely bring that into our conscious awareness, it is as if He were not there at all.

Some things to consider thinking about would be the last special thing you can remember that God did for you or all the blessings in your life. We can also think about His character. He is good, just, merciful, forgiving, long-suffering, patient, and wise, and He is actually a lot of fun to be with! God is your friend, so I recommend thinking of Him often and talking to Him about anything and everything! He is always interested in you and what you have to say!

Prayer: Father, I want to live in and enjoy Your presence. Help me do so by talking to You all the time and thinking of You often.

✷ Never Give Up! ✷

For a righteous man falls seven times and rises again . . .
PROVERBS 24:16

I have a nicely decorated sign in my home that says "Never, Never, Never Give Up!" Each time I see it, I am encouraged and reminded of the importance of being determined to keep doing what I know I am supposed to do. We all have times when we feel that we cannot go on and the temptation arises to give up. Satan would love it if we did, but we can decide to disappoint him. I once heard that the word "endure" means to outlast the devil. I like that thought! The apostle Paul teaches us to endure with good temper whatever comes (see Colossians 3:12). Sounds challenging, but we can do it!

If you are struggling today, or perhaps feeling weak in your resolve to press on due to problems that have lasted longer than you expected, I encourage you to set your mind and keep it set (see Colossians 3:2) that you will never, never, never give up! When we set our mind in the right direction, we are very difficult to defeat!

Even if you occasionally do have an emotional day, don't feel condemned—just get right back up and keep on keeping on! No matter how many times we fall, we can get back up, and God will be with us to help us reach our goals!

Prayer: Father, You are my strength, and I need You at all times. Help me to never give up and to regularly be refreshed in Your presence.

April 24

⁕ Defeating Doubt ⁕

Only it must be in faith that he asks with no wavering (no hesitating, no doubting)... JAMES 1:6

When you make a decision, don't start doubting yourself and then end up changing your mind several times until you become thoroughly confused. Don't let the fear of being wrong or making a mistake cause you to be indecisive. Do the best you can to decide and then go forward! Even if you make a mistake, it is not the end of the world. You can learn from your mistake and try again.

A double-minded man is tortured by his indecision.

Speak this: I will make prayerful decisions and then stand firm on what I have decided!

✷ Keeping the Peace ✷

If possible, as far as it depends on you, live at peace with everyone.
ROMANS 12:18

Recently someone was quite rude to me, and of course it hurt my feelings. I was tired because I had just returned from a conference, and that made me even more vulnerable. I had a decision to make! Would I stay angry, confront them, tell other people how they had treated me (gossip), or pray for them and be at peace?

I am sure you are familiar with the scenario I am describing, and when these things happen to us, we dare not follow our emotions. What we "feel" like doing and what God wants us to do are usually two very different things. I find it best to be quiet for a bit, let my emotions calm down, and think about the situation rationally.

Did the person hurt me on purpose, or were they perhaps under some sort of pressure that made them insensitive to my feelings? The individual who hurt me was having a very difficult day, and although they knew they were being rude and did apologize, they were having difficulty being kind to anyone. God's Word encourages us to always believe the best of every person (see 1 Corinthians 13:7), and if we are willing to do it, it is one of the best ways to keep our peace in situations like this.

Keeping the peace with others is very important and I highly recommend that you do so if it is at all possible. Confront those who mistreat you when God leads you to, but avoid being touchy and getting your feelings hurt easily. When you get your feelings hurt, forgive the offender quickly and just imagine all the times you may have hurt someone and needed God's forgiveness and theirs!

Prayer: Father, help me be at peace at all times. I want to always believe the best and forgive others just as You forgive me.

April 26

⁕ Let God Be Your Protection ⁕

Behold, I have indelibly imprinted (tattooed a picture of) you on the palm of each of My hands; [O Zion] your walls are continually before me. ISAIAH 49:16

Most of us spend more time trying to protect ourselves from being hurt than we do building good relationships. We erect invisible walls around our lives to keep people from hurting us, but God wants to be our wall of protection. When we wall others out, we also wall ourselves in. We often live isolated and lonely lives because we have been hurt in the past and we don't want to go through the same kind of pain again.

The Scripture above shows God's intimate concern for our protection. He is always watching out for us and will protect us if we trust Him to do so. No one will live their entire life and never be hurt by others, but God is able to comfort and heal us in all of our pain and affliction. It is much better to love and be hurt occasionally than to never love due to the fear of being hurt.

It is a natural human response to want to protect ourselves from pain, but God does not want us to live in fear. He wants us to enjoy one another and trust Him to heal us when we do get hurt. If you have been hurt badly in the past and find that you avoid close relationships or isolate yourself from others, I believe God is asking you to take down your walls of self-protection and let Him become your divine protection. This doesn't mean you will never get hurt, but it does mean you will be free!

Prayer: Father, help me put my trust in You for all of my protection. I am retiring from self-care and giving You the job of taking care of me!

⁕ Consider Your Ways ⁕

Thus says the Lord of hosts: Consider your ways (your previous and present conduct) and how you have fared. HAGGAI 1:7

The people in the book of Haggai felt they had sowed much and reaped little, and when they complained to God, He told them to consider their ways. They had actually been living in disobedience to God for eighteen years, building their own house instead of building His as He had instructed. If you don't like the harvest you have in your life, perhaps it would be wise to consider your ways. If there are areas of disobedience in your life, correct them immediately and I suspect things will change for the better.

Are you waiting for God to change something, or is He waiting for you to change?

Speak this: I will be promptly obedient to God at all times, and I will enjoy a blessed harvest in my life.

April 28

⁕ Stay Happy ⁕

A happy heart is good medicine and a cheerful mind works healing, but a broken spirit dries up the bones. PROVERBS 17:22

It is easy to focus on our problems and lose our joy, but I encourage you to stay happy no matter what, because God's joy gives us strength and has healing power. When you have a lengthy situation that is difficult, don't just pray for God to remove the trouble, but ask Him to keep you encouraged and joyful while you are waiting for Him to do what is needed.

One of the ways to stay joyful in hard times is to focus on something besides the difficulty. Pray for others that you know or take a walk or see a movie—do anything besides just be miserable. It also brings me joy to remember other things God has done for me in the past. It helps me know that if He did it once, He can do it again.

Prayer: Father, thank You for the gift of joy. Help me stay happy at all times and to think thoughts that will add to my joy instead of stealing it.

✷ Do What You Can Do! ✷

Who [with reason] despises the day of small things?...

ZECHARIAH 4:10

I recently started walking for exercise, and after about ten days I was up to three miles a day. A few more days went by and I started having pain in a groin muscle. It got so bad that I could only walk about three-quarters of a mile. I was tempted to quit altogether because I wasn't getting to do what I wanted to do, and I started thinking that walking that small amount wouldn't do any good. But I was wrong! By doing the little I could do, I eventually worked up to five miles a day.

If you cannot exercise three days a week but you can exercise one day, then start with that and see what happens. You may find that doing what you can do is an open door to eventually being able to do what you cannot do now! If you cannot study the Bible an hour every day but you can do fifteen minutes, then start with what you can do and watch it grow. Many people never get started with the things they want to do because they want to start at the finish line. My philosophy is this: "I may not be able to do everything, but I refuse to do nothing!" If you never get started in the right direction, you will never get to where you want to be!

Prayer: Father, I want to be active and always do what I can do. Help me see the value of doing even little things for Your glory. Help me take steps of faith, even if they are baby steps, and help me get to where I need to be.

April 30

* Believe *

. . . Did I not tell you and promise you that if you would believe and rely on Me, you would see the glory of God? JOHN 11:40

What we believe is our choice. God desires that we not only believe that He exists, but that we believe His Word. Trusting God to fulfill His promises will bring you into a state of rest. Those who have believed do enter the rest of God, according to Hebrews 4:3. When I am frustrated, worried, fearful, or upset in any way, I can always trace the problem back to wrong believing.

I keep a sign in my office that simply says "Believe." It reminds me to examine my heart and mind and be sure that I am placing my trust in God at all times. Joy and peace are found in believing (see Romans 15:13). Jesus said that if we would just believe, we would see His glory, which is the manifestation of His excellence in our lives. I am sure that you want to see the best that God has for you manifested in your life, as I do in mine.

If God instructs you to do (or not to do) something, believe and obey! When God states in His Word that He will take care of you and meet all your needs, believe it! Believe before you see. In God's kingdom economy, we always believe first and then we see the result of our believing. Right believing leads to right living! Right believing leads to a life of peace, joy, and fulfillment! My message to you today is very simple: *Believe!*

Prayer: Father, I know that all of Your ways are right and just. I believe Your Word is true, and I ask You to help me believe it at all times. Remind me to believe when I am starting to doubt, and help me walk in faith always!

✷ Let God Be Your Guide ✷

I [the Lord] will instruct you and teach you in the way you should go; I will counsel you with My eye upon you. PSALM 32:8

I think we all want to be sure that we are making right decisions, but if we are not careful, we can worry about our decisions and be double-minded and fearful. We have a better choice, and that is to relax and trust God to lead us.

The Holy Spirit is our teacher and our constant companion. He knows the mind of God and will reveal it to us as we lean on and rely on Him. Yesterday, I had a toothache and needed to go to a dentist, but I was out of town and didn't know anyone to go to. I started searching online to find a dentist and located one. He had a nice ad and was close to where I was staying, but I could not make up my mind to go to him just yet. In the meantime, I asked God to lead me, and soon my administrative assistant called to talk with me about an appointment I had asked her to cancel since I had a toothache. She said the woman she talked to recommended a dentist that she goes to, and when she gave me the name it was the same dentist I had looked at online. I believe that was God leading me. It was confirmation to go ahead and make an appointment. I did, and it turned out well!

It only takes a few seconds to ask God to guide you when you need to make decisions. Trusting God for His guidance will enable you to relax. You may simply sense in your heart a direction you should take and feel peaceful about a decision, or you may have some confirmation as I did with the dentist. However God chooses to guide, you can relax and trust Him to do it.

Prayer: Father, I choose to trust You to guide me through life and to help me with every decision. Teach me how to hear from You and relax concerning the decisions I need to make.

May 2

Think Like God Thinks

And do not be conformed to this world, but be transformed by the renewing of your mind, that you may prove what is that good and acceptable and perfect will of God. ROMANS 12:2 (NKJV)

God reminded me this morning to guard my thoughts and think as He does. That is a big goal, but it is one we should all aspire to daily. The more we think according to God's Word, the more of the Lord's joy we will experience.

God's Word teaches us the right way to think and tells us that we can choose our own thoughts by paying careful attention to them and casting down the ones that are not according to God's Word and will (see 2 Corinthians 10:5).

Every day that you keep pressing on is a day that you make progress!

Choose your thoughts. Don't let the devil use your mind as a garbage dump!

Speak this: I have the mind of Christ and I am learning to think as He does.

⁕ Change Your Approach ⁕

So do not worry or be anxious about tomorrow, for tomorrow will have worries and anxieties of its own. Sufficient for each day is its own trouble. MATTHEW 6:34

How do you approach life? Do you look at all the things coming in the future and start to panic or worry? Or do you live life one day at a time, refusing to borrow trouble from tomorrow?

Right now I have about six very important projects that I need to finish, and as I thought about them, I started to feel pressured. Then I realized that the projects were not pressuring me, but thinking about all of them at once instead of the one that needed to get done today was pressuring me. I have to remind myself often to take life one day at a time, and I thought you might also need that reminder today!

God will give you the grace you need for tomorrow when tomorrow comes, so enjoy today.

Prayer: Father, help me live my life one day at a time and to never waste today worrying about tomorrow. Thank You!

⁕ Living on Purpose ⁕

Therefore do not be vague and thoughtless and foolish, but understanding and firmly grasping what the will of the Lord is. EPHESIANS 5:17

God desires that we bear much good fruit (see John 15:1–5). That can only occur if we are people who live life "on purpose." Each day, we should prayerfully think through what we would like to accomplish that day and then purpose to do it. If we are vague and thoughtless, it is more likely that we won't accomplish much at all. Vague people wait to see how they feel before taking action, but purposeful people take the proper action no matter how they feel about it.

We live in a world of distractions, and even purposeful people need to be wise and not get off track. Many things scream for our attention, and yet it is up to each of us to decide what God would have us give our attention to. If I need to clean my house today, should I do that or go shopping with a friend who called at the last minute with an invitation? If I need to pay my bills and balance my bank account, should I do that or get distracted by television and sit on the couch most of the day? Many people live frustrated lives simply because they do not live on purpose.

When my day is over, I need to feel that I have accomplished something worthwhile. I want to have made progress in some areas of my life, and I believe that is a desire that God has placed in each of us. We feel fulfilled when we have confidence that we have done what we needed to do, but we feel frustrated if we feel we have just wasted the day. Even if we decide to rest all day, which is something that can also be fruitful for our overall health, we need to do it on purpose! In short, my advice is: Pray, plan, and stay focused on purpose!

Prayer: Father, I want to bear good fruit in my life, and I need Your help in planning and in following through. Help me not to get distracted by time-wasters that get me off track and frustrate me.

May 5

⁕ *Jesus Is Coming Soon* ⁕

Let all men know and perceive and recognize your unselfishness (your considerateness, your forbearing spirit). The Lord is near [He is coming soon]. PHILIPPIANS 4:5

Jesus has promised to come back again and take us to be with Him in Heaven for eternity. No one knows exactly when, but if we read what Scripture reveals about signs of the end times (see Matthew 24), we can easily recognize that the time is near. The apostles kept this truth in front of people because they wanted them to live as if they truly believed He was coming at any moment.

Is there anything you would change if you knew Jesus was coming tonight? If so, I recommend you change it now, because surely He is coming soon.

> Don't wait until it is too late to do what you should be doing now!

Speak this: I am anxiously waiting for the Lord's return, and I am living as if it could be at any moment.

⁕ Seated in Christ ⁕

And He raised us up together with Him and made us sit down together [giving us joint seating with Him]... EPHESIANS 2:6

When Christ accomplished the forgiveness of our sin and the riddance of our guilt, the Word of God states that He sat down in heavenly places at the right hand of God (see Hebrews 1:3). The fact that He sat down means that His work was finished and He entered God's rest. Through faith we are in Him, and we are also seated in heavenly places with Him. We have an opportunity daily to enter God's rest. We can work from a position of being seated. We can parent from a position of rest. We can run a business or pastor a church from a position of rest. We don't have to worry, fret, and be anxious, but we can trust God and enter His amazing rest!

When I sit in a chair, all my weight is taken off of me and goes onto the chair. If we imagine Christ as our chair, we can be relieved of weights and burdens by casting our care on Him. He has promised to take care of us and meet our needs, and we see that promise fulfilled in our lives as we believe, trust, and place our faith and confidence in Him and His Word.

I urge you to "sit down" and enter the rest of God. Be at rest internally. Let your mind and emotions rest by trusting God to do what needs to be done in you and in your life. Talk to God about anything that concerns you, let your petitions be made known to Him, thank Him that He is working in your life, and enjoy your day! If you begin to feel frustrated and weary at any time, just remind yourself that you need to take your place in Christ and rest in Him.

Prayer: Father, I am so privileged to be seated in heavenly places with You. Let this be a reality to me every day of my life. Teach me to do all that I do from a position of resting in You.

⁕ Heaven ⁕

And not only the creation, but we ourselves too, who have and enjoy the firstfruits of the [Holy] Spirit [a foretaste of the blissful things to come] groan inwardly as we wait for the redemption of our bodies [from sensuality and the grave, which will reveal] our adoption (our manifestation as God's sons). ROMANS 8:23

The Lord has been leading me to study eternity and Heaven, and I find it to be very encouraging. It seems that it will be more wonderful than we could possibly understand. God has planted eternity in our hearts (see Ecclesiastes 3:11). We seem to long for something better than what we experience here on earth. Even though we taste of the good things to come through our relationship with God, the Bible says that is only a down payment (see Ephesians 1:14).

Eternity is the place where time never ends, and each of us will slip into eternity when our time on this earth is finished. Believers in Jesus Christ will go to Heaven, and although there is a lot we don't know about it, the Word of God does tell us many encouraging things.

There will be no more crying or tears, no pain, sickness, or disease. There will be no sin or misery of any kind. We will know everything in Heaven, and we will love everybody. It is a beautiful city, with a crystal sea that flows out from the throne of God. The streets are made of pure gold, and the walls are decorated with precious stones of all kinds. Twelve gates give entrance to the city, and each one is made of one pearl! Even better than the beauty of the city is that we will live in the actual presence of God—He will be the light of the city.

Looking forward to eternity with God was what enabled the

early Christians to go through the persecution they suffered with such amazing faith, and it will also strengthen us. No matter how challenging life may be at times, we do look forward to the reward of Heaven. Let's enjoy the life we have now while looking forward to the good things to come!

Prayer: Father, I am grateful for my life now, and I look forward to spending eternity in Heaven with You. Thank You for all that You have done for me through Jesus!

May 8

⁕ Stay Happy ⁕

Rejoice in the Lord always [delight, gladden yourselves in Him]; again I say, Rejoice! PHILIPPIANS 4:4

Everything God's Word says is very important, but when I see something repeated twice in the same sentence, I pay extra attention. Paul said two times, "Rejoice in the Lord." I believe joy is the fuel we need to stay strong. According to Nehemiah, the joy of the Lord is our strength (see Nehemiah 8:10). When Satan attacks us in any way, it is more an attack aimed at stealing our joy than anything else. Jesus died that we might have joy (see John 10:10), but Satan works to steal it. We can maintain an attitude of joy in all circumstances if we will focus on Jesus rather the problem. Even if you are going through something right now, you can rejoice that you are *going through*, and you will come out victorious.

> Not all storms are in the forecast, but above the clouds the sun is always shining.

Speak this: I refuse to let the devil steal my joy. Jesus died so I could have it, and I will not give it up!

⁕ "If Only" ⁕

Moreover [let us also be full of joy now!] let us exult and triumph in our troubles and rejoice in our sufferings, knowing that pressure and affliction and hardship produce patient and unswerving endurance.

ROMANS 5:3

We often think that we could be happy "if only" we had fewer problems, or more advantages, but it is very unwise to put off being happy. Be full of joy now, because "now" is all that you have. We all hope for many tomorrows, but today is our only guarantee. This day is a gift from God and it would be tragic to waste it being unhappy.

Even if your circumstances are unable to provide your joy, let Jesus be your joy. Just imagine having your problems and not knowing Him! None of us enjoy dealing with painful situations in life, but we can rejoice and trust God's promise to work something good out of them (see Romans 8:28). We live in a world where the sin principle is at work, and we should face the fact that nothing is perfect here and it never will be.

God invites us into a life where, although we cannot avoid all difficulty, we can find a place in Him to live above it. The Bible calls it resurrection power! (See Philippians 3:10.) I urge you not to waste your time thinking that you would be joyful "if only" things were different in your life. Serve the Lord with gladness and always remember that the joy of the Lord is your strength!

Prayer: Father, You have given me many blessings and I want to always be joyful for You and what You have done for me. Forgive me when I put off being joyful until another time, and help me to always rejoice now!

✷ Be Careful About What You Say! ✷

I will not talk with you much more, for the prince (evil genius, ruler) of the world is coming. And he has no claim on Me. [He has nothing in common with Me; there is nothing in Me that belongs to him, and he has no power over Me.] JOHN 14:30

God frequently reminds me to be careful about what I say, especially when I am under pressure. Our Scripture for today reveals that at the time Jesus was entering His greatest suffering, He told the disciples that He wouldn't be talking much. I have always found that very interesting. He knew the power of words and apparently also knew how tempting it would be to say unwise things during difficult times.

Satan had no part in Him, and He wasn't going to give Satan an open door through speaking things that didn't agree with His Heavenly Father.

Are you going through difficulty right now? If so, make a decision to talk less and you might save yourself some trouble. Hold fast your confession of faith in God at all times (see Hebrews 10:23). Remember that the power of life and death are in the tongue (see Proverbs 18:21), and speak life at all times!

Prayer: Father, please help me speak words that are filled with life today and every day!

⁕ Specific Prayer ⁕

Do not fret or have any anxiety about anything, but in every circumstance and in everything, by prayer and petition (definite requests), with thanksgiving, continue to make your wants known to God. PHILIPPIANS 4:6

Prayer is not a religious obligation that we do out of duty, but a tremendous privilege. We are invited to come boldly to God and ask specifically for what we need and want, not only for ourselves, but we can intercede for others and their needs. I recommend putting some thought into what you want God to do for you and go to Him in faith with your requests.

I think sometimes we are afraid to be really specific in our requests, but God invites us to bring definite requests. If we ask amiss, God will not give us our request (see James 4:3, NKJV), but we don't need to be so afraid that we might be wrong in what we want that we don't even ask. You need not have fear in your relationship with God. He loves you, He understands you even better than you understand yourself, and He wants you to be completely confident and comfortable with Him.

My children are not shy about asking me for what they want, and they usually get it unless I feel it would not be good for them. We can trust God to be the same way with us. Knowing we are loved sets us free to be bold. Ask and receive that your joy may be full (see John 16:24).

Prayer: Father, thank You for the amazing privilege of prayer. Teach me to pray confidently and boldly, knowing that You love me and want me to be blessed.

May 12

⁕ Keeping God in First Place ⁕

Little children, keep yourselves from idols (false gods)—[from anything and everything that would occupy the place in your heart due to God, from any sort of substitute for Him that would take first place in your life]. 1 JOHN 5:21

We can make an idol out of just about anything or anyone. It could be a spouse, a child, a good friend, something you own, your home, or your career. When anything becomes more important to us than God, who always deserves first place in our lives, we must aggressively deal with it; we must put it back where it belongs. For example, if it happens to be your career, you would be better off to change careers if keeping the one you have means it takes you away from God. Keep in mind that one day everything on this earth will pass away, so don't spend your life worshipping something that is always in the process of turning to dust!

> God is the Alpha and the Omega, the Beginning and the End, and He must also be everything in between.

Speak this: I will not let anything take first place in my life other than God, and I will make any change necessary to be sure that is where He always stays.

✱ Righteousness ✱

God made him who had no sin to be sin for us, so that in him we might become the righteousness of God. 2 CORINTHIANS 5:21 (NIV)

Do you feel all wrong about yourself? I know that I did for much of my life, and it made me totally miserable. I frustrated myself trying to do lots of good things in hopes that I might feel better about myself, but it was never a permanent solution.

God offers us a new way of living through faith in Jesus Christ. He offers us righteousness as a gift, to be received through faith. We can feel right about ourselves, not because we do everything right, but because we have been made right by an act of God's great grace and mercy. The minute you believe this truth, the burden you've been carrying will lift off of you, and peace and joy will come.

Your sins were all paid for when Jesus took them upon Himself and took the punishment that you deserved when He died on the cross. See yourself washed clean and viewed by God as being right with Him. Believe God's Word more than you believe anything else and start living a brand-new way!

Prayer: Father, thank You for Your great grace. Help me receive it by faith and live without condemnation.

⁕ How to Resist Temptation ⁕

And when He came to the place, He said to them, Pray that you may not [at all] enter into temptation. LUKE 22:40

The disciples were instructed to pray that they would not *enter* temptation; they were not told to pray that they would not be tempted! Temptation comes to us all, and as a matter of fact, God's Word says that temptation is sure to come (see Luke 17:1). Even Jesus was tempted and yet He never sinned (see Hebrews 4:15). Temptation is not a sin if it is properly resisted!

We resist through prayer and discipline. One doesn't work without the other. We don't have enough discipline to resist on our own without God's help. We should pray and ask Him for help—for strength and grace—to overcome temptation, and when it does come, be prepared to resist and stand against it. God won't do it all for us, and we cannot do it all without Him. We are partners with God, and He is willing to help us with all temptation that we face if we ask Him.

No temptation comes to us that is beyond our ability to resist, because God always provides the way out (see 1 Corinthians 10:13). Know your weaknesses and pray diligently that when you are tempted, you will not enter into temptation!

Prayer: Father, thank You for making me strong to stand against temptation. Help me recognize and resist all temptation to sin!

✷ You Are Special ✷

So God created man in His own image, in the image and likeness of God He created him; male and female He created them.

GENESIS 1:27

You are special because you are made in the image of God. Nothing else on the earth—not trees or plants, fish or animals—was made in God's image, only man! God has free will and He has given us free will. We get to make choices about what we will do with our lives. Since you are created in the image of God, nothing can ever truly satisfy you but God. Serve Him with your whole heart, and remember that God carefully created you with His own hand in your mother's womb (see Psalm 139:13), and you are special!

You aren't weird because you aren't like other people—you are unique! And unique things have great value!

Speak this: God created me with a purpose and I am special!

May 16

⁕ Gratitude ⁕

At all times and for everything giving thanks in the name of our Lord Jesus Christ to God the Father. EPHESIANS 5:20

A thankful person is a happy person! If we want to increase our joy, all we really need to do is think more about what we have to be grateful for. Sadly, it is easy to fall into the habit of thinking about what we want, what we don't have, or what other people have that we wish we had. But that doesn't please God, and it steals our joy.

God's Word teaches that we should be anxious for nothing, and to pray about everything, with thanksgiving (see Philippians 4:6). I doubt that God has any interest in giving us more if we are already complaining about what we have or don't have. It seems to me that the more thankful and appreciative we are for what God has already done for us, the more He would be inclined to do. Think of five things today you have to be thankful for and voice your gratitude to God.

Prayer: Father, I am sorry for the times I've complained about my life. I am blessed, and I ask You to help me remember how good You are to me at all times.

✷ Be Excellent ✷

Whatever may be your task, work at it heartily (from the soul), as [something done] for the Lord and not for men. COLOSSIANS 3:23

Being excellent simply means that we do the best we can with what we have. God is excellent, and He has called us to be excellent also. So we should never be satisfied to just do what we have to do in order to get by. We should always go the extra mile and do an excellent job at whatever we are tasked to do.

Mediocrity seems to be normal in society today, but it isn't the will of God. If we are going to do a job, we can and should give it our best. We can take excellent care of all that we have. We can have excellent attitudes, treat people as valuable, and realize that we represent God at all times.

It is important not only to do the best you can when people are watching, but to do so when nobody is watching. God sees all that we do and we would be wise to remember that our reward comes from Him.

Prayer: Father, I know that You are excellent in all Your ways. Help me be an excellent person who brings glory to You.

May 18

⁕ Be Yourself ⁕

Having gifts (faculties, talents, qualities) that differ according to the grace given us, let us use them... ROMANS 12:6

I wasted many years of my life trying to be someone I wasn't. Due to insecurity, I tried to be like other people who had qualities and gifts that I did not have, and it was a waste of time. God will never help us be anyone but ourselves, so I encourage you to learn to be the best "you" that you can be!

God created you with His own hand carefully and intricately (Psalm 139:13–15). You are not a mistake! By God's design we are all different, and we need not compare ourselves with others or compete with them. I encourage you to stop looking at what you think you are not, and start seeing the gifts God has given to you and begin to use them.

We all have a part in God's amazing plan, and each of us is important. As long as we don't try to go beyond the grace (ability) God has given to us, we will be happy, fruitful, and enjoy our lives.

Prayer: Father, help me be the best me that I can be. Help me focus on my strengths and trust You to work through my weaknesses.

✷ Things Will Work Out ✷

And we know that all things work together for good to those who love God, to those who are the called according to His purpose.

ROMANS 8:28 (NKJV)

God wants to encourage you today to know that the things going on in your life right now that are not good or that you don't understand will work out for good! What is happening may not be good, but God is good, and because He is good, He can take a bad, unjust, or even tragic situation and work it out for good.

The painful things in life are only part of the ingredients in our life. There are other ingredients coming that, when mingled with the ones already present, will combine for a good outcome. Believe that you are on your way to good things!

Your pain will become your gain if you trust God.

Speak this: No matter what happens in my life, God will work all things out for good!

May 20

✷ Reasoning ✷

Lean on, trust in, and be confident in the Lord with all your heart and mind and do not rely on your own insight or understanding.

PROVERBS 3:5

Why?" seems to be the question that never goes away! There are many things that happen in life that we don't understand—that seem unjust, unfair, and even tragic. These are not times to confuse and frustrate ourselves through reasoning about things that are beyond our capacity to grasp mentally. These are times to trust God! Faith is not only for the things we do understand, but even more so for those that we don't understand. A life of faith requires some unanswered questions.

We live forward, but we only understand life backward. There are many perplexing things that we go through, and although we don't understand "why" at the time, we are often able to look back on them later in life and see more clearly. Whatever you might be going through right now, I urge you to find peace through trusting God without borders. We should not trust God until something happens that we don't understand and then lean on our own understanding; we should trust God *especially* when we don't understand. He sees all things from beginning to end and He is good, even when our circumstances are not!

Prayer: Father, help me trust You, especially when things happen that I don't understand.

✷ Standing Strong ✷

... Stand your ground on the evil day [of danger], and, having done all [the crisis demands], to stand [firmly in your place].

EPHESIANS 6:13

We are exhorted in God's Word to stand strong in Him at all times. When things are going well in our lives that is easy to do, but when difficulty and perhaps even crisis comes, our faith is tested. With God's help, we can always do what He leads us to do and then stand, which means to abide in Him and enter His rest concerning our situations.

We are limited in our ability to change things, but all things are possible with God. He can do in one moment what we could not do in a lifetime. God is faithful, and if we continue believing, we can be assured that He continues working in our behalf.

It is good for you to enjoy your life while God is working on your problems! Joy, laughter, and rejoicing give you strength to stand strong until your breakthrough comes. While Paul was in prison he said, "Rejoice in the Lord always... again I say, Rejoice!" (Philippians 4:4.)

Prayer: Father, help me be strong in You at all times. Help me enjoy every moment that You give me as I enter Your amazing rest.

✷ God Is Leading You ✷

And your ears will hear a word behind you, saying, This is the way; walk in it, when you turn to the right hand and when you turn to the left. ISAIAH 30:21

You might be trusting God to lead you, but it is time to graduate from believing that God *will* lead you to believing that He *is* leading you. I think that far too often we are so focused on what we hope God will do someday that we fail to see what He is doing right now. God is moving in your life today, so get excited and start moving with Him.

Each day, say several times, "I believe that God is leading me right now!" He might do so through something as simple as putting a thought in your mind about a direction you should take or having a friend say something that confirms what you were thinking of doing. Watch for God... He is working!

Where God guides, He always provides!

Speak this: God is leading me today, and I hear His voice.

✷ Facing Unexpected Storms ✷

And a furious storm of wind [of hurricane proportions] arose, and the waves kept beating into the boat, so that it was already becoming filled. MARK 4:37

Not all storms are in the forecast. Last week I started a four-session teaching seminar in Colorado, and after the first session, I noticed I had a sore throat. Each session it got worse, and by the final one I sounded like a squeaky mouse! Having very little voice power and facing a few thousand people who have come to hear you speak is not fun.

Things don't always work out the way we would like them to, but it is during those times that we need to continue trusting God and believe that He will work good out of our difficulty. I was teaching on the topic "Running Our Race and Finishing Strong," which is rather humorous if you think about it! I decided to squeak through the final message, and it turned out better than it would have if I had been completely well.

Don't get distracted by the storms of life. Stay focused and do what you need to do whether it is easy or difficult. The more we use our faith, the stronger it will become!

Prayer: Father, I thank You for Your strength in my weakness. When stormy circumstances come, help me stay focused on You and Your will for me.

⁕ Put On Righteousness ⁕

Stand therefore, having girded your waist with truth, having put on the breastplate of righteousness. EPHESIANS 6:14 (NKJV)

Satan is called the accuser of the brethren (see Revelation 12:10, NKJV), and so he is. He strives to make us feel guilty and condemned, and he wants us to carry the reproach of shame and blame. Thankfully, Jesus has provided us with righteousness (right standing with God) through our faith in Him.

We have been given righteousness, but we must put it on. That means we purposely wear it as a robe of confidence. Satan wants to separate us from fellowship with God. He wants us to shrink back in fear, but God invites us to come boldly to His throne (see Hebrews 4:16) and receive all the help we need for every situation in life. God helps us even though we make mistakes!

You are forgiven, and God remembers your sin no more (see Hebrews 10:17). Ask and receive, that your joy may be full (see John 16:24).

Prayer: Father, I am grateful that You sent Jesus to pay for my sins and to provide me with right standing with You. Help me confidently wear my robe of righteousness at all times!

⁕ Hold On to Your Dreams ⁕

For a dream comes with much business and painful effort, and a fool's voice with many words. ECCLESIASTES 5:3

Foolish people talk a lot about what they want out of life, but they don't always realize that dreams take time to develop and require lots of hard work and diligence. If you have a dream or a goal for your life (and I pray that you do), then I urge you to be committed and determined not to give up!

"Shooting star" successes rarely last, but things that develop little by little and are accomplished with hard work and patience do last. The foundation-laying years of a successful business, ministry, or life are not necessarily exciting, but they are absolutely necessary if we want something lasting.

Dream big dreams! God is able to do more than we can ask, hope, dream, or think (see Ephesians 3:20), so hold on to your dreams. Don't give up when you get weary or impatient. Endurance and steadfastness are the traits God looks for in His champions.

Prayer: Father, thank You for granting me strong determination and helping me endure whatever comes for the joy of finishing strong!

May 26

✷ *I Will Take Care of You* ✷

Casting all your anxieties on him, because he cares for you.

1 PETER 5:7 (ESV)

The Lord wants you to be confident today and every day that He will take care of you. He will never leave you, not even for one moment. He knows everything there is to know about you, including all of your faults, and He loves you completely anyway.

The Lord has a good plan for you today, and you can rest in the knowledge that all is well. Even if you are going through difficulty in your life right now, know that your Father is in the process of bringing you through it in victory and that all things will work out well in the end.

Go ahead and enjoy the day, because God is in control!

> God sees everything, He knows everything, and He is everywhere all the time.

Speak this: I am confident that God is taking care of me today and every day!

⁕ Choose Obedience ⁕

Then Peter and the apostles replied, We must obey God rather than men. ACTS 5:29

The apostles were being threatened with punishment if they continued to talk about Jesus, but they valued their reputation with God more than their reputation with man. This world is not our home, we are merely passing through, and while we are here it is important that we obey God at all times, even if that means that some people we know won't like our choice.

We will all face times in life when we must choose between doing what a friend or family member wants us to do and doing what we truly believe God wants us to do. Always choose God and strive to keep a clear conscience. Only do what you have peace about doing and you will have a contentment in your soul that no person can give you. Let God guide you and always do now what you will be happy with later on in life!

Prayer: Father, when I have to make a choice between listening to You and listening to people, give me the courage to always choose You and Your will.

May 28

⁕ Keep God First ⁕

But seek first the kingdom of God and his righteousness, and all these things will be added to you. MATTHEW 6:33 (ESV)

Keeping God first in our lives is something we must make an effort to do, because there are many things that try to crowd Him out. They are not always bad things. Sometimes they are good things, but not the best things for us. I have had times when I have let the ministry that God has called me to do to get in front of my personal relationship with Him. I worked *for* God, but wasn't spending much time *with* Him!

The only way our lives work right is if we willingly give God the place that belongs to Him, which is first place in all things. Our time, talent, finances, thoughts, and conversation are just some of the areas we need to keep God first in. Don't make the mistake of asking God to give you something, and when He does, letting the gift take your attention away from the Giver.

People frequently ask me how I keep my priorities straight, since I am a very active and productive person. I tell them, "I am always straightening them out." Take a look quite often at what is first in your life, and if it isn't God, make an adjustment!

Prayer: Father, anytime I let anything come before You in my life, please reveal it to me and help me make an adjustment!

✷ The Most Important Thing ✷

And He replied to him, You shall love the Lord your God with all your heart and with all your soul and with all your mind (intellect).

MATTHEW 22:37

I once heard a great woman of God say, "Love God and then do what you please." My initial thought was that if we all did what we pleased, we would do a lot of bad things. But if we truly love God, that would not be the case. Jesus said, "If you [really] love Me, you will keep (obey) My commands" (John 14:15). Out of our love for God, we want to please Him. We've become sons and daughters, not slaves.

A slave follows all the rules in order not to get into trouble, but sons and daughters learn the Father's heart and delight in pleasing Him. When we find an area of disobedience in our lives, or we feel that we cannot resist temptation to sin, instead of fighting the sin, we have a better option: We can draw closer to God, falling more deeply and intimately in love with Him, recognizing His amazing goodness. Then the sin will not be tempting or attractive. As we draw close to God, we are resisting sin and it finds no place to make its nest in our lives.

Prayer: Father, I want to please You at all times. Draw me to You, and teach me to know You better and to love You more.

✷ Dealing with Conflict ✷

If possible, as far as it depends on you, live at peace with everyone.

ROMANS 12:18

We all experience conflict in relationships at times, and when we do it is important for us to do all we can to restore peace. Conflict or strife left unattended to can ultimately become a major problem. The first thing to do in conflict is to examine your own heart and ask God to reveal your part in the problem. Humble yourself and do your best to make peace with everyone. Being right is highly overrated, but the value of peace can never be overrated. If you are angry with anyone, I urge you to be the peacemaker, for where there is peace, there is power and God's anointing.

The peaceful are the powerful!

Speak this: I will do my best to always be at peace with all people.

⁕ Generosity ⁕

. . . Remembering the words the Lord Jesus himself said: "It is more blessed to give than to receive." ACTS 20:35 (NIV)

Our tendency as human beings is to want to get something. We enjoy it greatly when we are given something. But God's Word teaches us that it is better to give than to get. When we get something, we only get the gift, but when we give something, we get joy! God is a giver, and if we truly desire to be like Him, then it is important that we develop the habit of generosity.

There are many ways to give. We can give help, encouragement, compliments, and material or financial gifts. We can also give mercy and forgiveness freely as God has given it to us. Most good things don't happen accidentally. We can purpose to do them, or "do them on purpose." Make a plan to give something today and every day. Be large-hearted, generous, abundant, and do more than you have to. Purpose to be a blessing everywhere you go, and you will find yourself being more blessed in many ways!

Prayer: Father, teach me to be a generous person at all times. Make me aware of the needs of others, and help me be willing to meet those needs.

June 1

✷ Letting Go of the Past ✷

Do not [earnestly] remember the former things; neither consider the things of old. ISAIAH 43:18

God offers us a new life, a new nature, and a new beginning. God seems to love new things, and His Word encourages us in many places to let go of the past. Perhaps you didn't get a good start in life, but you can have a great finish! God has a plan for your future, and it is a good one. Let go of what is behind you and press toward the good things that are ahead.

One of the best ways to let go is to stop thinking about the past and stop talking about it. The more we think and talk about a thing, the more impossible it is to forget it and move on. Whether your past was wonderful or tragic, it is over, and what you have left is today and the rest of your life! Give yourself fully and completely to the life God is offering you now. Today is the first day of the rest of your life, so make it a good day.

Prayer: Father, thank You for a new beginning. Help me let go of the past and embrace the future with enthusiasm.

✷ Choose Happiness ✷

Rejoice in the Lord always [delight, gladden yourselves in Him]; again I say, Rejoice! PHILIPPIANS 4:4

Something happened yesterday that was making me feel sad and unhappy as I thought about it, and I suddenly heard the Lord whisper, "Don't let anything make you unhappy."

I was reminded of how important joy is! The joy of the Lord strengthens us! Any kind of sadness, whether it is discouragement, depression, grief, or regret, weakens us and distracts us. It causes us to turn inward and meditate on how poorly we feel instead of serving God wholeheartedly.

Part of serving God with our whole heart is enjoying the life He has provided for us. God's Word states that we are to serve Him with gladness (see Psalm 100:2). There are frequently things we can choose to be sad about, but we don't have to be. We can choose to be happy!

Having a choice always means there is more than one option available to us. I urge you to choose to be happy. This is a day that God has given you, so don't waste it being sad!

Prayer: Father, I ask You to forgive me for any of my days I have wasted being sad. Please help me enjoy each day and rejoice in Your goodness to me.

June 3

✷ Getting Out of the Revenge Business ✷

Beloved, never avenge yourselves, but leave the way open for [God's] wrath; for it is written, Vengeance is Mine, I will repay (requite), says the Lord. ROMANS 12:19

When we are treated unjustly, our natural instinct is to want to lash out and hurt the person who hurt us. But God wants us to pray for our enemies and trust Him to repay us and bring justice into our lives.

A heart filled with bitterness and thoughts of revenge is a dangerous thing. It poisons our attitude and steals our peace and joy. Holding a grudge prevents us from growing spiritually and does not benefit us in any way. Let us use wisdom and put our trust wholly in our Lord, who is the rewarder of those who diligently seek Him (see Hebrews 11:6).

Are you holding a grudge, or is the grudge holding you?

Speak this: By the grace of God, I will never avenge myself, but I will trust God to be my Vindicator.

✷ Age Is Just a Number ✷

[Growing in grace] they shall still bring forth fruit in old age; they shall be full of sap [of spiritual vitality] and [rich in the] verdure [of trust, love, and contentment]. PSALM 92:14

Today is my birthday and I am seventy-four, but age is just a number; youth is a mind-set! I've decided I won't be "old." The number of my age will increase each year, but I will never be old!

Paul said that although his outer man was wasting away, his inner man was being progressively renewed day after day (see 2 Corinthians 4:16). Years were being added to his life, but he stayed young inside. He kept growing spiritually, and he continued to bear good fruit all of his life. We can do the same thing.

I have seen a twenty-year-old girl who was old, and I have seen a ninety-year-old woman who was young. It all depends on what is going on inside of you. How do you see yourself?

Keep a young attitude, make changes as you go through life, and don't desperately cling to old things that prevent you from doing new ones. I make plans for the future, and my plan is to never retire! I may rest more, but I will always be doing something that is worth doing.

Make a decision not to think "old," but instead think "young." Keep doing new things and stay on the cutting edge of an exciting life.

Prayer: Father, thank You for helping me always stay young. I trust You to renew my youth as I spend time with You.

⁕ Complete in Christ ⁕

And you are complete in Him, who is the head of all principality and power. COLOSSIANS 2:10 (NKJV)

Most of us feel at times that we should be "doing" more to be acceptable to God, but the truth is that we are made acceptable to God through our faith in Jesus (see Ephesians 2:4–8).

I have often felt that I needed to do or be more than what I am, and yet no matter how much I did, the feeling of being complete was never mine until I finally learned from God's Word that we are "complete" in Jesus. In Him, we are not lacking anything. In ourselves we are bankrupt, but in Him we are all that God requires.

Some disciples asked Jesus what God required in order to be acceptable to Him, and He responded, "This is the work of God, that you believe in Him whom He sent" (John 6:29, NKJV). Oh, how freeing and refreshing it is to finally know that we don't have to continually try to be more than we know how to be. We simply need to know God and put our trust in Him and allow Him to do what He desires to do in and through us.

Prayer: Father, thank You for making me complete through my faith in Jesus. Help me lean on You at all times and trust You in every situation.

⁕ Childlike Faith ⁕

Assuredly, I say to you, unless you are converted and become as little children, you will by no means enter the kingdom of heaven.

MATTHEW 18:3 (NKJV)

We are instructed in God's Word to come to Him as a little child. Children are usually simple in their approach to life, and they are trusting. Recently, my great-grandson, who is two years old, prayed for his mom, who was in bed, crying with back pain. He touched her and prayed this prayer: "Jesus . . . Mommy . . . ouchy . . . Amen!"

The pain left his mother's back right away!

It was not the eloquence of his prayer that got God's attention, but the simplicity and childlike faith that he displayed. God knows what we need before we even ask Him, and He is generous and ready to answer. He just wants us to come in simple, childlike faith and trust that He will do what needs to be done.

Whatever your concerns are today, take them to your Father in Heaven, who loves you with a perfect love, and simply ask for what you need. Release the burden to Him and enjoy your day.

Prayer: Father, I know that I tend to complicate things, but I truly want to enjoy childlike simplicity. Please help me grasp how good You are and how willing You are to help me if I will only ask!

⁕ Refreshed ⁕

He makes me lie down in [fresh, tender] green pastures; He leads me beside the still and restful waters. PSALM 23:2

We all need times of refreshing! We need times to step away from the ordinary routine of daily life and find a way to rest. I just finished taking five days away from my normal routine and did a variety of things that I enjoyed and that left me refreshed and ready to go back to work. I want to encourage you to schedule time like this into your life on a regular basis. It might be one day occasionally, or a few days every three months, but you need times of refreshing. You will be more productive and much happier if your soul is regularly refreshed.

A weary soul is weak, but rest restores our strength!

Speak this: I live a balanced life, and when I am weary, I take time to be refreshed.

⁕ Resisting the Urge to Move Too Quickly ⁕

The sheep that are My own hear and are listening to My voice; and I know them, and they follow Me. JOHN 10:27

I am a person who makes quick decisions. That can be really good much of the time, but it can also be a problem. Two times in the past two days, I made quick decisions without taking time to pray and see if the Lord had instructions for me, and both times I made decisions that ended up causing stress for myself later.

One time, I confronted a situation too fast and my timing wasn't good, and the other time I committed to do something that I had to back out of later. God corrected me for those actions, and I am glad that He did. When God corrects us, it is because He loves us and wants us to have the best life possible. Don't shrink from the chastening of the Lord, but welcome it as a sign of His care for you (see Hebrews 12:5–7).

God always wants to guide us, but the only way we can know if He approves or disapproves of an action we intend to take is if we wait a little while and see if we have peace or not. He usually lets us know within a short period of time, but He may be slower than we would like. If you tend to move too fast, slow down just a little when you have decisions to make and you will surely save yourself a lot of stress and difficulty.

Prayer: Father, please help me move in Your timing, not mine! Thank You for loving me enough to correct me when I need it.

June 9

✷ Greater Faith ✷

Yes, though I walk through the [deep, sunless] valley of the shadow of death, I will fear or dread no evil, for You are with me...

PSALM 23:4

When we experience trials in life, we usually ask God to deliver us from them. We want them to go away, and that is understandable. God often does deliver us as we stand in faith, but there are also times when He chooses to take us through them, and that requires a greater faith. It is easy on our emotions when we get what we want, but it requires great faith in God and steadfastness if we don't.

Whether God delivers us from something difficult or gives us the grace to go through it is up to Him, and we should receive His choice graciously, knowing that His way is always best. We receive strength in the struggle! When life is easy, we don't really make spiritual progress, but when we must stand firm, we grow!

We live life forward, but we understand it backward. In other words, we usually don't understand the "why" when we must go through a thing that is difficult, but we often do understand later on in life.

Be patient with God's choices and trust Him. His way is not our way, but it is *always* the best way!

Prayer: Father, I commit my way to You and I trust that You will work all things out for my good!

✷ Blessed Through Obedience ✷

But He said, Blessed (happy and to be envied) rather are those who hear the Word of God and obey and practice it. LUKE 11:28

I believe that God wants me to encourage you to take action and be obedient to anything He is asking you to do. Whether His instructions come from your study of His Word, or you feel He has put something specific on your heart that you are to do or not to do, it is important to obey. Blessings are always attached to obedience, and He doesn't want you to miss out on His best for you. Even if being obedient is difficult, it is worth it, not only for the sake of maintaining a clean conscience, but especially to honor God and show how much you love Him.

One act of obedience is better than a thousand good intentions!

Speak this: Because I love Jesus, I will obey Him, and He will bless me as He has promised to do.

✷ Relax ✷

Then they said to Him, "What shall we do, that we may work the works of God?"

Jesus answered and said to them, "This is the work of God, that you believe in Him whom He sent." JOHN 6:28–29 (NKJV)

Do you ever feel that no matter what you do, you should be doing something more? I know I have felt that way, and I have to remind myself that God is not pleased with me based on what *I* do, but on what *Jesus has done*!

The truth is that no matter what we do, it will never be enough, and that is why God sent His Son. He is not only enough, He is more than enough! Our goal should be to remain in faith at all times, and to avoid doing things in order to try to earn from God what He gives us freely by His grace.

Let us always do what we do for God to show our love for Him, and never to buy His love for us. God is not for sale!

Relax! Enter the rest of God, and refuse to live under the pressure of constantly feeling that you need to be "doing" something in order to be acceptable to God.

Prayer: Father, help me stay relaxed in my life and always remember that Your acceptance of me is not based on my record of good works but on receiving Your grace by faith. You are more than enough! Thank You!

✷ Avoid Strife ✷

He who has knowledge spares his words, and a man of understanding is of a calm spirit. PROVERBS 17:27 (NKJV)

Throughout Proverbs, there are frequent references to avoiding strife by being careful about what we say. We are encouraged to use excellent speech, to think before we speak, and not to talk too much.

Strife is said to be bickering, arguing, heated disagreement, and an angry undercurrent. God's Word teaches us that it is very dangerous and displeasing to God. Wrong words spoken in haste are very often the beginning of strife.

God's presence and blessing abide where there is unity, not strife and turmoil, so we should do all we can to remain peaceful at all times. God has changed me over the years, and I now prefer to be peaceful rather than right in situations that don't really matter anyway. Being right is highly overrated! We often get into arguments with people in an effort to prove them wrong and ourselves right, but it doesn't do any good except to perhaps feed our ego.

Peace is one of the most valuable things we can have, so let's do all we can to protect ours!

Prayer: Father, forgive me for the unwise words I have spoken that ended up causing strife. Help me do what I need to do to live in peace at all times!

⁕ Give People Freedom ⁕

Why do you stare from without at the very small particle that is in your brother's eye but do not become aware of and consider the beam of timber that is in your own eye? MATTHEW 7:3

Sometimes people make decisions that we don't agree with, but we must remember that each person has a right to make their own choices. It is especially difficult when the decision that they make affects us in some way that we don't like.

That happened to me recently, and although it has been difficult, I do realize that it is important for people to follow their own heart. If we want freedom, we need to give freedom!

Dave and I spent years trying to change each other before we realized how vital it is to let people be themselves and trust God to do whatever changing needs to be done. Are you trying to change anyone in your life? You can avoid a lot of frustration over the years if you will realize now that only God can change people! You can pray that God will give people a desire to change, and that He will help them change, but you cannot change them.

Prayer: Father, help me mind my own business and not get upset when other people make decisions that I don't like.

✷ Treat Everyone Equally ✷

My brethren, pay no servile regard to people [show no prejudice, no partiality] . . . JAMES 2:1

I have learned in my life that it is important to God that we treat all people with respect and honor. They are all equally loved and valued by Him, and we should do the same. We have a tendency to treat people better if we think they may be able to do something for us, or if they are seen as important in the eyes of the world, but that isn't the way God desires for us to behave. God "shows no partiality" (Acts 10:34) and He is good to all people. As you go about your daily business, strive to be good and respectful to everyone you come in contact with, remembering that each of them is important to God.

People may not always remember what you said, but they will remember how you made them feel.

Speak this: I will always strive to treat all people respectfully and remember that they are important to God.

✷ *When You Are Dealing with Pain* ✷

He was despised and rejected and forsaken by men, a Man of sorrows and pains, and acquainted with grief and sickness...

ISAIAH 53:3

If you are in pain of any kind, Jesus knows how you feel! I hurt my back three days ago and I have been in a lot of pain. I have received some medical help, but my faith is in God for complete healing. Always remember that all healing comes from Jesus. He is our compassionate Healer! He may work through some type of medical care, but He and He alone is the source of healing!

Even though we seek professional help when we are sick or in pain, we should keep our eyes on Jesus to make us whole, and when we are well again, be sure to give Him the praise. Thank God in the midst of trouble, and trust and thank Him that His healing power is working in you. God's Word says to thank Him at all times, in all things (see 1 Thessalonians 5:18). You may not be thankful for your pain and discomfort, but you can be thankful that God is with you and that He will cause all things to work together for your good as you continue loving Him and doing His will (see Romans 8:28).

When you are sick, it is an especially good time to pray for others you may know who are sick. During our own pain, we tend to have greater compassion for others who are also hurting. Prayer is sowing seed into the lives of others, and seed always produces a harvest. So keep on trusting God and expect to get better and better every day!

Prayer: Father, I ask You to heal me from all sickness, pain, and disease. I trust You to be my healer and I give You praise for my restoration.

✷ Receive Mercy ✷

Let us then fearlessly and confidently and boldly draw near to the throne of grace (the throne of God's unmerited favor to us sinners), that we may receive mercy [for our failures] and find grace to help in good time for every need... HEBREWS 4:16

God is full of mercy and loving-kindness! He is extending His mercy to you right now, but you must believe it and receive it in order for it to benefit you. When we sin, we don't need to punish ourselves, because Jesus already took our punishment and He now offers us His mercy. Amazing!

Mercy would not be mercy if it could be deserved, because it is said to be kindness that exceeds what could be expected. If you are suffering from guilt, shame, and condemnation, God is reaching out to you now and offering you mercy. Don't turn away because you know you don't deserve it. Receive it and let it make you fall more in love with Jesus than ever before.

We need mercy every day, and God has provided it because His Word says that His mercy is new every day and His faithfulness is great and abundant (see Lamentations 3:23). Our sin will never exceed God's mercy because where sin abounds, grace abounds much more (see Romans 5:20).

Prayer: Father, thank You very much for Your amazing mercy. Teach me how to receive not only mercy but also all of Your gracious benefits.

Resist the Devil

So be subject to God. Resist the devil [stand firm against him], and he will flee from you. JAMES 4:7

Although people don't necessarily enjoy thinking about the devil, it would be a mistake to not be aware of his attacks and strategies. He is the source of all evil and wages war on God's kingdom and God's people. We have authority over him, but authority that is not used becomes useless. Jesus rebuked and resisted the devil, and we need to do the same thing.

We don't need to live our lives with our mind on the devil, but we do need to be discerning concerning his attacks and be ready to resist him. God's Word teaches us to resist the devil at his onset (see 1 Peter 5:9) and to be firm in faith. Don't be passive and unaware of your enemy!

Some things I advise you to watch for are temptations to sin, any kind of strife or offense, and any unresolved anger or unforgiveness toward others. These are all tactics of the devil designed to bring disunity with God and people. Satan is the instigator of turmoil. He sets us up to be upset! One of the best ways to resist him is to always walk in peace with God, yourself, and other people.

Prayer: Father, thank You for giving me authority over the devil. Grant me discernment to always recognize his work and to resist him immediately in Your name!

✷ Nothing Is Hidden from God ✷

Nothing in all creation is hidden from God's sight. Everything is uncovered and laid bare before the eyes of him to whom we must give account.
HEBREWS 4:13 (NIV)

If we would keep in mind that God sees everything we do all the time and that nothing is hidden from Him, it might motivate us toward better behavior! Would we gossip about others if we kept in mind that God is listening? Would we mistreat others if we remembered that God was watching? It is wise to remember that one day we will all give account to God of our behavior, so let us live now as if we believe that He is watching, because He is!

There is not one thing that is ever hidden from God.

Speak this: I will do my best at all times to live and behave as if I truly believe that God is watching.

✷ Guess Who Loves You! ✷

For great is Your mercy and loving-kindness toward me...

PSALM 86:13

God loves you! Don't let any difficulty that comes your way, no matter how much it hurts or how long it lasts, make you think that God doesn't love you.

The devil wants to deceive us and make us believe God doesn't love us, but he can't do it if we know the truth! We are encouraged in the Bible to let nothing separate us from God's love. And nothing in life, no matter how threatening or difficult—not even death itself—should separate us from the love of God (see Romans 8:38–39).

Knowing that you are loved gives you confidence and enables you to enjoy your life, and the devil doesn't want that. He wants you to cower in fear and be miserable at all times. Lift your head up today and boldly declare, "God loves me!" Speak it out of your mouth and meditate on it throughout the day. God's love is unconditional, and that means that even your sins and failures never prevent Him from loving you!

Prayer: Father, thank You for Your amazing love. Help me be fully aware of Your love and walk in the confidence it gives me at all times.

✱ Let Go of Fret ✱

Cease from anger and forsake wrath; fret not yourself—it tends only to evildoing. PSALM 37:8

God's will for us is peace, but in order to have it, we must avoid fretting over things that don't go the way we would like them to. Worry, anxiety, and fretfulness are all from the same family of torments. They are designed by the devil to steal our peace and cause us to waste our time. Fretting over a thing never improves it. It doesn't change it, but it does change us. When we fret and worry, we become irritable and self-absorbed in our problems, and we lose sight of the blessings that we have.

As I look through my journals, I find peppered throughout opportunities to worry over first one thing and then another. The opportunities it seems are endless, but it is up to me whether I say yes or no to worry. I cannot prevent the devil from tempting me, but I can resist the temptation and save myself a lot of trouble and misery.

If you are fretting over anything today, you have an opportunity to cast your care on God and watch Him take care of you. He cares about everything that concerns you and is waiting for you to invite Him to go to work in your behalf. Don't waste your time and energy fretting, because "it tends only to evildoing," as the Scripture says. You can have a great day even in the midst of difficulty by simply trusting God and waiting expectantly to see Him work in your behalf.

Prayer: Father, forgive me for the time I have wasted fretting over things that I cannot change. Right now I say no to worry and I wait on You. Thank You for helping me!

✷ Healing ✷

There are those who speak rashly, like the piercing of a sword, but the tongue of the wise brings healing. PROVERBS 12:18

I am recovering from a hip replacement surgery, and I have been amazed to watch the healing power of God work in my body. It has only been three weeks since the surgery, and I have very little pain and am walking quite well.

If you are in need of healing in your body, I encourage you to believe that God is working in you right now and that every day you are getting better and better in every way. God has placed healing power inside of us, but it is important that we cooperate with it. Use wisdom, get the rest you need, take care of yourself, and be very positive in how you talk about your physical condition.

Use wisdom with your words and talk about how you believe God is working His healing in you, instead of talking about how bad you feel and giving voice to all kinds of unfounded fears. God has a good plan for you, including healing in all areas of your life, but in order to have God's will, we need to agree with Him.

The power of life and death is in the tongue (see Proverbs 18:21), and with each word that we speak, one or the other is released. You have the ability to release God's power in your life today by speaking words of life. God's healing power is working in you right now—believe it and speak it and watch yourself get better each day.

Prayer: Father, I thank You for healing me. I trust that You are working in me right now and that every day I get better and better in every way.

✷ Stir Up Your Gift ✷

Therefore I remind you to stir up the gift of God which is in you through the laying on of my hands. For God has not given us a spirit of fear, but of power and of love and of a sound mind.

2 TIMOTHY 1:6–7 (NKJV)

Have you let your problems cause you to lose focus on your gifts and talents? Are you so busy dealing with challenging people and circumstances that you have stopped developing, or perhaps even using, the gifts that God has placed in you? If so, you are playing right into the devil's hands. You see, he doesn't want you to use the abilities God has given to you, but he does want you to lose them. He doesn't want the rest of us to benefit from your capabilities!

I felt that I should encourage you today to stir up your gift. Be responsible to do what God shows you to do about your problems, but then cast your care on Him and get back to your true purpose in life.

Learn to live life on purpose for a purpose every day!

Speak this: I will develop and use the gifts and abilities that God has placed in me.

June 23

⁕ When Things Don't Go As Planned ⁕

O keep me, Lord, and deliver me; let me not be ashamed or disappointed, for my trust and my refuge are in You. PSALM 25:20

Learning to properly deal with disappointment is part of spiritual maturity. We all experience disappointment in our lives, but we can make a decision to get "reappointed," to let go of what didn't work out for us and focus on something new. For example, if I planned to go to lunch with a friend and she had to cancel, I can either spend the day disappointed because my plan didn't work out, or I can pray about what else God might want me to do and believe my steps are ordered by the Lord.

Our disappointment doesn't come as much from our circumstances as it does from our misplaced believing. Trusting God is something we can choose to do all the time, especially when things don't work out the way we planned. Proverbs 16:9 says, "A man's mind plans his way, but the Lord directs his steps . . . " If we believe that, then it is not difficult to let go of our disappointment and believe that God has something better in mind for us than what we knew to plan or ask for.

Even when we are disappointed in ourselves, we can trust God to help us learn from our mistakes and do better in the future. Don't let disappointment rule your emotions. God has a good plan for you even if you don't know what it is, so trust Him and go ahead and have a good day.

Prayer: Father, help me put my trust in You at all times, especially when things in my life don't work out the way I planned. I cast my care on You and wait on Your plan to develop in my life.

⁕ Thankful ⁕

Thank [God] in everything [no matter what the circumstances may be, be thankful and give thanks], for this is the will of God for you [who are] in Christ Jesus [the Revealer and Mediator of that will]. 1 THESSALONIANS 5:18

I am convinced that being thankful is one of the most powerful things we can do. I believe that complaining and murmuring weakens us, but gratitude empowers us. Very few days are perfect, but every day we can find something to be thankful for if we will only look.

I am recovering from a hip replacement surgery, and for the past nine days, I have had a stomach virus (yuck!). But at the same time, I can truly say that God is giving me grace for each day, and good things are happening. I am recovering from the surgery even faster than normal, and I know that the stomach thing won't last forever. I am full of hope, and that is a good reason to give thanks!

It is important for each of us to realize that everyone goes through difficult times. Our lives are usually a mixture of abasing and abounding (see Philippians 4:12). The apostle Paul said that he had learned to be content either way. I am sure in the learning process he discovered that complaining did no good at all, but thankful contentment allowed him to be unmoved by his circumstances, which is certainly a "power position."

Prayer: Father, I am sorry for all the times in my life I have complained. Please help me to be thankful every day in every situation.

⁕ Be Happy and Enjoy Life ⁕

The thief comes only in order to steal and kill and destroy. I came that they may have and enjoy life, and have it in abundance (to the full, till if overflows). JOHN 10:10

I love to see my children be happy and enjoy their lives, and I believe God feels the same way about His children. I have always been a "worker," and although work is a good thing, it does need to be balanced with rest and play. The society we live in seems to push us to accomplish more and more, and it is easy to fall into the trap of thinking that the more we work and produce, the more valuable we are.

Life is a gift from God and should be thoroughly enjoyed. I really enjoy my work, but I have also learned to enjoy many other aspects of life. I want to serve the Lord with gladness (see Psalm 100:2). My goal is to enjoy *everything* that I do. I am especially learning to enjoy the simple things of life—taking a walk, having a cup of coffee with a friend, looking out the window and watching it snow, listening to good music, and thousands of other things.

I am inviting you to join me in my journey of learning to be happy at all times and enjoying every aspect of life. Together we can serve the Lord with gladness and enjoy Him more than ever before by enjoying the life He has provided for us.

Prayer: Father, thank You for the life You have given me. Help me enjoy it thoroughly each day no matter what I am doing.

✷ Created in God's Image ✷

So God created man is His own image, in the image and likeness of God He created him; male and female He created them.

GENESIS 1:27

The fact that you were created by God means that He wanted you. If you had just evolved from an animal or any other lower life form (as many scientists would have you believe), then you would merely be an accident of nature; you would have no definite divine design. But God does want you—you are special to Him and He designed you carefully and purposely with His own hand in your mother's womb (see Psalm 139:13). He breathed the breath of life into you and has already written in His book all the days of your life. You are loved!

God created you and you are His masterpiece!

Speak this: God created me in His own image. I am special, and I have a God-ordained destiny.

✷ Living Life on Purpose ✷

Therefore do not be vague and thoughtless and foolish, but understanding and firmly grasping what the will of the Lord is.

EPHESIANS 5:17

Are you living the life you truly want to live? If not, is it because you allow your life to rule you instead of you ruling it? When God placed Adam and Eve in the Garden of Eden, He instructed them to subdue it and be fruitful. God has given us a free will and He wants us to use it to choose His will for us. When we make choices according to the will of God, He empowers us to live a life that is truly amazing.

What do you want to accomplish today? Pray, make a plan, stay focused, and go for it! Put your time into what you want to do and don't let circumstances and people derail you. Fight for yourself! Fight for your right to follow your heart instead of being controlled by outside forces.

Be determined; be strong. Don't be vague and thoughtless, but have a plan and work your plan. God, through Christ, has provided a way for us to live an amazing life, but we need to continually make choices that agree with God. You have one life to live, so live it fully and refuse to drift along, letting other people and circumstances make your decisions for you.

Prayer: Father, show me Your will for me and help me be courageous enough to make choices that agree with You. I want the life that You want for me!

⁕ Patience ⁕

For you have need of steadfast patience and endurance, so that you may perform and fully accomplish the will of God, and thus receive and carry away [and enjoy to the full] what is promised.

HEBREWS 10:36

We all have things that we want right now. I am still limping a little bit from my hip surgery and I don't want to. I want to walk perfectly normally *now*! However, the doctor told me yesterday that it would happen but it would take time. How often have we all heard that in our life? "It is going to take time!"

I have two choices: I can wait patiently or I can wait miserably. The choice is mine, but either way I will wait. Patience is not the ability to wait; it is the ability to wait well... to wait with a good attitude and trust God's timing to be perfect. What are you waiting for right now? How are you waiting?

Let's make a decision to honor God by waiting patiently, with a smile on our face, knowing that each day that goes by we are closer to the desire of our heart. God has given us the ability to enjoy all phases of life if we will only decide to do so.

Prayer: Father, help me trust Your timing in my life and honor You by waiting patiently for the fulfillment of my desires.

✷ God Thinks About You ✷

How precious and weighty also are Your thoughts to me, O God! How vast is the sum of them! PSALM 139:17

It is pretty amazing to realize that God thinks about us! His thoughts toward you and me are more in number than the grains of sand (see Psalm 139:18). I am convinced that God has never had even one bad thought about you in your entire life! He believes in us and He always believes the best.

God didn't create us and then throw us out into the world to try and manage on our own. He promised to be with us always and to watch over us with loving care (see Psalm 121:5). His Holy Spirit is our guide through all of our life. Take a moment to remember that God is thinking about you right now!

When everyone else gives up on you, God still believes in you!

Speak this: God has me on His mind, and all of His thoughts about me are good.

✳ Finding Freedom Through Facing Truth ✳

And you will know the Truth, and the Truth will set you free.

JOHN 8:32

God's Word is truth, and living according to it is what sets us free from bondage and misery of every kind. The Holy Spirit is called the Spirit of Truth (see John 16:13), and it is His job to guide us into all truth.

Like most of us, I lived a life of deception for many years. I believed things that were not true according to God's Word, and those things kept me imprisoned in sin, guilt, shame, insecurity, fear, and many other miseries. When I began to seriously study God's Word, and the Holy Spirit started leading me into truth, some of it was very exciting and, to be honest, some of it was very painful.

Hearing that all of my sins were forgiven was exciting, but learning that I was selfish and self-centered was painful. Learning that God wanted to meet all of my needs was exciting, but learning that I had a heart filled with bitterness was painful. In order to find freedom, we cannot just take the parts of God's Word that are exciting—we must be willing to take the parts that may be painful to us personally as the Holy Spirit leads us into truth.

Each thing I learned about myself, although often quite uncomfortable, did indeed move me one step closer to freedom. I urge you not to hide from the truth. Ask the Holy Spirit to guide you into all truth, and when He does, face it boldly and you will be changed!

Prayer: Father, I ask You to guide me into all truth. I want to live truly and have no deception in my life. I trust You to set me free!

✷ Say Goodbye to Guilt ✷

All we like sheep have gone astray, we have turned every one to his own way; and the Lord has made to light upon Him the guilt and iniquity of us all. ISAIAH 53:6

Jesus not only took our iniquity upon Himself, but He also took the guilt, and we are free from both. To believe that our sins are forgiven and then remain guilty and condemned makes it clear that a person does not properly understand God's Word. How can we feel guilty about something that the Bible clearly says God forgives, forgets, and removes as far as the east is from the west? (See Hebrews 10:17–18; Psalm 103:12.)

Feeling guilty is our carnal way of trying to pay for our sins, but we cannot pay for something that has already been paid for. Jesus paid and we are debt free! This does not mean that we don't feel sorry for our sins. We may even feel a grieving in our hearts because of our iniquities, but a guilty condemnation is the devil's tool to keep us from making progress and bearing good fruit for God.

Conviction of sin is from the Holy Spirit and is intended to lift us out of sin, but condemnation is counterproductive because it presses us down and burdens us with feelings of overwhelming guilt.

The only way we can be useful to God is if we know what He has done for us, who we are in Him, and the power that is available to us as believers in Him. Jesus paid for our sins and in Him there is no condemnation (see Romans 8:1). Make a decision to stop wasting precious time and energy feeling guilty about something that God has forgiven and forgotten.

Prayer: Father, thank You for Your great grace and mercy. Your complete forgiveness of my sin is astounding. Help me walk in the freedom that You have provided for me in Jesus.

✷ Fear Not ✷

Fear not [there is nothing to fear], for I am with you . . .

ISAIAH 41:10

I have been dealing with a situation that I definitely don't want to deal with anymore, and this morning, as that same situation presented itself once again, I felt fear grip my heart. The next thing that happened was God interrupting my misery and reminding me that fear is the worst thing I can do. Why? Because fear says I am not sure that God is with me and I don't know if He will help me; therefore, I have to try and handle the situation on my own and I have no idea what to do.

There are numerous places in the Word of God that simply read, "Fear not, for I am with you." God doesn't say what He is going to do or when He will do it; He simply wants it to be sufficient that He is with us, and knowing that, we should be able to trust that all things will turn out well in the end.

We can do all things through Christ who is our strength (see Philippians 4:13), but we have to keep reminding ourselves of that fact when we feel weary and overburdened. "I will not fear" is the believer's only proper response to fear. The next time fear knocks on your door, answer with faith. Know that God loves you and that He is with you and He has a plan even if you don't know what it is.

Prayer: Father, I know that fear will knock on my door, and when it does, let me answer with courage. Make me fully aware of Your presence at all times and let that be enough to overcome fear.

July 3

✷ Chosen by God ✷

Before I formed you in the womb I knew [and] approved of you [as My chosen instrument]... JEREMIAH 1:5

God told Jeremiah that before He chose him to be His prophet, He knew and approved of him. To me, that means that God knew everything Jeremiah would ever do, right or wrong. He knew every mistake that Jeremiah would ever make and still He chose him. This truth should give each of us confidence concerning whether or not we are someone that God can use. God doesn't choose us because of our perfection. If we love Him and are willing to let Him work with and through us, that is all He requires.

God uses what the world sees as worthless.

Speak this: God knows everything there is to know about me, and He still chooses to be in relationship with me.

⁕ Generosity ⁕

. . . Be mindful to be a blessing, especially to those of the household of faith . . . GALATIANS 6:10

Our old nature is greedy, but our new nature as children of God craves to be generous. Each day we must decide which desire we will pursue and follow. Greed steals our lives, according to Proverbs 1:19, so we need to actively resist it. We can never defeat any sin by fighting with it or merely using self-will to resist, but we can overcome it by turning away from it and to something else.

I believe that generosity is the antidote for greed. If we purpose to be generous and live each day looking for ways to be a blessing to others, then we won't be greedy because there will be no place for it in our lives. Start each day by asking God to show you what you can do for Him that day. Ask Him whom you can bless. The world is filled with sad and needy people who crave a kind word or some encouragement, or who have a need that we could easily meet.

The more we do for others, the happier we will be. Instead of being greedy and going through the day trying to get more and more for ourselves, we have another option. We can be generous, and our generosity will give hope and send up cries of thanksgiving to God from those who are blessed.

Prayer: Father, I want to learn more about the beauty and power of generosity. Show me people who are needy today and grant me the grace to help them.

⁕ Decisions ⁕

[For being as he is] a man of two minds (hesitating, dubious, irresolute), [he is] unstable and unreliable and uncertain about everything [he thinks, feels, decides]. JAMES 1:8

Decisions are very difficult for some people to make because they are fearful of making the wrong one. Although I am generally fairly confident, I have had my own experiences with being double-minded and I can verify that it is a miserable place to be. God has taught me that if I make a mistake, He can redeem it, and that we can never be positive we have made the right decisions until we move forward in them and see how things turn out.

I often say, "Step out and find out." The response usually comes back, "What if I make a mistake?" The good news is that mistakes are not the worst thing that can happen in the world, and sometimes they are even good for us. Mistakes can be an education, because we learn what not to do again. Most of us fail our way to success. In other words, we make quite a few mistakes as we travel through life, but if we don't give up, we will reach our destination anyway and will have gained a great deal of humility along the way.

Do the best you can to make a solid decision. Pray about your decision, and consider whether or not what you are doing is wise. Does it give you peace? If your decision is something that has you emotionally excited, let your emotions subside before you finally decide. These are a few guidelines to making good decisions, but when all is said and done, you still have to do something, and it is always better to do something than to spend your life doing nothing because of fear.

Prayer: Father, grant me the courage to be decisive. Guide me in decision-making and help me to move forward with confidence.

✷ Enjoy the Day ✷

Behold, what I have seen to be good and fitting is for one to eat and drink, and to find enjoyment in all the labor in which he labors under the sun all the days which God gives him—for this is his [allotted] part. ECCLESIASTES 5:18

Today is a gift to you from God, and you can choose to enjoy it or to waste it being unhappy. If you are like most of us, I am sure you could find several things to be unhappy about if you just look for them. But I am also sure that being unhappy about them won't change them, so why waste your time? When this day is gone, you can never get it back, so use it wisely and enjoy it fully.

Enjoy the journey because that is what life is all about.

Speak this: I will not waste this day, but I will enjoy it fully and completely.

⁕ One Mouth—Two Ears ⁕

Understand [this], my beloved brethren. Let every man be quick to hear [a ready listener], slow to speak, slow to take offense and to get angry. JAMES 1:19

Most of us will readily admit that our mouths at times have caused us grief and sorrow. If only we would pay attention to the apostle James' encouragement to listen more than we talk, we would be so much better off. I suppose if God had wanted us to talk more than we listen, we would have two mouths and one ear, but that is not the case.

I have always been a big talker and have often committed to listen more and talk less; however, my commitments have been short-lived because the mouth seems to be a wild animal with a mind of its own. The Bible says that no man can tame the tongue (see James 3:8). We need God's help!

I have learned to pray daily about my mouth. I ask God to put a guard on it so I don't sin with my tongue (see Psalm 141:3) and to let the words of my mouth and the meditations of my heart be acceptable to Him (see Psalm 19:14). God's Word is filled with Scriptures about the importance of our words. Let us always remember that we have one mouth and two ears, which is a good indicator that we should listen more than we talk.

Prayer: Father, I cannot tame my own tongue, but I do ask You to help me think before I speak and listen more than I talk.

⁕ Wandering Desire ⁕

Better is the sight of the eyes [the enjoyment of what is available to one] than the cravings of wandering desire . . . ECCLESIASTES 6:9

Instead of letting our desires roam all over the place, wanting first this thing and then another, we should learn to enjoy what we have. Discontentment is a temptation for everyone, but it is a heart filled with gratitude for what we have that God delights in. There is nothing wrong with wanting something, but it is wrong to let the desire for what we want to outweigh the thankfulness for what we have.

Ask God for what you want, but never forget to enjoy what you have.

Speak this: I have thousands of things to be thankful for and I appreciate each of them.

July 9

⁕ Strong in Every Situation ⁕

...Let not your [minds and] hearts faint; fear not, and do not tremble or be terrified [and in dread] because of them.

DEUTERONOMY 20:3

To faint is to relax and loosen our courage and give up. I believe that fainting begins in the mind, because we think about the difficulties we either are in or fear we will be in, and we begin to dread the things we are facing and start to faint.

God wants us to be courageous all the way through every situation, and He never wants us to dread things that are coming up in our lives. Dread is a close relative of fear and it weakens us. When you are tempted to dread, to faint and give up, ask God to strengthen you. He said that those who wait on Him will not faint or grow weary (see Isaiah 40:31).

God never allows more to come on us than we can bear (see 1 Corinthians 10:13), so there is no need to dread things. What we need to do may not be pleasant or easy, but through Christ we can do it!

Prayer: Father, I ask that You keep me strong in every situation. Help me to go all the way through and not to faint or get weary and give up.

⁕ Silence ⁕

Come to Me, all you who labor and are heavy laden, and I will give you rest. Take My yoke upon you and learn from Me, for I am gentle and lowly in heart, and you will find rest for your souls. For My yoke is easy and My burden is light.

MATTHEW 11:28–30 (NKJV)

Our souls need to rest. We need internal rest. Rest from planning, thinking, reasoning, worrying, and all other internal activity. We need solitude and silence and inactivity, but we rarely get enough of it. I must admit that I am not good at doing nothing. I find myself planning what I want to eat, or what I will do with the rest of my week, or how I can entertain myself.

Sometimes God has to make us lie down by still and restful waters (see Psalm 23:2). I have been recovering from a hip replacement surgery, and between not being able to move much and being on pain medicine that dulled my mind as well as my body, I found myself spending large amounts of time sitting and simply looking out the window. This was a novelty for me, but one I actually enjoyed because I got internal rest that I needed.

Try to have some time of complete solitude each week. Sit somewhere beautiful and peaceful and just "be." Believe it or not, we don't always have to "do" something. Actually, if we will take regular time to "be," our "doing" will be more productive!

Prayer: Father, teach me to let my soul rest and not feel I always have to be involved in a flurry of activity.

July 11

✷ *Before It's Too Late* ✷

Lord, remind me how brief my time on earth will be. Remind me that my days are numbered—how fleeting my life is.

PSALM 39:4 (NLT)

There is nothing worse than regretting something we did (or didn't do) when it is too late to do anything about it. I want to encourage you to show appreciation to the people in your life who mean a lot to you, and do it now! Procrastination may have good intentions, but it prevents obedient action. Why put off until later what needs to be done today? It is often the devil's method of causing us to live in regret over things we intended to do but just never got around to. Say "I love you" while you still can. Say "I'm sorry" while there is time. Say "Thank you" for today's blessings today!

Never put off until tomorrow what needs to be done today!

Speak this: I am a person of action, and I don't put off the things I know I need to do.

✷ Be a Blessing Today ✷

But to you who are listening I say: Love your enemies, do good to those who hate you, bless those who curse you, pray for those who mistreat you. LUKE 6:27–28 (NIV)

We have two things to give everyone we come in contact with—the blessing or the curse. If God expects us to bless our enemies, how much more should we be ready and willing to bless our family, friends, and acquaintances? Each of us comes in contact with many people every day, and we have the opportunity to give people what their soul craves. We can bless them! We can do them good with our words, attitudes, time, facial expressions, and material possessions.

Think of it: You can bless people today! You can also curse people, but hopefully we all want to avoid doing that. We can curse a person with something as simple as ignoring them. When we do that, we make them feel belittled and devalued.

A few days ago, I walked into a room where several people had gathered, and right away a man approached me with a friendly greeting; however, I had no interest in talking with him, so I said a very quick hello and moved away. I did what was best for me, but as I look back, I am sure he felt my rejection and disinterest. I could have blessed him by spending a few minutes with him and showing interest in him, but I was too selfish to do it.

I have set a new goal for myself, and that is to be a blessing to everyone I meet. I believe it is the way God wants us to live, and I also believe it is the doorway to personal joy.

Prayer: Father, forgive me for each time I have cursed someone when I could have blessed them. Help me change and be a blessing everywhere I go.

✷ Forgiven ✷

I acknowledged my sin to You, and my iniquity I have not hidden. I said, "I will confess my transgression to the Lord," and You forgave the iniquity of my sin. PSALM 32:5 (NKJV)

Do you acknowledge your sin and ask for forgiveness but still continue to feel guilty? If so, perhaps you don't understand how complete and amazing God's forgiveness is. He not only forgives us, but He forgets our sin (see Isaiah 43:25). I suggest you stop talking to God over and over about things He has forgotten. If you have truly repented, then your sins are definitely forgiven from God's standpoint, but maybe you need to *receive* the forgiveness and forgive yourself! Remember, Jesus took your punishment, so you don't have to punish yourself by feeling guilty and condemned.

God's forgiveness is total and complete...receive it!

Speak this: When I sin, I immediately acknowledge my sin, I repent, and I receive God's complete and total forgiveness.

✷ Declare ✷

I will declare the decree of the Lord... PSALM 2:7

When something is decreed, it is written down, and when it is declared, it is spoken. The psalmist David said that he would declare the decree of the Lord. In other words, he spoke out loud the Word of God over his life, circumstances, and friends and family. I do the same thing, and if you have never done it, I strongly encourage you to make a spiritual habit of doing so.

Words have power and we should use them wisely. You might start a day like this: "I declare that I will see God's goodness in my life today. I will be good to others and be obedient to God. My sins are forgiven, I receive God's mercy and favor in my life today and every day."

The Word of God is filled with promises, and you can declare any and all of them. Fill the atmosphere you dwell in with the promises of God. It will encourage you and increase your faith.

Be careful not to declare things over your life that you don't want. For example: "I am afraid I will get that flu that is going around," or "I'm probably going to lose my job." Live in agreement with God and watch Him do wonders in your life.

Prayer: Father, help me choose my words carefully. I want to speak life and not death.

✷ Abide in Love ✷

I have loved you, [just] as the Father has loved Me; abide in My love [continue in His love with Me]. JOHN 15:9

Today God reminded me to always abide in His love. Being consciously aware of God's love is one of the most important things we can take time to do. His love strengthens and heals us. It makes us secure and it adds value to us as individuals. Don't let anything separate you from the love of God!

Beware when you sin that you don't lose the awareness of God's love. It is easy to let guilty feelings rob us of it when we feel that we have failed. God never stops loving us for one moment. Actually, the truth is that when God shows us our sins, that is His love in action. He chastens those whom He loves (see Revelation 3:19).

The devil works tirelessly to steal our awareness of God's love from us through deception. He knows how powerful God's love is. He is called "the accuser of the brethren" (see Revelation 12:10). He reminds us of our mistakes and tries to convince us that God doesn't love us or that God is angry with us, but remember that the devil is a liar! God loves you, and that is final!

Prayer: Father, teach me to abide in Your love! You don't love me because I deserve it but because You are love. Thank You for loving me!

✷ God Is with Us in Our Weakness ✷

Though he falls, he shall not be utterly cast down, for the Lord grasps his hand in support and upholds him. PSALM 37:24

I think our weaknesses bother us more than they bother God. He already knew every mistake we would make even before we were born, and He chose us anyway. Guess what? God is not shocked by your failures! Anytime we fall or fail, He is present to pick us up and help us get going in the right direction once again.

I have four children, and when they were little, they fell down often, especially while learning how to walk. Never once did I get angry with them because they fell, but I always rushed to help them up. If this is our reaction to our children, how much more will God react mercifully to us?

> God knows about the mistakes we will make even before we do, and He has our rescue planned!

Speak this: When I fall, I will get up again because God will help me!

✷ God Has Your Answer ✷

My son, attend to my words; consent and submit to my sayings...
For they are life to those who find them, healing and health to all their flesh. PROVERBS 4:20, 22

God's Word holds the answer to all of our problems. I like to see God's Word as an antidote for anything that tries to poison our lives. If a snake bit me, I would rush to the hospital for an antidote. I would want to counteract the poison as soon as possible. There are countless things that poison our souls—things such as bitterness, selfishness, greed, and insecurity.

For bitterness, God gives us the ability to forgive those who have hurt us. For selfishness, He gives us the ability to love others. For greed, He gives us generosity. And for insecurity, He gives us His unconditional love. These are just a few of the answers we find in God's Word.

Should you ever feel that your soul has been poisoned with things like I have mentioned—or even others like hopelessness, fear, guilt, shame, worry, anxiety, or loss of joy—rush to God for the antidote!

Prayer: Father, thank You for Your Word! I don't want to live with my soul filled with poison, so I ask for Your help because I believe You have my answer.

⁕ Be Yourself ⁕

For as in one physical body we have many parts (organs, members) and all of these parts do not have the same function or use, so we, numerous as we are, are one body in Christ (the Messiah)... Having gifts (faculties, talents, qualities) that differ according to the grace given us, let us use them... ROMANS 12:4–6

Just as our body parts are all different, we are also different from one another. Don't fall into the trap of trying to be anyone other than who you are. God was able to do very little with or through me until I stopped trying to be some other person and became content with being me.

I tried to be the homemaker my neighbor was, but gardening and making my family's clothes just wasn't me. I tried to be soft-spoken like my pastor's wife, but that didn't work either. I tried to be more relaxed and easygoing like Dave, but that was difficult also. After years of frustration and failure, I finally realized that I had to be "me," because everyone else was already taken! God wasn't going to help me be someone else because He had created me the way He wanted me to be.

We all need to make improvement in some areas of our lives, but we must be the people God created us to be, and that means we'll always be a little different than most of the other people we know. God obviously loves variety, and He wants us to enjoy ourselves and not compare ourselves with other people.

Prayer: Father, help me embrace the person You want me to be. Help me enjoy myself and live free from the tyranny of comparison.

⁕ Distractions ⁕

Let your eyes look right on [with fixed purpose], and let your gaze be straight before you. PROVERBS 4:25

We probably experience more distractions in our lives today than at any other time in history. The world is indeed a busy and a noisy place. All the electronics that we own are enough by themselves to do a thorough job of distracting us; however, to get anything accomplished, we need to focus on our purpose. I am simply reminding you today to be persistent in not letting people and things distract you from the will of God for your life. Today matters, so be sure you don't waste it on nonessential things.

Discipline is what we need to help us become who we want to be.

Speak this: Each day I stay focused on my goals, and I don't allow useless distractions to steal my time.

⁕ Be Stable ⁕

He who dwells in the secret place of the Most High shall remain stable and fixed under the shadow of the Almighty...

PSALM 91:1

Have you ever been happy and calm and then let someone else who is in a bad mood change you? Most people have, but we don't have to be "most people." Today, I am going to be with someone that I love, who is often given to temperament shifts. I know that it is important for me to be an example to this person and remain stable no matter what they do.

You might also be in a relationship with someone or work with someone who is moody and unstable. The best way to be prepared to deal with them properly is to spend time with God, receiving His strength. When we dwell in the secret place (God's presence), we grow in stability.

Don't let other people dictate your behavior. Why should you be in a bad mood just because someone else is? Stay happy and be an example of godly behavior to all those around you.

Prayer: Father, help me remain emotionally stable at all times. Don't let other people or my circumstances change me!

July 21

✱ The Indwelling Christ ✱

I have been crucified with Christ; it is no longer I who live, but Christ lives in me... GALATIANS 2:20 (NKJV)

This morning I told the Lord I felt a little disconnected from Him, and He quickly reminded me that I am never disconnected because He lives in me. We don't always feel the presence of God, but He is always in us. It is important for every believer to stay "God-inside minded." We live by and through Him. He is our wisdom, strength, peace, righteousness, and everything else we will ever need. We never have to go in search of Him because He is not hiding and has not left us. We simply need to believe that Christ in us is the hope of glory (see Colossians 1:27). He is our hope of living a life worth living and one that is pleasing to Him.

One of the names by which Jesus is called is Immanuel, which means "God with us"! (See Matthew 1:23.) He promised to be with us always (see Matthew 28:20). Meditate on the fact that God lives in you and you are never disconnected from Him no matter how you feel. Satan wants us to feel alone and abandoned, but he is a liar, and the truth always makes us free.

Prayer: Father, I am amazed that You have chosen me as Your home. Help me be conscious and aware at all times that You live in me!

⁕ Face Your Fear ⁕

Have not I commanded you? Be strong, vigorous, and very courageous. Be not afraid, neither be dismayed, for the Lord your God is with you wherever you go. JOSHUA 1:9

The fear of what might happen is often worse than what actually does happen. Fear is very tormenting, but it has no real power over us if we face it courageously, knowing that God is with us. We may not know what to do about our difficulties in life, but God always knows what to do, and He will show us at the right time. He gives us the grace we need to deal with things in life when we actually need it, not before we need it. If we look into the unknown future, most of the time fear is waiting for us, but if we keep going forward, the fear will run from our courage.

Face your fears and they will vanish.

Speak this: When I feel fear, I will keep moving forward. I will not let fear rule my life.

⁕ The Blessing ⁕

The Lord shall command the blessing upon you in your storehouse and in all that you undertake. And He will bless you in the land which the Lord your God gives you. DEUTERONOMY 28:8

The Bible frequently refers to "the blessing." We find in studying these words that it is an extremely powerful thing. Because we're blessed by God, His blessing is in us to give to others. Recently, God has been leading me to begin each day by blessing my family, naming each of them personally and blessing myself as well. I also bless our homes, health, the day, our partners in ministry, and many other things.

When we bless someone, we are, in essence, saying, "May all of God's good plan for you come to pass." I have been so deeply impressed by the importance of giving the blessing that I usually do so when I first awake, before getting out of bed. I am finding that starting my day with blessing in my thoughts and words makes the day better.

When we bless others, the blessing comes back to us. Not only should we bless those whom we love and admire, but God also commands us to bless our enemies so that we might inherit a blessing from Him. When we bless our enemies, we place them in God's hands and trust that His best for them will be worked out in their lives, including the recognition and repentance of their sins.

Be aggressive in releasing the blessing each day and you will be in agreement with God, for He indeed is the one who blesses.

Prayer: Father, teach me to bless and never to curse. You have blessed me, and I want to always release Your blessing to others. I want them to experience Your good plan for their lives. Bless each thing we lay our hands to do. Thank You!

Happy Anywhere

I [the Lord] will instruct you and teach you in the way you should go; I will counsel you with My eye upon you. PSALM 32:8

This morning I wrote this in my journal, and I thought we could turn it into our devotional for today:

> I love You, Father, Son, and Holy Spirit. You are good every moment. I have just returned from a monthlong trip, and it is good to be home. But, thankfully, I can be happy anywhere as long as I am close to You. I am glad to be back with my children and in my regular routine. Nothing is better than family and the simplicity of daily life.
>
> I lean on, rely on, and put my trust in You, Lord. Strengthen me today for my walk with You and let me represent You well in each thing that I do.
>
> Today is a great day and I choose to live it in Your presence!

Prayer: Father, draw me into Your presence today and every day. Help me be aware of You! Use me for Your glory, and let me help someone today.

⁕ Be at Peace ⁕

. . . Let your adorning be the hidden person of the heart with the imperishable beauty of a gentle and quiet spirit, which in God's sight is very precious. 1 PETER 3:3–4 (ESV)

Today I am fighting a little battle with worry. There are three different issues that I could be concerned about, but I know that God has called us to peace.

Perhaps you too have something today that you could worry about, but what good would it do?

When anything tries to steal our peace, we can choose to be peaceful on purpose. Peter wrote that we should crave peace, pursue and go after it (see 1 Peter 3:11). A peaceful spirit is precious to the Lord! When we are at peace and quiet inside, we can hear from God, and that is what we need anytime we have a situation to solve. Worry won't solve it, but God always has our answer.

Lay aside your burdens today and trust God to take care of whatever concerns you. He loves you and is waiting to help you.

Prayer: Father, I choose peace today. Grant me the grace not to worry or have any anxiety about anything.

✷ No Parking ✷

For though the righteous fall seven times, they rise again, but the wicked stumble when calamity strikes. PROVERBS 24:16 (NIV)

Some people keep going when life is difficult, but others park at the point of their pain. They decide to stay where they are instead of pressing through the difficulties. When they do, they always miss the best life that God has for them. Terah, Abram's father, headed for Canaan, but settled in Haran (see Genesis 11:31). I wonder how much Terah missed in life because he settled. It is interesting to note that we don't hear anything about Terah after that. You are important to God's plan, so don't park…just keep moving forward!

Don't park your life at the point of your pain!

Speak this: When the going gets tough, I will keep going! I'm going all the way with God.

July 27

✷ Silence ✷

For God alone, O my soul, wait in silence, for my hope is from him. PSALM 62:5 (ESV)

My favorite part of the day is early in the morning when I get up before anyone else and the house is totally silent. I spend that time with God, and I find that the silence strengthens me and helps me get focused for the day. I spend some time just sitting and enjoying it.

Our world today is very noisy, busy, and at times stressful. When you feel stressed or frustrated, go somewhere that is silent and just enjoy it for a few minutes; I believe you will find that your soul begins to calm down. Inner peace and quiet are vital for hearing from God or sensing the direction He wants us to take.

Outer silence helps promote inner silence. Learn to love silence and you will be more inclined to hear the still, small voice of God. At a time when Elijah desperately needed to receive direction from God, he had to wait until all the noise passed, and only when he was in a gentle stillness did he hear the still, small voice of God speaking to him (see 1 Kings 19:11–12).

Prayer: Father, help me learn to love the silence so I can hear Your voice and sense Your presence.

✷ Think Good Thoughts ✷

. . . Whatever is true, whatever is worthy of reverence and is honorable and seemly, whatever is just, whatever is pure, whatever is lovely and lovable, whatever is kind and winsome and gracious, if there is any virtue and excellence, if there is anything worthy of praise, think on and weigh and take account of these things [fix your minds on them]. PHILIPPIANS 4:8

I was tired when I first got up this morning, and I was having a difficult time keeping my thoughts in line with the instructions in the Scripture for today. We don't just automatically have all lovely thoughts, and there are times when we must diligently direct our thoughts in the right direction.

Several times, I actually had to say to myself, "No, I will not think like that. I will think good things." It seemed as if the flaws of anyone I knew were coming to my mind, one after another, but through the help of the Holy Spirit and some diligence, I won the battle. The "attack" on my mind lasted about five or ten minutes and then it was over.

We must be firm in faith against the enemy when he attacks, and as we are, he will soon go away. When Jesus was being tempted in the wilderness, He withstood each lie of the devil, and finally the devil went away to wait for a more opportune time (see Luke 4:13). We never know when ungodly thoughts may try to gain access into our minds, but we do know that as we stand firm, we'll always win the battle.

Prayer: Father, help me recognize when my thoughts are not pleasing to You and give me the grace to think on things that are lovely and pure.

✷ Wholeness ✷

And Peter said unto him, Aeneas, Jesus Christ maketh thee whole . . .
ACTS 9:34 (KJV)

Jesus offers us salvation, and that means wholeness. He didn't die so we could be partially healed in one or two areas of our life; His will for us is complete healing and wholeness! Jesus wants to heal us spiritually, mentally, emotionally, physically, socially, and financially. He is concerned about everything that concerns us, and we don't have to settle for anything less than being made whole and complete. If you have any area in your life that is lacking, ask Jesus to heal you in that area, as well as all other areas.

Jesus wants to make you whole—not leave you with a hole in your soul!

Speak this: Jesus can heal me everywhere I hurt, and I won't settle for less than His best!

⁕ The Shield of Faith ⁕

Lift up over all the [covering] shield of saving faith, upon which you can quench all the flaming missiles of the wicked [one].

EPHESIANS 6:16

The devil attacks us in a variety of ways, but we can always have the victory if we will lift up the shield of faith against him at the onset of his attack. Recently, early in the morning, he attacked my mind with critical thoughts about several people I know, and this morning it was fear and worry. Both times, the Holy Spirit made me aware of what was happening and I released my faith in God by remembering the faithfulness of God and trusting Him to take care of everything that was attempting to annoy me. I also replaced the wrong thoughts with good ones, because that is one way that we overcome evil with good (see Romans 12:21).

When the devil is attacking, we dare not be passive and do nothing. We must come against him. We submit ourselves to God and His Word, and we resist the devil and he flees (see James 4:7). No matter what lie the devil is whispering to your mind, don't believe him, but instead wield (use) the sword of the Spirit that is the Word of God.

Replace thoughts of criticism with thoughts of humility and love. Replace fear and worry with trust and confidence. Faith is a shield and it will protect us in every battle if we will "lift" it up by simply declaring our trust in God.

Prayer: Father, always reveal to me when the devil is attacking me and remind me of relevant Scriptures to replace the evil thoughts he is suggesting. Help me lift up my shield of faith at all times. Thank You!

⁕ *Test of Character* ⁕

Beloved, do not be amazed and bewildered at the fiery ordeal which is taking place to test your quality, as though something strange (unusual and alien to you and your position) were befalling you. 1 PETER 4:12

In school we are never promoted to the next grade until we pass our final exams, and we expect to have to take and pass them. Students usually prepare extra hard for finals. Why then are we so surprised when we encounter difficulties in life that test the quality of our character?

We can pray to be able to love everyone, but how do we respond when we encounter someone who is very difficult to love? We can pray to be generous, but are we willing to give even when it is inconvenient for us? We may not be picked for something that we really want to do—things like the baseball team, the worship team, class president, or a promotion at work. When that happens, how do we respond? Are we able to be happy for those who were chosen and trust God that He will always do the best thing for us at the exact right time?

The ability to do something does not mean that we have the character to do it. We might need more growth in God before we are promoted. God gives each one of us talents and abilities, but our character must develop over a period of time, and a test of character is one of God's favorite tools to use in helping us. Always remember to stay happy and be thankful and your time will come!

Prayer: Father, help me pass each test of character that comes my way. I want to represent You well and always trust that You will promote me at the right time. In Jesus' name, thank You!

⁕ Testimony ⁕

But constantly and earnestly I bore testimony both to Jews and Greeks, urging them to turn in repentance [that is due] to God and to have faith in our Lord Jesus Christ [that is due Him].

ACTS 20:21

Paul had the privilege of sharing his testimony with people and introducing them to Jesus, but he also shared the things he had experienced and how God was always faithful. People usually love to share their testimony of victory, but when I share mine, I like to also take time to share the tests I encountered along the way. People want us to be honest with them about our journey in life. Many of us have experienced God's life-transforming power, but it surely was not easy to get from where we started to living in victory.

If you are attempting to serve God and you're experiencing trials and tribulations, you can be assured that you will end up with a good testimony of victory if you don't give up. We never have a *test*imony without a test. Receive the strength of the Holy Spirit and face your challenges boldly. We truly can do all things through Christ who is our strength (see Philippians 4:13), but it is important to keep a good attitude and take steps of faith all along the way.

The next time you are facing a challenge (test), don't be afraid of it and don't let it defeat you. Declare in faith that, with God's help, you will pass the test and end up with a testimony of victory!

Prayer: Father, I trust You to grant me strength to face every difficulty I encounter. Help me keep a good attitude and always be thankful in every situation. Thank You!

August 2

✷ One Step at a Time ✷

I [the Lord] will instruct you and teach you in the way you should go; I will counsel you with My eye upon you. PSALM 32:8

If you are anything like me, you like to see things happen fast. You don't want to wait for things, and you get frustrated when you have to. God doesn't move on our timetable, but on His own. He has a plan, and He won't be rushed. He promises to guide us through life, but He does it one step at a time. We get excited when God reveals something to us or gives us direction, but we quickly realize that we need to trust Him for the next step also. God will always give you the grace (favor and power) that you need, but you can't store it up and put it in the bank. Trust God for help one step at a time. Keep doing the last thing He showed you to do and the next thing will be revealed right on time.

God is never late, but He is usually not early either.

Speak this: I trust God to guide me one step at a time.

✷ Recovering Lost Things ✷

For the Son of Man came to seek and to save that which was lost.

LUKE 19:10

Jesus came to seek and save lost sinners, but He also wants to help us recover everything that we have ever lost that He intended for us to have. I lost my childhood through abuse, but God started giving it back to me while I was in my fifties! It is never too late to take back the things the devil has stolen from us. I learned to believe as a little child, to have fun like a child, and to trust as a little child. My natural father abused me, but I have a Heavenly Father now who loves me and has promised to meet all of my needs, and so do you.

Have you lost your childhood, confidence, security, joy, peace, hope, trust, boldness, or anything else? If you have, then Jesus wants to give it to you now. Jesus has already provided for our complete restoration through His death and resurrection, and we simply need to realize it and pray expectantly for those things to be restored.

Everything from God comes through faith, so I recommend that you release your faith for anything you need. God can do more than we can think, or even imagine, and nothing is impossible for Him, so pray boldly. He loves you and wants you to be completely whole.

Prayer: Father, I ask boldly for the restoration of all that the devil has taken from me in my lifetime. Help me stand firm in faith and refuse to do without the things You sent Jesus to provide for me. Thank You!

August 4

The Privilege of Prayer

Pray without ceasing.
1 THESSALONIANS 5:17 (ESV)

I woke up this morning thinking about my prayer life and wondering if it is as good as it could be. In light of that, I spent some time studying prayer and was reminded of several things:

1. We may pray anytime, anywhere, about anything! As we pray our way through the day, we are praying without ceasing.
2. Prayer need not always be long. Short, sincere prayer filled with faith is sufficient.
3. In addition to praying your way through the day, having a special place where you like to pray is also good.
4. Ask in faith, believe you have received your request, and God will answer (see Mark 11:24).
5. Pray according to God's will, not your own will.
6. Pray at all times with thanksgiving (see Philippians 4:6). No matter what we need, we always have much to be thankful for.
7. The fact that we pray is much more important than the methods we follow!
8. When you pray, be aware that God is definitely listening.

Prayer: Father, thank You for the privilege of communicating with You in prayer. Teach me to pray more effectively and to be led by Your Spirit in all my prayers.

✷ Your Helper ✷

And I will ask the Father, and He will give you another Comforter (Counselor, Helper, Intercessor, Advocate, Strengthener, and Standby), that He may remain with you forever. JOHN 14:16

Probably one of the most frequent prayers that I pray is "God help me." I am not even always sure what I need help with, but I am aware that without God's enabling power, I will not succeed at anything. It is wonderful to know that we have a Divine Helper, the Holy Spirit, who is with us and in us at all times.

I encourage you to ask for help as many times every day as you want to. God never tires of hearing your voice and listening to you tell Him that you need Him. We need His help in big things but also in little things. We need His help in things that we don't know how to do, but we also need His help with things we have done a thousand times before. He is our success!

Here are some things I frequently ask God to help me with: Representing Him well everywhere I go. Keeping my thoughts in line with His Word. Saying only things that are filled with life and power. Getting my contact lens in. Fixing my hair and getting properly dressed for the day. Making the right choices. Not overeating! Exercising! And literally everything else you can imagine.

I strongly encourage you to lean on God at all times and voice your dependence on Him by asking for help throughout the day.

Prayer: Father, I ask You to help me in all things, at all times. I can do nothing without You and I am totally dependent upon You! Thank You for being my Helper!

August 6

⁕ Our Secrets Make Us Sick ⁕

When I kept silence [before I confessed], my bones wasted away through my groaning all the day long. PSALM 32:3

We should never try to hide our sin from God. He knows everything we do, but we need to bring it out in the open and talk to Him about it. Hidden things have power over us, but once the darkness is exposed to the light, it dissipates. King David committed adultery and had the woman's husband killed. He mistakenly waited a year before he finally confessed his sin. He was miserable until he confessed, and we will be too. Let's always be open and honest with God about everything. You can talk to Him about absolutely anything!

> Our sin is no surprise to God—He knew what we were going to do before we did it.

Speak this: I will not try to hide anything from God.

✷ A Time Not to Talk ✷

I will not talk with you much more, for the prince (evil genius, ruler) of the world is coming. And he has no claim on Me. [He has nothing in common with Me; there is nothing in Me that belongs to him, and he has no power over Me.] JOHN 14:30

Jesus was nearing the time of His suffering and death, and He told His disciples that He would not be talking much with them any longer. I believe that when we are under pressure, or having a particularly difficult time, it is often best to choose to be quiet, for we might be tempted to say something that we will later regret.

We often tell our children, "If you can't say something good, then don't say anything at all." There will be times when we need to follow our own advice. When I don't feel well, or am extremely tired, or have had a stressful day, or am going through a tough time, I am likely to say things that contain no positive power and may even open a door for the devil to increase my misery. The Bible teaches us that we must be satisfied with the consequences of our words (see Proverbs 18:20), and if we are going to be, then we need to be very careful what we say!

Our words have consequences, and we need to use them wisely. Jesus knew that He was approaching a very important time in His life and He was determined not to give Satan any power over Him through unwise words.

Let this be a reminder that being quiet is sometimes the best thing to do. It might save you a lot of trouble later on!

Prayer: Father, help me be quiet when I am in danger of saying things that I will regret later on. Teach me to think before I speak!

⁕ Always ⁕

I am the Lord, and I do not change... MALACHI 3:6 (NLT)

God is always the same; He is the Rock on which we can stand. He will be with us always, He always forgives, He will always love us unconditionally, He is always for us, and He is always faithful! I urge you to focus on these promises and the word "always," and realize how comforting it is to know that we can always count on God.

Even if we become faithless, God remains faithful. As humans, we often change toward people when they change toward us, but God does not do that. He is who He is, and nothing we do (or don't do) changes that fact. It is awesome to think about how God is *always* with us, and therefore, we are never alone... we are never without hope and strength.

It is equally wonderful to remember that anytime we acknowledge our sin and are willing to turn from it, He *always* forgives us completely. He removes our sin and does not even remember it anymore. If you are hanging on to the guilt of old sins, you need to stop remembering what God has forgotten.

On the days when you feel that nobody loves you, and perhaps you even feel very unlovable, you can be assured that God *always* loves you. He has promised to love you with an everlasting love (see Jeremiah 31:3).

When everything around you is shaking and nothing seems stable, remember that God never changes and you can always depend on Him.

Prayer: Father, thank You that You are always the same and I can rely on You. Help me always remember that You are always with me and always for me!

✷ Take What Is Yours ✷

Every place upon which the sole of your foot shall tread, that have I given to you, as I promised Moses. JOSHUA 1:3

The Bible teaches us that God has provided everything we need for life and godliness (see 2 Peter 1:3). He has promised, but we need to take action as the Holy Spirit leads us. It says in 2 Peter 1:5 that we must add our diligence to the promises and exercise our faith. God told Joshua that the land was his, but he needed to step out and take it. If you are expecting the promises of God to manifest in your life while you do absolutely nothing, you are mistaken. Pray and release your faith to see God's promises come to pass, and then do anything God shows you that you need to do.

Step out and find out what God has for you!

Speak this: I will step out in faith and possess all that God has for me.

✷ Do It! ✷

Why do you call Me, Lord, Lord, and do not [practice] what I tell you? LUKE 6:46

God's Word makes it plain in several places that we are not to be hearers only, but that we need to do what we hear (see James 1:22). It is dangerous for one to think that they are spiritually mature because they attend a lot of church services, have a large library of Christian books, and read their Bible regularly. The proof of our true spiritual maturity is seen in our fruit.

Actions speak much louder than words. To know something does us no good at all unless we do what we know to do. Jesus washed His disciples' feet as an example to them and then said they would be blessed if, knowing these things, they did the same (see John 13:17).

We don't want to be hypocritical, but that is exactly what we are when we tell others to do what we are not doing ourselves. I recall a time when I had a problem and I was praying and asking God, "What do You want me to do, Lord? What do You want me to do?" He replied to my heart, "Do what you would tell someone else to do if they were in this same situation and asked your advice!" Ouch! Life would often be much simpler if we would follow our own advice.

Take this opportunity to ask yourself what you know to do that you aren't doing, and then correct it by taking faith-filled action. God is ready to help you if you will take the step of faith to be obedient.

Prayer: Father, help me always do what I know to do.

✷ God Knows Our Thoughts ✷

But He was aware all along of their thoughts... LUKE 6:8

It is sobering to realize that God always knows all of our thoughts! Our blessings and our problems are rooted in either right or wrong thinking. We reap what we sow, and that is a spiritual law that we cannot avoid. Thoughts are seeds that produce a harvest in our lives.

If we want to have more peace, or be more joyful, we will need to improve our thoughts. If we want to be able to do more, then we must not think and meditate on what we cannot do and how weak we are. You cannot change your life without changing your thoughts.

The Bible even says that God knows when we sit down and when we get up, and He knows our thoughts from afar (see Psalm 139:2). Keeping in mind that none of our thoughts are a secret from God may help us be more willing to think according to His will. Your thoughts do matter. They turn into your words, your attitudes, your moods, and your behavior.

Before you get up in the morning, practice "on purpose" thinking. Think according to what you want to have, not according to what you have always had in the past. God is doing a new thing in your life and He wants you to think accordingly.

Prayer: Father, thank You for reminding me that You know all of my thoughts. Please help me think things that will be pleasing to You and that will release Your power into my life.

⁕ Comparison ⁕

Let us not be vainglorious and self-conceited, competitive and challenging and provoking and irritating to one another, envying and being jealous of one another. GALATIANS 5:26

Most of us are tempted to compare ourselves with others. We may become jealous of what they can do and begin to think that unless we do the same as them, we are not as good as they are.

I was recently reading a book on prayer, and some of the things the writer said he experienced in prayer are things that have never happened to me. I started to wonder if I should "try" to do what he was doing, the way he was doing it. You have probably experienced this same thing at some time in your life.

I am grateful that God has taught me that we are all individuals and He uses each of us in different ways, including prayer. I might feel an urgency to pray frequently about something that another person never prays about, and that is as it should be. God will never help us be someone else, because He wants us to be fully who He created us to be. Someone may be an example to us, but only Jesus is our pattern for living our life.

I encourage you to avoid comparisons and wasted effort, trying to be what you will never be. God enjoys you, and you should enjoy being yourself.

Prayer: Father, help me always be the best version of me that I can be. Lead me in what You want me to do and help me not to compare myself with others.

✷ Do Good Things in Secret ✷

But when you give to charity, do not let your left hand know what your right hand is doing. MATTHEW 6:3

When God gives us the grace to do a good deed, we should not tell others in order to have them think well of us, nor should we even think repeatedly about the good we have done. If we are willing to do a good deed in secret, God will reward us openly. I think that we often lose our reward because we cannot resist the temptation to tell about what we have done. Never tell about the good deeds you do unless you are certain your motive is right for doing so.

> Do good deeds for others without needing applause and God will smile!

Speak this: I will do good deeds in secret and be excited to see my reward from God!

✷ Refusing to Dread ✷

A happy heart is good medicine and a cheerful mind works healing, but a broken spirit dries up the bones. PROVERBS 17:22

I just returned home from doing a conference in Virginia. I am fully unpacked from the trip, and it's already time to pack for the next one! There is a temptation to dread it, but I refuse to do so. Dread steals the life and enjoyment out of things, and it is foolish to dread doing something that we will inevitably have to do anyway.

I believe Jesus wants us to enjoy our lives to the fullest, and to me that means every part of my life, especially the everyday ordinary things. Enjoying life begins with right thinking, and we can choose to think right on purpose. Thoughts of dread only drain our energy and they never produce anything good.

How much time do you waste dreading things that you need to do? Why not make a decision to stop dreading and start enjoying? Life is a gift from God, and He meant for it to be enjoyed and appreciated. I believe that one of the ways we can say "Thank You" to Jesus for what He has done for us is to enjoy every moment that He gives us.

Prayer: Father, grant me the grace I need today to do everything I do with joy and gratitude. Help me to never dread anything but to be strong in You and approach each task boldly.

✷ The Dream Thief ✷

A dream comes with much business and painful effort...

ECCLESIASTES 5:3

Having a dream for your life is one thing, but seeing it fulfilled is quite another. Many people have goals and dreams, but in comparison, not many stick with them all the way through to the finish and fulfillment.

First, we must realize that Satan is a dream thief and he not only works against us himself, but also through other people. Sometimes the people closest to you are the ones who are the most discouraging to you. They are too familiar with you to see who you can become and what God can do through you.

Our dreams are not fulfilled because someone waves a magic wand over us and—*Poof!*—everything we ever thought possible just happens. Dreams come to pass with a lot of hard work, responsibility, and a refusal to quit and give up. There are times of growth and progress, which of course are exciting, but there are also setbacks and times when things seem to be going nowhere. There are even times of being lonely—when you feel that nobody understands what it is like to be in your position.

It is important to celebrate any progress you have and not let the setbacks and waiting discourage you too much. Hang on to your dreams and be willing to sacrifice now for what you hope to have in the future. Trust God and lean on Him at all times and He will bring it to pass!

Prayer: Father, help me not to give up on the dreams You have put in my heart for my future. Strengthen me in difficult times, and help me believe that You are working, even when nothing seems to be happening.

✷ When to Give Advice and When Not To ✷

He who, passing by, stops to meddle with strife that is none of his business is like one who takes a dog by the ears. PROVERBS 26:17

Most of us are not doing a great job of managing our own affairs, yet we are tempted to get into other people's and try to give them advice they have not asked for! If you want more peace in your life, one of the ways to get it is to make sure that you don't get into other people's business (including your adult children). Very few even truly want our advice even if they ask for it, and they certainly don't want it if they have not asked for it. If someone does ask for our advice, we can give it, but even then, we should not try to convince them that we are right!

If you want more peace, mind your own business!

Speak this: I will take care of my own business and stay out of other people's.

⁕ No Place Like Home ⁕

[Yes] we have confident and hopeful courage and are pleased rather to be away from home out of the body and be at home with the Lord. 2 CORINTHIANS 5:8

As I write these words, I am sitting in a hospital room with my mother and one of my daughters. My mom will be going home to be with the Lord sometime in the next few hours. She is a few weeks away from turning ninety, and has lived a difficult but long life. I am excited for her to be going home, because there is no place like home.

While we are here on the earth, we are "strangers" and "aliens," according to God's Word (see 1 Peter 2:11). We are literally just passing through. We are in the world, but we don't belong to it (see John 17:13–16). It is not our home.

The apostle Paul said, "... To live is Christ [His life in me], and to die is gain ..." (Philippians 1:21). We all want to live a long life, but it is also wonderful not to be afraid of or dread leaving this life and stepping into one that will be far, far better. As I said, my mom has had a very difficult life, but after today, she will have no more crying, no tears, no pain, no sadness or sorrow. She won't be wrinkled and crippled, she will be young and more beautiful than we can imagine. She will be completely free!

I thought earlier that some angels are probably already assigned to bring her home, and perhaps my dad and brother, as well as her mom and dad and sister and three brothers, have already been alerted that she will be coming home today and are waiting to greet her. Her mansion is ready, and maybe Jesus Himself will take her to it! I am, of course, using my imagination, but I just wanted to share with you that I have a strong sense that her home-coming today will be celebrated with great joy!

Prayer: Father, I am grateful for the hope of Heaven and living in Your presence for all eternity. Help me live my life in a way that is pleasing to You while I am waiting to come home!

✷ A Dangerous Word ✷

Then Pharaoh called for Moses and Aaron, and said, Entreat the Lord, that He may take away the frogs from me and my people . . .

EXODUS 8:8

Due to disobedience to God, the land of Egypt experienced a plague of frogs. Frogs covered the land and filled the houses. They were literally everywhere! Just imagine how that would be. Pharaoh asked Moses to pray that the Lord would take the frogs away and stated that he would be obedient to do what God had asked, which was to let the Israelites, who had been slaves in Egypt, go free.

Moses said, "When do you want me to pray?" and Pharaoh answered, "Tomorrow" (see Exodus 8:10). Why would anyone want to keep the frogs another day? Why didn't he say, "Pray right now"?

"Tomorrow" is a dangerous word at times. We put things off until tomorrow that should be done today. We procrastinate! It may be a task that needs to be done or an apology we need to give. We may even need to confront an issue in our own character, and yet we keep putting it off until tomorrow. We wait for a more convenient or comfortable time and, in the process, it often never gets done.

Instead of being "tomorrow people," let's be "now people"! We will all be much happier if we do now what needs to be done and stop wasting time by procrastinating.

Prayer: Father, help me be aggressive and always do what needs to be done today!

✷ Stay on Track ✷

Let your eyes look right on [with fixed purpose], and let your gaze be straight before you. PROVERBS 4:25

I am leaving soon on a ministry trip to Europe where I will teach nine times. I want to be totally prepared for all of the teaching sessions when I leave, so I made a plan to stay home all day today and finish the messages I had not yet completed. I finished all of them except for one and started being double-minded about whether or not I wanted to finish or quit working and do something more relaxing. Does that sound familiar?

I knew that the best choice was to stay on track, so I did. When I finished the last message, I felt a huge sense of relief that everything was done and I was ready to go. I was so glad that I was finished and I didn't have to face tomorrow with the project still needing to be done. I still have time to relax, but now I can do it with joy rather than a feeling that I really should have stayed on track.

The next time you find yourself in a similar situation, I urge you to ask yourself how you will feel later if you quit halfway to your goal. A job half done doesn't feel as good as a job completed!

Prayer: Father, help me stay focused and on track when I have a job to do. I want to be a person who finishes what I start.

⁕ Be Trustworthy ⁕

Argue your cause with your neighbor himself; discover not and disclose not another's secret. PROVERBS 25:9

God's Word teaches us not to gossip or to be talebearers (see Proverbs 20:19). We should make the commitment to do unto other people as we want them to do unto us. I certainly want others to keep my secrets, and I am sure that you do too. We need to sow good seed in the lives of those we know so we may have a good harvest in our own life. I am not sure why it is so tempting to tell things, but most of us delight in saying, "Did you know...?" and then sharing a secret that we really should keep. Let's be the kind of people who can be trusted!

People will tell you secrets if you can be trusted to keep them.

Speak this: I always keep people's secrets because I want them to keep mine.

⁕ Little by Little ⁕

And the Lord your God will clear out those nations before you, little by little . . . DEUTERONOMY 7:22

We all want changes in our lives, and hopefully, we all desire to change and be more like Jesus. God wants this for us too, but we need to be patient, because He delivers and changes us little by little.

As we study God's Word, we are transformed into His image from glory to glory, according to the Bible in 2 Corinthians 3:18. God could work faster, and we would all love it if He did, but He has His own reasons for doing things the way He does. We would be wise to trust Him and stay in peace. It often feels to us that nothing is happening in our lives, but God is always working! God is working in your life right now!

Sometimes He takes us the longer and more difficult way to our destination because He wants to teach us something along the way. God is good and only wants the best for us, so we can always trust that His timing is perfect. He may not be early, but He will never be late.

Prayer: Father, help me trust Your perfect timing in my life and keep a good attitude while I am waiting.

✷ Transition ✷

To everything there is a season, and a time for every matter or purpose under heaven. ECCLESIASTES 3:1

Things change in our lives and it is important that we learn to navigate them with grace. I've been letting go of some responsibilities at the ministry in order to give myself to other things, and even though I want this change, part of me resists it. Letting go of things we have invested time and effort into is not always easy, but it always becomes necessary at some time in life.

We raise our children and put a great deal of time and effort into it, and when the time comes for them to move away from home and live their own lives, many parents find it very difficult making the transition. Our bodies change and get older, and that isn't always easy. We want to always be able to do what we have always done, but it never works that way. I used to play golf and bowl, but now I cannot do either because of a problem with my wrist!

Let's pray to make changes gracefully, and I believe God will help us. Don't be sad about what you are letting go of, but instead be happy about what you're reaching toward. New seasons can be exciting and refreshing if we have a good attitude toward them.

Prayer: Father, help me navigate the changing seasons of my life with grace and peace. Thank You!

⁕ All for Jesus ⁕

Whatever may be your task, work at it heartily (from the soul), as [something done] for the Lord and not for men.

COLOSSIANS 3:23

If you desire to develop a closer relationship with God, there is a simple way to do so. Begin practicing doing everything you do for Him, especially the common daily tasks that you normally just try to get done so you can move on to other things. Before each task—whether it's grocery shopping, cleaning out the garage, getting dressed to go out for the day or paying your bills—do it with the thought in mind that you are doing it with and for God. You can tell God that you are doing the task at hand for Him, to worship and glorify Him.

Most people fall into the habit of dividing their spiritual life from their secular life, but that is a mistake. We tend to think that God is only interested in our spiritual life, but He is interested in and wants to be included in everything that we do. Once I understood this truth, doing life with God became very exciting.

God is not just in the church building or in your time of prayer and Bible study. He is always with you everywhere, all the time, and should not be ignored. Don't be discouraged if you find that it takes time to develop this habit; just keep at it and you will discover a deeper closeness developing between you and the Lord.

Prayer: Father, I am grateful that You are interested in everything I do. Help me to remember that You are present at all times and to do all that I do with and for You.

⁕ Check Your Attitude ⁕

And be constantly renewed in the spirit of your mind [having a fresh mental and spiritual attitude]. EPHESIANS 4:23

The kind of attitude we have determines a great deal about the outcome of our lives. Or, as you may have heard it said, "Your attitude determines your altitude." It determines how far and how high you can go in life. Our attitude belongs to us, and no one can force us to have a bad one unless we choose to! Don't let someone else's bad attitude poison yours! When circumstances are bad, keep your attitude good and God will help you in marvelous ways.

Refuse to have a bad attitude and even sour things will become sweet!

Speak this: Having a bad attitude won't make my circumstances better, but it will make me bitter!

⁕ Say Your Prayers and Cast Your Cares ⁕

Pray at all times (on every occasion, in every season) in the Spirit, with all [manner of] prayer and entreaty... EPHESIANS 6:18

If we would follow God's advice to say our prayers and cast our cares, our lives would be much more peaceful and enjoyable. But if we pray and worry, we negate the effectiveness of prayer.

When we pray, we invite God to take charge of the things that concern us and to work on our behalf, and tremendous power is made available. It is God's power and all things are possible with Him. Our worry, anxiety, and care won't solve our problems. If they do anything at all, they only make them less endurable and more painful. We are instructed in God's Word to cast all of our cares on Him, for He cares for us affectionately and watchfully (see 1 Peter 5:7).

Casting our care is evidence that we truly trust God. It shows humility on our part when we refuse to worry and be anxious about the things we have given to God in prayer. Our refusal to worry says that we know we cannot solve our own problems and we are waiting on God to work. Saying your prayers and casting your cares must go together if you want to see God's power at work in your life.

Prayer: Father, teach me not to worry and be anxious, but to cast all of my care on You after I have prayed and asked You to solve my problems.

One Thing at a Time

I have strength for all things in Christ Who empowers me [I am ready for anything and equal to anything through Him Who infuses inner strength into me; I am self-sufficient in Christ's sufficiency]. PHILIPPIANS 4:13

I am in a very busy time right now, and I find that some mornings, I feel a bit overwhelmed. I am sure that we all feel that way at times. Thankfully, if we approach life one thing at a time and refuse to worry about anything beyond what we are facing each day, we can do all things that we need to do through Christ who gives us strength.

God gave the Israelites manna one day at a time and they were strictly forbidden from trying to gather what they would need for anything beyond the day they were in. You might be looking to the future and wondering if you will be able to handle the things that are ahead, but I assure you that you can. God's strength is always sufficient, and as we receive it by faith, our own strength is renewed. Always lean on God and not on yourself and you will be amazed at what you can do.

Prayer: Father, give me strength and help me live one day at a time and be assured that when tomorrow comes, You will give me strength for that day also.

August 27

⁕ *Keep Your Passion for Jesus* ⁕

So, because you are lukewarm and neither cold nor hot, I will spew you out of My mouth! REVELATION 3:16

When our relationship with Jesus is new, it is often filled with passion and enthusiasm, but it is possible as time goes by to let it become commonplace and dull. That is a serious mistake! We should keep ourselves stirred up, and not allow ourselves to become so familiar with the amazing things that God does for us that we are no longer enthusiastic about them. Once I recall asking God, "Why don't You do the exciting things in my life that You once did?" and He said, "I still do the same things, but you have become accustomed to them and are no longer amazed!" Let's not be lukewarm, but instead let's keep our passion for Jesus.

> Familiarity is dangerous—it takes the passion out of things that were once special!

Speak this: I refuse to become lukewarm in my relationship with God—I will keep my passion for Jesus!

✵ Spiritual Growth ✵

You must submit to and endure [correction] for discipline; God is dealing with you as with sons. For what son is there whom his father does not [thus] train and correct and discipline?

HEBREWS 12:7

I said something yesterday about someone that I should not have said. I talked about a fault I think they have, but God's Word teaches us to cover other people's faults in love (see 1 Peter 4:8). I immediately felt the conviction of the Holy Spirit.

Receiving correction and discipline from God is necessary for spiritual growth. God corrects us because He loves us and desires for us to be all that we can be in Him. Just as discipline is vital in order for a natural child to grow and develop into a healthy adult, so spiritual correction is necessary in order for us to grow into the men and women that God wants us to be, with conduct that is pleasing to Him.

Receive correction graciously, because it is intended for your good. Thank God that He cares enough about you to help you grow. And never be condemned when you feel convicted about wrong behavior. Being able to feel conviction is a sign that you are spiritually alive and growing!

Prayer: Father, help me always receive Your correction and discipline with a thankful attitude. I trust You and I want to be all You want me to be.

⁕ The Helper ⁕

Let me assure you, it is better for you that I go away. I say this because when I go away I will send the Helper to you. But if I did not go, the Helper would not come. JOHN 16:7 (ERV)

Jesus sent the Holy Spirit to be with us always. The Holy Spirit is a person with all of the personality traits that any person has, and He deserves our attention. Jesus told His disciples they would be better off when He went away because He would send the Holy Spirit to be with them and in them. I am sure they thought, *How could anyone be better than Jesus?*

Jesus had a flesh-and-blood body as we do, and He could only be in one place at a time, but the Holy Spirit can be everywhere, all the time, helping each of us simultaneously. Because the Holy Spirit is always with us, we are never alone and we need not fear. He not only helps us, but He comforts and strengthens us.

The Lord offers us many blessings, and our part is to receive them by faith. Believe the Holy Spirit is with you right now and that He will never leave you. Ask for His help and strength throughout the day. Talk with Him and enjoy close fellowship with Him.

Prayer: Jesus, thank You for sending the Holy Spirit. I am thankful to know I am not alone and will always have the divine help that I need.

⁕ What Makes a Person Great ⁕

You have also given me the shield of Your salvation; Your right hand has held me up, Your gentleness has made me great.

PSALM 18:35 (NKJV)

What makes a person truly great? It is the presence of God in his life—not his accomplishments. Our identity should be found in God, not in what we do. In the Gospel of John, John referred to himself five times as the disciple whom Jesus loved. He didn't refer to himself by name. Why not? Because his identity was defined by Jesus and nothing else.

I have always been a hard worker, and I am motivated by accomplishment and reaching my goals. That trait is my natural temperament, but I have had to learn that my worth and value are not in what I do but in my relationship with God.

Our value is found in belonging to God, not in what we do for Him!

Speak this: I do what I do because I love Jesus, not in order to get Him to love me!

✷ Sowing and Reaping ✷

... For whatever a man sows, that and that only is what he will reap. GALATIANS 6:7

The law of sowing and reaping works in every area of our lives, but today I would like you to think about it in regard to how you take care of your physical body. Are you sowing healthy habits so you will have good health now and in the years to come? I am quite sure that you want to be healthy and feel well, but you may not be aware of how necessary it is for you to make healthy choices daily in order to reap a healthy life.

I encourage you to eat food that is filled with good nutrition and avoid eating and drinking excessive amounts of sugar, caffeine, and chemical-laden, prepackaged options. Get good sleep, drink lots of clean water, and exercise regularly. You may have groaned when you read this and realized that doing so would require discipline and some lifestyle changes on your part; however, I can assure you that the benefits you will reap are well worth any sacrifice you make.

You only have one body, and if you take care of it, it will last a long time and help you enjoy your life. If you don't take care of it, you will be sorry later on that you didn't. Don't wait until it is too late to do the right thing. Sow good health habits now and you will be strong, energetic, and enthusiastic about life.

Prayer: Father, help me make good health choices. Teach me how to take good care of myself so I will feel my best and serve You better.

✷ Unity ✷

Behold, how good and how pleasant it is for brethren to dwell together in unity! PSALM 133:1

I recently had the privilege of seeing the heads of two large religious groups, who have been at odds for over five hundred years, agree to work together for the sake of unity. The atmosphere was filled with God's presence as these two men of God shook hands and declared their love and trust of one another.

They have agreed to disagree agreeably about the things they don't agree on and to magnify the things they do agree about and work around those things. Unity brings peace, and that is where we find God's blessing and His anointing. This is the same whether it is in our homes, workplaces, or churches. We must have unity if we want to enjoy life and see God's power work in our midst. However, unity doesn't automatically come because we want it—we must all be willing to work for it.

Humility is a vital ingredient for those who treasure unity. We need to realize that no one of us is always right about everything. Wisdom listens genuinely to what other people have to say, and wisdom loves peace (see James 3:17). Make a decision to be a maker and maintainer of peace. Those who do are called the sons of God (see Matthew 5:9).

Prayer: Father, help me be a peacemaker in my home, workplace, and church. I want to avoid strife and learn to love and value all people. Help me always see the good in people.

September 2

✷ A Love Affair with God ✷

Love the Lord your God with all your heart and with all your soul and with all your mind and with all your strength.

MARK 12:30 (NIV)

The Christian life is not about following rules and regulations, but it is about a love affair with God. It is about doing life with Him, and knowing that He is more important than anything else. Keeping God first in all that we do is something we will have to do on purpose because the world is filled with many things designed to distract us from Him. God wants us to be blessed and enjoy the things He gives us, but we must not let anything else cause us to forget Him. I urge you to think about Jesus, talk about Him, talk to Him, and acknowledge Him in all your ways.

> If you keep God first in all you do, He will keep you first in what He does.

Speak this: Jesus is the center of my life, and I can do nothing without Him!

✷ Jesus Is Our Healer ✷

Bless the Lord, O my soul, and forget not all His benefits: Who forgives all your iniquities, Who heals all your diseases.

PSALM 103:2–3 (NKJV)

Perhaps you are in need of healing, and if you are, then I want to remind you that Jesus is our Healer. He may work through a doctor, or medicine, or a medical procedure, or He may grant you a miracle, but be sure of this: Jesus is our Healer!

Always look to Him first when you are sick or in pain. Ask for His healing and direction in your situation. Even while being treated medically, continue to trust God to use whatever means He desires to heal you. Jesus took our sicknesses and diseases, and by His stripes we are healed and made whole (see Isaiah 53:5).

With Jesus, every day we get better and better in every way!

Speak this: God's healing power is working in me right now, and every day I get better and better in every way.

✷ Imperfection ✷

But God demonstrates His own love toward us, in that while we were still sinners, Christ died for us. ROMANS 5:8 (NKJV)

Yesterday, in a moment of hot temper, I said something I should not have said, and of course, once I calmed down, I felt bad that I had behaved foolishly. I immediately asked God for forgiveness and apologized to Him. Today, I am rejoicing in the fact that God does not demand perfection from us in order to receive His love.

A person who pressures him- or herself to be perfect is properly referred to as a "perfectionist," and they usually live under a great deal of pressure and disappointment simply because reaching perfection while here on earth is an unattainable goal. Our loving Father knows this, so He sent Christ to die for our sins (imperfections). The truth is that our sins are paid for before we ever commit them!

I urge you to believe that God loves you unconditionally at all times and your fellowship with Him does not need to be interrupted by your imperfections (sins). When you make mistakes, admit them, talk openly with the Lord about them, be willing to turn from them, and remember that it was for people just like you and me that Jesus died!

Prayer: Father, thank You that I don't need to live under the pressure to be perfect. I want to do everything right, but when I fail, help me remember that Your love for me does not diminish.

✷ Sorrow and Rejoicing ✷

Rejoice with those who rejoice [sharing others' joy], and weep with those who weep [sharing others' grief]. ROMANS 12:15

I have noticed that my children and my close friends always call me right away to share any good news they have and any grief or sorrow they are experiencing. I woke up this morning to two text messages, one from my daughter and another from a good friend. Both of them were about difficulties they were going through. I felt sorrow for their challenges, but I rejoiced that they feel close enough to me to share them with me.

I believe God feels the same way about us. He is delighted when we run to Him to share any joy or sorrow that we have. I am so grateful that we can talk to our Heavenly Father about absolutely anything! Sharing the things that are meaningful to us with those we love is what builds deeper relationship.

God cares about everything that concerns you, and He wants to be included in every detail of your life. He is indeed the best friend you will ever have!

Prayer: Father, I thank You that I can come to You with everything that happens in my life, and that You are always interested in me. I rejoice in being able to share my life with You.

✷ Developing Your Potential ✷

Every place upon which the sole of your foot shall tread, that have I given to you . . . JOSHUA 1:3

Every person has untapped potential that needs to be developed. The way we develop it is to take steps of faith. God told Joshua that He had already given him all the land, but he had to step out and take it. Are you stepping out into new things as God guides you, or shrinking back in fear?

Not seeing ourselves as God does is one of the reasons that some people never develop their potential. We can't develop what we don't believe we have! You have tremendous potential and God will use you to do amazing things if you will trust Him and take steps of faith. Stepping out into the unknown and into things we have not experienced is challenging but it leads us to fulfill our destiny.

God told Joshua to be strong and courageous (see Joshua 1:9) because He would be with him everywhere he went, and God is with you also. When you step out, you are not stepping out alone, and should you stumble and fall, God will be there to pick you up.

Prayer: Father, help me develop the potential that You have placed in me. Help me take bold steps of faith even when I feel afraid. Thank You for always being with me.

✷ Don't Be Discouraged with Yourself ✷

And I am convinced and sure of this very thing, that He Who began a good work in you will continue until the day of Jesus Christ [right up to the time of His return], developing [that good work] and perfecting and bringing it to full completion in you.

PHILIPPIANS 1:6

If you feel that you are not where you should be spiritually, you are not alone. I think most people can easily become discouraged with themselves when they compare their behavior with that of Jesus or even other more mature believers. When we study the Bible, or perhaps read a good book about Christian character, God's goal is to urge us forward, not to make us feel condemned because we have not arrived yet. God is working in you! He will continue doing so until Jesus returns. There is no need to compare yourself with anyone else.

Enjoy where you are, and soon you will be where you want to be!

Speak this: I'm growing in spiritual maturity because God is continually working in me. He will complete the good work that He has begun in me!

⁕ *Benefits* ⁕

Bless (affectionately, gratefully praise) the Lord, O my soul, and forget not [one of] all His benefits. PSALM 103:2

When most people apply for a job these days, one of the first things they ask is, "What are the benefits?" They want to know about health insurance benefits, retirement benefits, and vacation benefits, among other things. Benefits are important to us, and according to the Scripture above, relationship with God comes with many benefits.

He provides insurance but calls it "assurance," and it covers any kind of problem you could encounter. He assures us that our sins are forgiven and our needs are met. He protects us from our enemies and gives us strength to do all things.

He gives us retirement benefits because He promises to guide us until we die (see Psalm 48:14, Isaiah 46:4). As far as vacation benefits are concerned, He gives us rest and relaxation for our souls if we will come to Him when we are weary (see Matthew 11:28).

You can rest today and every day in the knowledge that as you serve God, you have every benefit anyone could possibly want. Let us not forget one of all of His many benefits!

Prayer: Father, thank You for Your many benefits. I am extremely grateful for Your goodness to me.

✳ Faith Cannot Coexist with a Guilty Conscience ✳

The just shall live by faith . . . HEBREWS 10:38

We receive all the great promises of God through faith, and it is very important for us to remain in faith at all times. We are told in Scripture that righteousness is revealed, which leads us from faith to faith (see Romans 1:17). We are to live by faith! However, that is impossible to do if we don't walk daily in the righteousness that is ours through Christ.

Condemnation and a guilty conscience are opposed to faith. When we feel bad about ourselves or guilty over something we have done wrong, it is difficult to go boldly to God in faith and receive the help we need. There is a simple answer to this problem!

We all do things that are wrong, but we all have the opportunity to admit our sins, repent of them, and then confidently believe that God has completely forgiven us and remembers our sins no more.

If you have been living with a guilty conscience most of the time, I urge you to take a stand against it and start believing what God's Word says: There is no condemnation for those who are in Christ Jesus (see Romans 8:1).

Prayer: Father, thank You for the gift of righteousness in Christ. Help me to know who I am and to resist any and all thoughts of condemnation.

September 10

✷ Goal Setting ✷

But as for you, be strong and do not give up, for your work will be rewarded. 2 CHRONICLES 15:7 (NIV)

I believe God has created us in such a way that we cannot be satisfied and fulfilled unless we have goals that we are working toward accomplishing in our lives. They may be short- or long-term goals, but we need goals. Our goals give us purpose, and the accomplishment of them gives us something to look forward to.

I am a very goal-oriented person, and I have found that having dreams and desires and reaching for them daily gives me purpose in my life. We always want to make sure that our goals are God-inspired and that they align with His will for us, and then we should lean on Him to help us accomplish them.

Reaching our goals requires hard work, diligence, patience, and a determination not to give up, but these qualities eventually produce a wonderful reward. We all have a lot of potential (untapped ability), and it is exciting to work with God and watch Him help us develop them. You can do amazing things if you will simply set goals and stay focused on reaching them.

Prayer: Father, help me accomplish amazing things today and every day. Help me put my energy into something that will produce good fruit and bring a satisfying reward.

✷ A Humble Mind ✷

Let this same attitude and purpose and [humble] mind be in you which was in Christ Jesus: [Let Him be your example in humility].

PHILIPPIANS 2:5

All men are created equal, and therefore we should be cautious about beginning to think that we are better than anyone else. It is very unwise to look down on others, while exalting ourselves in our own mind. It is easy to develop prideful mind-sets about some people and form low opinions of them, when in reality, we know nothing about them at all. Everyone has a story, and if we took time to get to truly know them, our opinions would change drastically.

Never form an opinion about anyone unless you have taken the time to truly know them.

Speak this: I will not form hasty and premature opinions about people I don't really know.

⁕ *The Power of Peace* ⁕

He who is slow to anger is better than the mighty, he who rules his [own] spirit than he who takes a city. PROVERBS 16:32

Jesus teaches us that He has given us His very own peace and that we should stop allowing ourselves to become upset and disturbed (see John 14:27). I have learned that the more peaceful I am, the more powerful I am. I am stronger in every way when I hold my peace in each situation. As the Scripture above shares, the person who can rule his spirit is, in reality, stronger than someone who would have the ability to capture an entire city. That is an amazing statement and one that we should seriously consider.

We encounter situations almost daily that are designed by Satan to frustrate and upset us. Hold your peace and you will maintain your power! The apostle Paul teaches that if we go to bed angry instead of resolving issues that are upsetting us, we give the devil a foothold in our lives (see Ephesians 4:26–27).

Let the peace of God rule in your heart as an umpire (see Colossians 3:15). Don't allow unbridled emotions to rule you and steal your peace.

Prayer: Jesus, thank You for giving me Your peace. Help me choose to walk in it at all times!

⁕ How to Bless Yourself ⁕

The merciful, kind, and generous man benefits himself [for his deeds return to bless him], but he who is cruel and callous [to the wants of others] brings on himself retribution. PROVERBS 11:17

We all have many opportunities daily to either be kind and good to someone or to be callous to their needs and ignore them. What we choose to do helps determine the level of our own blessings. God's Word clearly teaches us that when we are kind and generous toward others, our good deeds return to bless us.

How I treat others has become very important to me over the years. It has always been important to God, but sadly, it wasn't always important to me. I am grateful that He has changed me in this area of life, because I am much happier when I purposely look for ways to bless other people rather than having myself on my mind all the time.

I often say that we cannot be happy and selfish at the same time! Do you want to increase your blessings? If so, then be on the lookout for the needs of others and take action to help them. Whether they need a smile, a hug, an encouraging word, or some kind of help that will require your time or money...be ready to help! As you do, you will benefit yourself.

Prayer: Father, forgive me for being selfish and help me learn the power of generosity. Show me the needs of people and what I can do to help them.

✷ Being God's Friend ✷

And the scripture was fulfilled that says, "Abraham believed God, and it was credited to him as righteousness," and he was called God's friend. JAMES 2:23 (NIV)

Do you have a friendship with God? I pray that you do, for that is God's desire! Yes, He wants to be your friend! We may see God in many different ways. Perhaps as a Father, a Master, our Lord, our Helper—and He is all of these things, but He uses the term "friend" as a way of saying that He desires a close and intimate relationship with each of us.

I think a lot about this invitation of friendship, and I've gathered all the biblical information I can about what that means and how to develop it. I like the thought of "doing life with God." We should involve Him by inviting Him into all that we do and developing a conversational relationship with Him. God wants to talk to you, and He will talk back. He speaks to us in many ways and through many different avenues, but He does speak and we should expect Him to. How can we possibly be the friend of God if we don't have conversation?

The Bible is filled with records of people who prayed, and it is also filled with numerous accounts of God speaking to His people. Jesus said that His sheep know and hear His voice (see John 10:27). We learn to hear from God by studying His Word and by experience. I encourage you not only to talk to Him about everything, but to learn to listen and expect Him to speak to you.

God is your friend and He has promised to be with you always, until the end of time! You are never alone!

Prayer: My God and my friend, thank You for inviting me into a close friendship with You. I ask You to teach me about this friendship and help me develop it.

✷ Sharing with Others ✷

And he replied to them, He who has two tunics (undergarments), let him share with him who has none; and he who has food, let him do it the same way. LUKE 3:11

There are millions of needy people in the world. It is my opinion that we should not hang on to things we are not using just in case we ever happen to need them. There may be some things that belong in that category, but most of us have hundreds of things stored in closets and on shelves that have not been used in a long time, and even if we did need them, we probably would not know where they were. Why not pass those things on to someone in need and trust God to give us what we need, when we need it? Pack up the clothes and shoes you are not wearing, and all other useable items, and take them to a church or an organization that will distribute them for you.

When we are generous, I believe God smiles!

Speak this: I will give to those in need in the same way I would want someone to give to me if I were in need.

✷ Grace for Your Place ✷

But by the grace of God I am what I am, and his grace to me was not without effect... 1 CORINTHIANS 15:10 (NIV)

The apostle Paul knew what his assignment from God was, and he worked at it diligently. He worked hard, but God gave him the grace to do it. When we have grace for the place we are in, we find that we can do very difficult and challenging things with peace and joy.

Jesus said that His yoke is easy to bear (see Matthew 11:30). This means that, as long as we are in the will of God, no matter how difficult the assignment, we can do it with a good attitude.

When we are out of our place, or trying to do something that is not God's will for us, then there will be no grace. If you are in a difficult place, but you believe it is where God wants you to be, then receive His grace (His power and ability) by faith today and let Him bring ease to your soul.

Prayer: Father, thank You for making my burden light and easy to be borne. Help me not to complain about my place in life and let me serve You with gladness.

Resist the Devil

For a wide door of opportunity for effectual [service] has opened to me [there, a great and promising one], and [there are] many adversaries. 1 CORINTHIANS 16:9

We should be fully aware that when we make a decision to serve God and seek to do good, the devil will try to hinder and impede our progress. However, we can resist him and complete our assignment from God by being filled with a holy determination to never give up. Satan hates and despises anything good because he knows that we overcome evil with good (see Romans 12:21). In other words, we overcome him because he is the author of all evil activities. When people do nothing, evil continues to spread, but when we rise up in the power of God and resist Satan's evil by doing good, he loses ground and his activities are weakened.

I want to encourage you to set your mind and keep it set (see Colossians 3:2) on your assignment from God. Do all the good that you can, as often as you can, in every place that you can. Be a blessing to others, help them, encourage them, and be kind to them. Seek to do good to others (see 1 Thessalonians 5:15), and don't let Satan discourage you and cause you to give up just because you find the way difficult at times.

The apostle Paul said that afflictions and difficulties would be unavoidable in our position (see 1 Thessalonians 3:3). We don't need to be disturbed or surprised by it, we just need to know that God is always with us and in us, and He that is in us is greater than he that is in the world (see 1 John 4:4).

Prayer: Father, grant me grace to never give up on doing good and making progress in doing all that You have assigned me to do. Thank You!

September 18

✱ How to Avoid Trouble ✱

... Make it your ambition and definitely endeavor to live quietly and peacefully, to mind your own affairs, and to work with your hands, as we charged you. 1 THESSALONIANS 4:11

We can save ourselves a great deal of mental anguish and trouble by learning to stay out of the affairs of other people. Most of us are too free with our advice and we often give it when the truth is that nobody really wants it.

God's will for us is peace, and if we read the Scripture quoted above, we find that peace and minding our own affairs are linked together. I am sure you are like me in that you have enough of your own affairs to tend to without getting involved in other people's. Of course, if people ask for and truly want our advice or help, we should be ready to help them, but we should do so with an attitude of humility.

Most of us are quick to judge others who are not like us or who don't make the decisions that we would, but it would help each of us to remember that God instructs us not to judge at a glance or superficially (see John 7:24). Only God truly knows people's hearts and motives, and only He is qualified to judge righteously. When the Holy Spirit makes me aware that I am allowing judgmental thoughts to linger in my mind, I often say to myself, "Joyce, this is none of your business," and I let it go. Ask God to help you mind your own business!

Prayer: Father, I am sorry for all the times I have judged people and gotten into their affairs without being invited. Forgive me and help me mind my own business. Amen!

✷ God's Choices ✷

But God chose the foolish things of the world to shame the wise; God chose the weak things of the world to shame the strong.

1 CORINTHIANS 1:27 (NIV)

God delights in choosing and using people that the world would ignore and call useless. He does it so nobody can take the glory or the credit for what He does. Those who think they are intelligent and strong are often put in their place when they witness God using someone they would have rejected and assumed was incapable of doing anything noteworthy. If you have been slighted by the world, don't discount yourself from being used by God. His strength is made perfect in your weakness!

God doesn't need your ability; He needs your availability!

Speak this: I believe God can work through me, and that I can do great things for His glory.

⁕ *The Day of the Lord* ⁕

For you yourselves know perfectly well that the day of the [return of the] Lord will come [as unexpectedly and suddenly] as a thief in the night. 1 THESSALONIANS 5:2

The apostles taught the people frequently about the second coming of Christ. They were reminded to live unselfishly (see Philippians 4:5), to watch and pray, and to look for His return at any moment. I think this is something we need to be reminded of more often in our lives today.

We don't want to be like the five foolish virgins whom we read about in Matthew 25 who fell asleep while waiting for the bridegroom, and then when he did come, they were unprepared. We should live with expectancy and be alert and active doing our best at all times.

What would you change in your life if you believed that Jesus was coming for you today? Whatever it might be, it would be wise to change it now and not put it off. We should live at all times to please the Lord and do everything we do unto Him and for His glory.

Prayer: Father, thank You for reminding me that Jesus will be coming soon. Help me be fully prepared to meet Him. Help me live every day as if it were my last, doing my best at all times. Thank You!

✷ More Than a Conqueror ✷

Yet amid all these things we are more than conquerors and gain a surpassing victory through Him Who loved us. ROMANS 8:37

Every day of my life isn't perfect and neither is yours. We all have times when we experience tribulation and affliction, but even then, we still have the victory because Jesus loves us.

What does it mean to be "more than conquerors"? I believe it means that we know we will have victory and that all things will end well even before we have a problem or challenge. We can live with the confidence that God is always on our side and that by following His guidance, we will always triumph over difficulty.

I urge you not to merely look at your problems, thinking and talking about them over and over, but think about your breakthrough that is already planned by God and is sure to come at just the right time. Begin thanking God for it as if you already have it, and be persuaded beyond doubt that nothing in this world can ever separate you from God's love.

Prayer: Father, thank You that through You, I am more than a conqueror. Help me look forward to my breakthrough instead of looking at my difficulties in life.

✷ Dealing with Disappointment ✷

Why are you cast down, O my inner self? And why should you moan over me and be disquieted within me? Hope in God and wait expectantly for Him . . . PSALM 42:5

When we experience disappointment in life, it can develop into depression unless we quickly put our hope in God and believe that we can begin again and experience victory.

While working on a book recently, I lost several hours of work by accidentally hitting a delete key on my computer. I actually made a series of errors that prevented me from being able to get the work back. I was disappointed, to say the least! I had a choice to make. I could remain upset and let my disappointment turn into a bad mood that would ruin my day, or I could put my hope in God and simply begin again.

I decided to trust that I would do a better job on the lost section of my work than I did the first time and not let my disappointment defeat me. No one wants to be disappointed, but at least with God on our side, we can get "reappointed."

If you have experienced a recent disappointment, I encourage you to make a choice to not let it become a worse problem than it is. Don't let it turn into discouragement and then perhaps depression. God is ready to help you begin again if you will let go of the past and press on.

Prayer: Father, I trust You to help me turn all disappointments in life into new beginnings. Don't let me waste one of the precious days that You give me in discouragement over the past!

Choose Excellence

Then this Daniel was distinguished above the presidents and the satraps because an excellent spirit was in him, and the king thought to set him over the whole realm. DANIEL 6:3

This morning, I was walking past a parking lot, and I noticed that someone had cleaned the empty cans out of their car and just left them where their car had been parked. Whoever did that was not an excellent person, and although they may never make the connection, their behavior may inhibit them from enjoying the successful life they would like to have. God promotes excellent people, those who go the extra mile and do their best in everything they do. Don't leave messes for other people to clean up, but treat their property the way you would want yours to be treated.

God is excellent, and as His representatives, we should be excellent too!

Speak this: I will do my best at everything I do. I will not compromise. I will walk before God with excellence and integrity!

✷ Justice ✷

For the Lord delights in justice and forsakes not His saints; they are preserved forever... PSALM 37:28

Anytime we are mistreated, we feel that we are owed something. We want to be paid back for the pain we have encountered. I spent many years trying to collect from people who had hurt me, but it never worked. God is the only one who can properly pay us back for our past injustices. He makes wrong things right!

If you have been hurt and feel that you have been cheated out of what you should have had in life, I strongly encourage you to wait on God and trust Him for your recompense and reward. The Lord will pay you back and it will be a sweet victory. He never forsakes or forgets those who put their hope in Him.

We overcome evil with good, so stay busy doing as much good as you can while you wait on God's justice in your life. Don't let bitterness take root in your soul—pray for the people who hurt you. As you do, God will do amazing things in your life.

Prayer: Father, grant me the grace and patience to wait on You for justice in my life.

✷ Cease from Anger ✷

Cease from anger and forsake wrath; fret not yourself—it tends only to evildoing. PSALM 37:8

There is plenty in life to get angry about. Life is not always fair, and people certainly don't always treat us the way they should, but anger never solves the problem. Actually, anger makes our problems worse. God's Word says that when we are angry, we should not sin (see Ephesians 4:26). Your question may be, "Then what am I supposed to do when I am mistreated?" The answer is, "Trust God."

We all feel angry when things happen to us that are unfair and unjust, but we can feel anger and still not allow it to lead us into sin. Feeling anger is not a sin, but what we do with our anger can be sinful if we let it. Instead of acting on our anger and lashing out at the people who hurt us and then becoming bitter, we are taught in the Bible to trust God and pray for our enemies (see Matthew 5:44). It may seem difficult, but it is the only approach that keeps us peaceful and eventually brings justice into our lives.

Like many of you, I have been hurt in life, and I wasted a lot of years being bitter, angry, and resentful, but thankfully, there is another option. We can choose to cast our care on God and believe that He will always make wrong things right. No one enjoys being hurt, but we always triumph in Christ Jesus!

Prayer: Father, give me the patience to wait on You to deal with my enemies. Help me respond properly when I feel angry by immediately forgiving the person who hurt me and putting my trust in You to make wrong things right.

✷ *The Benefits of Trust* ✷

He shall not be afraid of evil tidings; his heart is firmly fixed, trusting (leaning on and being confident) in the Lord.

PSALM 112:7

There are many wonderful benefits that we experience from trusting God, but one of the most important is that we no longer need to live in fear. There are many things in life that we cannot handle, but God can handle anything, and He will always help us and show us what we need to do if we put our trust in Him.

Fear is the normal human response to any kind of bad news, but thankfully, we can make a choice to trust God rather than going with how we feel. When we trust God, we not only shut the door on fear, but we release peace and joy in our lives. Trust relieves stress, and that helps our health and our relationships. Trust also releases God to work in our lives and brings solutions to the problems that we need help with. Trust is very beneficial, and it is God's desire that we trust Him at all times, in every situation.

Prayer: Father, please help me grow in trusting You.

⁕ Be Wise ⁕

Be diligent to know the state of your flocks, and look well to your herds. PROVERBS 27:23

When my mom was in her eighties and still alive, she had a bad habit of thinking she could spend whatever she saw on her bank statement, so she did. She wasn't good at looking ahead and managing her money in such a way that she would have enough for the whole month. Sadly, many people are like that and it causes problems for them—sometimes big problems. We should always be diligent to know what we have to spend and how much we owe. God expects us to be people of integrity who pay our bills on time. If we manage what we have well, God will give us more!

Don't spend money that you don't have and then you'll have plenty to spend when you truly need to.

Speak this: I am diligent to be well informed about my finances, and I don't waste money.

September 28

✷ Relax ✷

So we see that they were not able to enter [into His rest], because of their unwillingness to adhere to and trust in and rely on God [unbelief had shut them out]. HEBREWS 3:19

There are plenty of things that happen in daily life that we can let upset us unless we choose not to. Yesterday we had a water leak in one of our pipes and were told that we may have a more serious problem throughout the house! Today our credit card company canceled our card, saying it had been compromised; when that happens it always involves a lot of work to change any autopay bills. In both instances, my first human reaction was to get frustrated, which always leads to being tense, but thankfully, as God's children we have another option.

Being upset doesn't solve our problems, and being tense doesn't help us in any way, so why do it? I was reminded by the Holy Spirit to relax and believe that God would help me do what I needed to do.

Is there anything you are frustrated about? Is it causing tension in your life? If so, why not just relax on purpose? Take a breath and let everything inside relax while you remind yourself that God is with you and He is for you, and with Him, you can do whatever you need to do (see Philippians 4:13).

Prayer: Father, help me relax and enter Your rest in every situation that I encounter in my daily life. Thank You for guiding me at all times and helping me.

✷ What Do You Think of Yourself? ✷

Do two walk together except they make an appointment and have agreed? AMOS 3:3

Your self-image is like a photo you carry of yourself in your wallet. How you see yourself is a determining factor in what you accomplish in life, so it's important to learn to see yourself as God sees you.

God created you, and you are special to Him. He has a good plan for your life, and He loves you unconditionally. You may only think of what you do wrong and what you think you are not, but God sees what you will be as you and He work together to bring good changes in you.

You may not be where you should be, but if you are a Christian, you are a new creature in Christ and you are in the process of changing daily. Rejoice in how far you have come instead of being sad about how far you have to go. Have a daily appointment with God and come into agreement with Him to see yourself as He does and it will put a smile on your face and His!

Prayer: Father, help me see myself through Your eyes, as the new creature You have made me to be. Help me let go of the old things and take hold of Your new plan for me.

✱ Loss ✱

And God will wipe away every tear from their eyes; there shall be no more death, nor sorrow, nor crying. There shall be no more pain, for the former things have passed away.

REVELATION 21:4 (NKJV)

I heard the news today that a close friend and colleague died. She was thirty-seven years old, married with two children. She was a committed Christian and a very lovely young lady. One of the most difficult things to deal with in life is loss that seems to make no sense to us, but I am grateful that even in the midst of a tragedy like this one, we can still trust God.

I am sure that you have experienced some type of loss yourself, and I want to encourage you to resist an unhealthy reasoning that never leads to answers, but to more and more questions. Your loss may not be the death of someone you love, but the pain of some kind of loss comes to us all.

Don't ever allow loss to tear you away from God. In your pain draw closer to Him and trust Him to heal your wounded heart.

Prayer: Father, thank You for comfort and for healing my wounds.

✷ Be Careful What You Say ✷

I said, I will take heed and guard my ways, that I may sin not with my tongue; I will muzzle my mouth as with a bridle while the wicked are before me. PSALM 39:1

The psalmist David must have had true insight into the power of words, because he often speaks about the importance of not sinning with our tongue. It may be hard to face, but many of the things we say are sinful. Whatever is not of faith is sin (see Romans 14:23), so anything we say that is filled with doubt, fear, unbelief, etcetera is sinful, and that is only the beginning of the list I could make. We are God's representatives, and as such, we speak for Him. Our words judge us in front of the world and we need to be careful what we say at all times, but especially when we are before nonbelievers.

> What comes out of your mouth originates in your heart, so if you listen to yourself, you can learn a lot about yourself!

Speak this: My words contain power, so I will be careful about what I say!

October 2

⁕ Think Big ⁕

Enlarge the place of your tent, and let the curtains of your habitations be stretched out; spare not; lengthen your cords and strengthen your stakes. ISAIAH 54:2

God's Word teaches us that He can do much more than what we can dream, imagine, or think (see Ephesians 3:20), so why not think big? Surely we don't believe that God wants us to live narrow lives with barely enough to get by in life. He is a big God and wants to provide more than enough of all that we need.

Always be content with what God is providing, but at the same time, think big about your future. God wants to use you in a *big* way, bless you in a *big* way, and help you in a *big* way! Don't let your own small thinking keep you trapped in a little life.

Prayer: Father, thank You for reminding me to think big! Let me think Your thoughts and dream Your dreams.

⁕ Give Thanks ⁕

Give thanks in all circumstances; for this is God's will for you in Christ Jesus. 1 THESSALONIANS 5:18 (NIV)

I recommend forming a habit of giving thanks the moment you wake up each day and continuing to do so throughout the day. A thankful person is a happy person! I have also noticed in my own life that I have more energy when I am thankful.

It is easy to fall into the trap of focusing on what is wrong with life and the people we deal with, but that is not what God desires, and it steals our joy and energy. Each of us has many things to be thankful for, but the first thing to thank God for each day is His love and salvation through Jesus. What an amazing gift God has freely given us!

Thank God at all times, including circumstances that you don't like. Give thanks that you don't have to go through your challenges alone because God is always with you. You are more than a conqueror in Christ (see Romans 8:37), and He always causes you to triumph in Christ Jesus (see 2 Corinthians 2:14).

Prayer: Father, I thank You for Your amazing goodness and for Your help and presence in my life.

October 4

⁕ Who Is Directing Your Life? ⁕

. . . It is not in man [even in a strong man or in a man at his best] to direct his [own] steps. JEREMIAH 10:23

It is hard for us to realize that we don't have the ability to run our own lives and have them turn out well. Coming to that realization usually requires that we make many mistakes and find out the hard way that we need to humble ourselves under God's mighty hand and ask for His help and guidance in all things.

If things are not going well in your life, perhaps it is because you are making your own plans and expecting God to bless them. I certainly wasted many years doing that, but I've learned to ask for God's help and to acknowledge Him in all of my ways (see Proverbs 3:6).

Humble people do not think more highly of themselves than they ought to, and they fully realize that even on their best day, they still need God's wisdom concerning any decision or plans that they make.

Prayer: Father, I am sorry for all the times I have made my own plans without consulting You. Forgive me and grant me Your wisdom at all times.

✷ Choice Overload ✷

If any of you lacks wisdom, let him ask God, who gives generously to all without reproach, and it will be given him. JAMES 1:5 (ESV)

I recently read that the average supermarket carries 48,750 items. I think that is choice overload. Most people would say that life is stressful these days, and I believe one of the reasons why is that we have so many choices in most things that it causes confusion, and we may end up making no decision at all. What to watch on TV? There are so many choices. What to wear? There are so many clothes in our closets that we become confused about which outfit to put on. I want to encourage you to pray, asking God for guidance, and then believe you have it and make a decision. Don't let the choices available to you become a stressor in your life!

> Simplifying your life is one of the best ways to remain peaceful!

Speak this: God gives me wisdom to make good choices.

✷ *God's Mark Is on You* ✷

In Him you also trusted, after you heard the word of truth, the gospel of your salvation; in whom also, having believed, you were sealed with the Holy Spirit of promise. EPHESIANS 1:13 (NKJV)

A seal is a stamp, a mark of ownership or of approval. It says: This person belongs to me; they are mine. Paul wrote his letter to the Ephesians and used the phrase "sealed with the Holy Spirit" in chapters 1 and 4. In his second letter to the Corinthians, he used the same language.

Both of those cities (Ephesus and Corinth) were centers for the lumber industry. The logs would arrive on rafts and be held in the harbor where buyers would come and choose the logs they wanted. After making their choice, they paid a little earnest money and cut a notch in the logs that now belonged to them.

The logs might sit in the harbor for a long time before they were claimed, but no one tried to take them because they had the owners' seal or mark on them.

We are sealed with the Holy Spirit, and that means we are protected by God, who is our owner. We may be in this world for a while, waiting for Christ to return and take us to our home in Heaven, but even though conditions may become quite difficult in the world, we can be at peace because we are marked! We have been chosen by God, paid for by the blood of Christ, and branded and sealed with the Holy Spirit. We are safe!

Prayer: Father, thank You for sealing me in the Holy Spirit and keeping me safe from harm.

⁕ The Brokenhearted ⁕

The Lord is close to those who are of a broken heart and saves such as are crushed with sorrow for sin and are humbly and thoroughly penitent. PSALM 34:18

When we have sinned, we often feel brokenhearted over what we have done. We are disappointed in ourselves and may feel that God is angry with us. He is not angry, and He has not left us. When we humble ourselves and talk to God about our sin, we can receive His complete forgiveness. You may feel far away from God right now, but He is close to you!

God is not mad at you!

Speak this: I confess my sins, telling all, and God completely forgives me!

✷ Experience God's Love ✷

[That you may really come] to know [practically, through experience for yourselves] the love of Christ, which far surpasses mere knowledge [without experience] . . . EPHESIANS 3:19

I sense the Holy Spirit urging me this morning to meditate on how much God loves me, and I want to urge you to do the same thing. God doesn't love us because we deserve it, but simply because He is love, and He delights in loving us.

Although we walk by faith and we don't base what we believe on mere experience or what we see with our natural eyes, it is nonetheless encouraging and energizing when we do see and experience the manifestation of our faith. God's Word teaches us to pray to experience His Love, and to be conscious and aware of His Love (see 1 John 4:16; Ephesians 3:19).

Watch daily for all the ways in which God reveals His love for you. It may be in giving you favor, or providing something you enjoy, or giving you great joy. He can reveal Himself in countless ways, and learning how to recognize them is not only an exciting adventure, but it also feeds and builds our faith.

God loves you more than you can imagine. He loves you every moment of your life, and He is reaching out to you right now with His healing and energizing love. Receive it!

Prayer: Father, teach me to recognize all the ways in which You reveal Your love to me. Let me experience it, enjoy it, and share it with other people.

✷ Be Happy ✷

Rejoice in the Lord always [delight, gladden yourselves in Him]; again I say, Rejoice! PHILIPPIANS 4:4

Stop waiting for someone or something to make you happy, and take responsibility for your own happiness. The type of attitude we choose to have toward people and life is a major factor in determining our level of happiness. We can focus on what people don't do and what we don't have, or we can focus on what people do for us, their value to us, and how many blessings we do have in life. It is a choice! We cannot sit idly by and "wish" we were happy, blaming people, life, and perhaps even God because we aren't. You have as many reasons to be happy as most people do, so get started today!

Stop giving someone else the responsibility to keep you happy.

Speak this: I am not going to waste another day being unhappy. I will rejoice and be glad.

⁕ Answered Prayer ⁕

Then one of them, upon seeing that he was cured, turned back, recognizing and thanking and praising God with a loud voice.

LUKE 17:15

In God's Word we read about ten lepers who asked Jesus to heal them, and He did; however, only one came back to give thanks (see Luke 17:11–15). This is a great reminder to be sure that our petitions don't outweigh our praise!

This morning I made a list of all the prayers I could think of that God has answered for me this year. I did it to remind myself of how good God is, how powerful prayer is, and to once again thank Him for the amazing privilege of prayer.

Just think about it: We can go to God and ask for anything and then cast our care on Him. Prayer is so much better than worry and anxiety. I encourage you to ask, because you can't get an answer if you don't ask (see James 4:2). I also encourage you to regularly give thanks! Be specific and perhaps make a list of the prayers God answers for you. I like keeping notes because I can refer to them to refresh my memory concerning the goodness of God. Recalling to mind the good things that God has done for us increases our faith to trust Him even more.

Prayer: Father, thank You for all the prayers You have answered for me. Help me to be thankful and to never forget Your goodness.

✷ I Wish I Wouldn't Have . . . ✷

Do not [earnestly] remember the former things; neither consider the things of old. ISAIAH 43:18

This morning I thought, *I wish I wouldn't have done that yesterday!* Immediately, the Lord lovingly chastised me, reminding me that looking back at something I cannot change is energy-draining and merely produces stress. The only thing we can do about the past is learn from it.

I don't mean to say that we should not be sorry for the things we do wrong or that hurt people, but it is very important to deal with them and then move on quickly. Regret is self-defeating. It does nothing to change the past, but it does steal today's energy!

Pray about the things you are sorry for and ask God to redeem your mistakes by working something good out of them, but refuse to live with regret. Peter made a big mistake by denying Jesus at a crucial time, but after he wept bitterly about it (see Luke 22:62), it is never mentioned in the New Testament again. He was sorry, but he moved past it in the power of the Holy Spirit. I urge you to make the same choice anytime you're tempted to get stuck in the regrets of yesterday.

Prayer: Father, thank You that I don't have to live in the past. Help me fully embrace the future You have for me. Thank You!

⁕ Plan to Be Positive ⁕

Surely your goodness and love will follow me all the days of my life . . . PSALM 23:6 (NIV)

The psalmist David frequently said positive things, and we can plan to do the same. Each day plan to say at least five positive things within two hours after you get up. I believe it will improve your mood and you will see good results.

It is easy to listen to all the negative talk that is abundant in society today and to become negative also, but if you *plan* to be positive, you are more likely to be that way. Make your list right now and get started changing your day!

> The more positive you are, the better you will like your life.

Speak this: God is good to me, and I am looking forward to this day!

⁕ Variety ⁕

In the beginning God created the heavens and the earth.

GENESIS 1:1 (NKJV)

From the first verse of the Bible, we are told that God is creative. He not only creates things, but within groups of things, we see a large variety. Not all trees, flowers, animals, or people are the same. Actually, the variety is quite amazing.

I have found in my own life that I need variety. If I do the same thing or eat the same thing over and over again for long periods of time, I begin to get bored with it. You may be feeling that your life has gotten a little stale, and it is very possible that all you need is to change things up! Be creative and introduce more variety into your life. We are created in God's image, and if He enjoys variety, then we will too.

I always spend time with God, but I don't always do the same thing during that time. I walk every morning for exercise, but I don't always take the same route. I enjoy a variety of foods, the company of different people, and wearing a variety of clothing styles.

I encourage you to introduce plenty of variety into your life and don't be afraid to try new things.

Prayer: Father, thank You for all the variety that You have created. Help me think creatively and enjoy many different things.

October 14

✷ Finish What You Begin ✷

Better is the end of a thing than the beginning of it, and the patient in spirit is better than the proud in spirit. ECCLESIASTES 7:8

For the past two days I have been thinking about the importance of finishing what we begin. Perhaps you have some new goals that you're excited about, but we all know that it is easier to plan and begin than it is to finish. I want to share three keys I have found to be helpful in accomplishing a goal.

First, it is important to count the cost. Think through what your goal will require in order for you to finish. How much work will be involved? Is there a financial cost, and if so, are you prepared to pay it?

Second, set your mind and keep it set on finishing. When you get weary of working and not seeing the end result yet, don't give up. This is when you need real discipline. Keep your thoughts positive about reaching your goal, and don't start entertaining thoughts that you just can't do it.

Third, be patient! Nothing worth doing is ever accomplished without patience. That means you may need to do the right thing for a long time before you see the result you desire. But reaching your goal will be well worth the wait.

Prayer: Father, help me be a finisher in life!

⁕ It Is All Up to Me ⁕

Except the Lord builds the house, they labor in vain who build it... PSALM 127:1

There are few things in life more stressful than thinking, *It's all up to me!* My stress level is rising just saying it. Jesus said, "Apart from Me...you can do nothing" (John 15:5). He is just waiting for us to humble ourselves and ask for His help, because when He gets involved, life gets much easier.

We need help, and Jesus sent us the Holy Spirit, who is the Helper! He is also a gentleman and will not push His way into our lives. I encourage you to ask for the help you need and receive it, that your joy may be full (see John 16:24).

"Help me, Lord!" should be the most frequently uttered prayer.

Speak this: I need God's help in everything I do. I can do nothing without Jesus!

✷ Listen ✷

I will listen [with expectancy] to what God the Lord will say, for He will speak peace to His people . . . PSALM 85:8

I think most of us talk more when we pray than we listen. We need to listen, because God often reveals very simple answers to some of our most complex problems. I believe God speaks to us in many different ways. He might speak through what the Bible calls the still, small voice. I explain that as a *knowing* in your heart of what you are to do. He may speak through another person, through your own thoughts, a circumstance, an article you read, or a sermon you hear. The ways that God speaks to us are probably countless, but we often don't recognize His voice either because we are narrow-minded about how He will speak, or we simply don't listen.

When you pray, be sure you do so with a listening ear. Keep your spiritual ears tuned to your Master at all times. As you hear Him, He will lead and guide you into what will produce peace in your life. Part of the definition of the word *hearing* is "to be listening." I believe God is speaking, but are you listening?

God wants to reveal things to you that you need to hear. Pray about everything and be sure you watch and wait for Him to speak.

Prayer: Father, I delight in hearing Your voice. Teach me how to listen!

✷ God Recycles Damaged Things ✷

Therefore, if anyone is in Christ, he is a new creation. The old has passed away; behold, the new has come. 2 CORINTHIANS 5:17 (ESV)

Recycling is something that has developed over the past couple of decades and is now a big business. We are all encouraged to put certain types of trash in special trash containers for recycling. It is good to take used and even damaged things and create something new from them. We may think this is a modern idea, but God has been doing it as long as time has existed.

There is nothing about you or your past that God cannot restore and make something new out of. He actually uses those people that the world views as completely without value and throws away. Look forward to your future and never think it is too late for you to have a good life.

God recycles our trash.

Speak this: God is restoring anything in my life that is damaged. He makes all things new!

October 18

⁕ *The Mind of the Spirit* ⁕

. . . The mind of the [Holy] Spirit is life and [soul] peace [both now and forever]. ROMANS 8:6

The mind is a beautiful thing. Thoughts are constantly running through it, and they minister life or death to us, depending on which ones we choose to keep.

One of the ways that God speaks to us is through our thoughts, but of course we cannot assume that every thought we have is from God. How can we discern which ones are and which ones are not? The mind of the flesh (or our carnal nature) is "sense and reason without the Holy Spirit" (see Romans 8:6 [AMP]) and it produces thoughts that are filled with death. These thoughts produce every kind of misery known to man. But thoughts from God minister life and peace to us.

When we truly know the character of God, we quickly recognize thoughts of the Spirit because they are filled with the fruit of the Spirit. For example, God often gives me thoughts of things I can do for other people, and as I meditate on those thoughts, I sense joy and enthusiasm. At times I have thoughts running through my mind of something a family member or friend is *not* doing for me that I think they should do, and those thoughts begin to make me angry and unhappy, so I definitely know they are not "God-thoughts."

I woke up this morning and lay in bed for a while pondering how the quality of my life today would depend on the thoughts I choose to think, and I want to remind you to join me in maintaining a beautiful mind that is filled with thoughts of the Spirit that minister life.

Prayer: Father, please help me think thoughts that You approve of and quickly cast down the ones that You don't approve of. Thank You!

✴ Jesus Understands ✴

For we do not have a High Priest Who is unable to understand and sympathize and have a shared feeling with our weaknesses and infirmities and liability to the assaults of temptation, but One Who has been tempted in every respect as we are, yet without sinning. HEBREWS 4:15

Most of us at times feel that no one understands us. We may feel separated from others because we are not like them or because they are strong in areas in which we are weak. This can be a lonely feeling, but in reality, we are never alone. Jesus is always with us and He understands us.

Not only does Jesus understand our weaknesses and what we go through when we're tempted by the devil, but He understands everything about us. People certainly did not understand Jesus when He walked the earth. Even His own family didn't understand Him, but He was content knowing that His Father in Heaven totally understood each thing about Him and all that He experienced during His life here on Earth.

There is nothing about you that the Lord is not aware of, and He cares about everything that concerns you.

Prayer: Father, thank You for understanding me and accepting me! Help me remember that You are always on my side even when others are not.

✷ Trust God with Your Pain ✷

He heals the brokenhearted and binds up their wounds...

PSALM 147:3

It is fairly easy to trust God for something that you want, but what about trusting God when life hurts? Are you willing to trust God with your pain? When I am hurting, I find that my faith is tested. We don't like pain, and we usually don't understand why we have it. We may find it difficult to see beyond it, let alone believe that anything good can come out of it. However, God does promise that He will heal our wounds, and that He will take our pain and turn it into something good as we continue trusting Him (see Genesis 50:20). If you are hurting right now, I encourage you to offer your pain to God and ask Him to use it for His glory and work it out for your good!

With the right attitude, your pain can become your gain!

Speak this: I will trust God at all times, and His praise shall continually be in my mouth.

✷ Guardian Angels ✷

Bless (affectionately, gratefully praise) the Lord, you His angels, you mighty ones who do His commandments, hearkening to the voice of His word. PSALM 103:20

This morning I was thinking about how dangerous complaining is. God is so very good and we have thousands of things to be thankful for, yet we often complain. We have angels who are ready to help us, but they listen to and act on God's Word, not our complaining.

I'm in Florida and the weather this week has been cooler than normal, and when I look back, I realize I have voiced a lot of complaints about it. I expected it to be warmer and have not been happy that it wasn't. When I left home it was 18 degrees, and it's been 60 here in Florida, but I wanted it to be warmer! I am quite ashamed of my behavior now that I realize what I have been doing.

I have much more to be thankful for than I have to complain about, and so do you. If you find yourself tempted to complain today about anything, do yourself a favor and instead of giving voice to it, find something good to talk about! Your angels are waiting to help you, so keep speaking God's Word and trusting Him.

Prayer: Father, forgive me for complaining and help me keep my mouth filled with gratitude for Your goodness in my life.

✷ Increase ✷

May the Lord give you increase more and more, you and your children. PSALM 115:14

The Lord put the word "increase" in my spirit a couple of days ago and I keep thinking about it. There are many areas of my life where I would delight in seeing increase, and I am sure you feel the same way. I believe God is bringing increase to our ministry this year and that we will be able to help more people. He is urging me to declare increase over my ministry, our partners, my children, Dave and myself, and our home.

Here are just a few of the areas we can expect to increase: favor, peace, joy, laughter, knowledge of God, greater intimacy with Jesus, creativity, and productivity. Energy, enthusiasm, passion, and zeal are at the top of my list. An increase in wisdom is at the top of my list also, as well as knowledge, discernment, prudence, and discretion. You can make your own list, but be sure you have Scripture to back it up. For example, if you are a giver, then declaring financial increase is scriptural (see Malachi 3:10–11).

When we declare a thing, we are speaking out what God's Word says. We are agreeing with God. Words have power, and we should use all of ours for a beneficial purpose rather than a useless waste of time. Be filled with expectancy for increase in all areas of your life.

Prayer: Father, I am excited about seeing increase. I want to be able to help more and more people and be equipped for every good work.

⁕ God Enjoys You ⁕

For the Lord your God is living among you. He is a mighty savior. He will take delight in you with gladness. With his love, he will calm all your fears. He will rejoice over you with joyful songs.

ZEPHANIAH 3:17 (NLT)

It is often hard to comprehend that God enjoys us, but He does. He also wants us to enjoy Him. I once heard it said that our highest calling is to enjoy God. I am learning to make sure I enjoy God every day, all throughout the day, and I have taken a step of faith and decided to believe that He enjoys me. I wasted many years feeling most of the time that He was not pleased with me because of my imperfections, but I no longer believe that lie.

Just as we see the flaws of our children and yet we still enjoy them, God does the same thing with us.

> Roses have thorns, but they are still beautiful and we enjoy them.

Speak this: God sees all of my flaws and He still loves and enjoys me!

✷ Stop Being Mad at Yourself ✷

Before I formed you in the womb I knew [and] approved of you [as My chosen instrument], and before you were born I separated and set you apart, consecrating you; [and] I appointed you as a prophet to the nations. JEREMIAH 1:5

God told Jeremiah, who was allowing his fears to hold him back, that He had known and approved of him even before Jeremiah was born. He had not yet done anything right or wrong, but God approved of him.

The devil wants us to live with a vague feeling that God is not pleased with us and perhaps is a little angry with us, but that is not true. God loves us and is constantly working in our lives to help us grow in Him, to constantly become more and more like Him.

We do things that are wrong, but if our heart is right toward God and we are repentant and willing to learn, that is all God requires. Don't be mad at yourself because you think you are a disappointment to God. He knew each of us intimately even before we were born and He loves us with an everlasting love.

Prayer: Father forgive my sins, and help me develop a healthy and godly relationship with myself as well as with You.

✷ The Seasons of Life ✷

To everything there is a season, and a time for every matter or purpose under heaven. ECCLESIASTES 3:1

I want to urge you to enjoy every season of your life, because each one contains something beautiful that you don't want to miss. Life, it seems, is always changing, as well as the people around us. We also change as the years go by. Let's embrace each change and look for the blessing in it, because our times are truly in God's loving and capable hands.

Each new season in life means new adventures!

Speak this: Change is good and it keeps life fresh and exciting.

October 26

⁕ Find the Good in Everything ⁕

But test and prove all things [until you can recognize] what is good; [to that] hold fast. 1 THESSALONIANS 5:21

Recently, we were in a hotel on the twenty-seventh floor and the fire alarm went off. I was in my pajamas lying in bed when we received a call that we had to evacuate the building. The elevators automatically stop working when there is a threat of fire, so that meant we had to walk down twenty-seven flights of stairs. I would like to say that I behaved perfectly and did not complain at all, but I did do a little murmuring.

It came to my heart that I could be thankful that I was able to walk down the twenty-seven flights of stairs instead of murmuring that I had to do it. I believe we can find something good to focus on in every situation if we will look for it.

The apostle Paul said that we should thank God in everything no matter what the circumstances are, and by doing so we will not quench (suppress or subdue) the Holy Spirit (see 1 Thessalonians 5:18–19).

Look for the good things in life and focus on them! You will be much happier, and God will be able to do much more in your life.

Prayer: Father, help me always find the good in everything and magnify that!

✷ Trusting People ✷

Love bears up under anything and everything that comes, is ever ready to believe the best of every person, its hopes are fadeless under all circumstances, and it endures everything [without weakening]. 1 CORINTHIANS 13:7

Recently I dealt with a situation in which one person told me something negative and unpleasant about another person, and I had to make a choice about what to believe. Surely, you have also been in this same situation. It is easy to go through life being suspicious of people, because we have all had some bad experiences in which people have disappointed and hurt us. However, it is totally unfair to judge people based on an experience that we had with someone else.

Long ago, I became weary of being suspicious most of the time and I decided to always believe the best of others. I want to encourage you to do the same. Always give people the benefit of the doubt, and never believe something bad about them unless you positively know it to be true.

Believing the best saves you many hours of mental misery!

Speak this: I will follow God's advice and always believe the best of everyone!

✷ Winning over Worry ✷

Casting the whole of your care [all your anxieties, all your worries, all your concerns, once and for all] on Him, for He cares for you affectionately and cares about you watchfully. 1 PETER 5:7

God's Word teaches us not to worry, but at times we are all tempted to do it anyway. As a mother, I want all of my children to be happy at all times, and when they are not, I tend to get concerned about them and I want to fix whatever the problem is. I find myself in that situation today, and I am busy reminding myself that worrying and fretting does absolutely no good. It is actually a total waste of time.

Even though we may know the Word of God, we often have to remind ourselves of it by meditating on it or looking up Scriptures we know, reading them again and again. God's Word contains power that will help us do what we know we should do, and it will comfort us in our concerns.

God's Word is medicine for our souls. It calms our emotions and gives us peace of mind. Anytime you are worried about anything, I encourage you to turn to God's Word for the strength you need to let it go!

Prayer: Father, I know that You don't want me to worry, but to trust You at all times. Help me learn to never waste my time on worry.

✷ The Privilege of Prayer ✷

. . . You do not have because you do not ask. JAMES 4:2 (NKJV)

I frequently read books on prayer because I want to stay stirred up to pray throughout each day. Prayer is one of the most powerful things we can do, and it produces great results, as long as it is offered in faith.

It has been said that every failure in life is the result of a failure to pray. God is ready to save, help, heal, and restore, but someone has to pray in order for Him to work. That is rather amazing if we think about it.

God, who can do absolutely anything, waits for us to pray! He hears the faintest cry and answers even childlike, simple prayers. Prayer need not be eloquent or even long, it just needs to be sincere and offered in faith that God hears and answers. Why should we live weak and powerless lives when we have all power available to us through asking and receiving?

God is good and He wants to do more for us than we can even imagine. I urge you to pray bold, courageous prayers. God is waiting to do greater things if we will ask Him to.

Prayer: Lord, my prayer is that You will teach me to pray and help me understand more fully how powerful prayer is.

October 30

⁕ Be Patient—God Is Still Working! ⁕

Better is the end of a thing than the beginning of it, and the patient in spirit is better than the proud in spirit. ECCLESIASTES 7:8

When you get frustrated because you feel that nothing is happening in your life, or that your prayers are not being answered, just remember that as long as you believe and put your trust in God, He is still working! Your "suddenly" is coming soon. You may wait a long, long time, but then *suddenly* God will show you the result of all He has been doing for a long time.

The fulfillment of your hopes and desires will come at the right time and in the right way, so be sure to enjoy your journey. Being patient makes the journey much more pleasant than being impatient!

> Being impatient does not make things go faster, it only makes you miserable!

Speak this: God is never late; therefore, I will trust His timing in my life.

✷ Resisting Self-Righteousness ✷

Also He spoke this parable to some who trusted in themselves that they were righteous, and despised others. LUKE 18:9 (NKJV)

I have had to repent lately of the sin of self-righteousness. It is a sin that is rooted in pride and one that we often fail to see in ourselves. The apostle Luke tells us a story about a man who saw a tax collector and thanked God that he wasn't like him and listed his wonderful qualities (see Luke 18:9–14), while listing the sins of other people.

Recently, someone I know very well was found to be hiding secret sin and was actively involved in deceiving many people. Not only was my heart broken for the man and the body of Christ, but I also found myself being very angry and then thinking, *I can't believe people do things like this; I could never do that*. That kind of thinking is unwise and rooted in self-righteousness.

God's Word teaches us to be careful when we think we stand, lest we fall (see 1 Corinthians 10:12). It is important to judge righteously according to God's instructions (see John 7:24) but never to judge self-righteously. Let's be led by the Holy Spirit in how we deal with the sins of other people, while maintaining a spirit of humility, lest we also fall.

Prayer: Father, forgive me for the sin of self-righteousness and help me not to be self-deceived.

✷ *Enjoy Today* ✷

Give us this day our daily bread. MATTHEW 6:11 (NKJV)

This morning, soon after getting up, I started thinking about the many things I needed to do not only today, but also during the remainder of the week. I immediately started feeling pressured! Thankfully, the Holy Spirit quickly reminded me that I needed to take one day at a time. As soon as I changed my focus from the entire week to this day, I felt the pressure lift.

God has designed us to live one day at a time, and He gives us grace for the day we are living. He will give us grace for tomorrow when tomorrow comes. Jesus teaches us not to worry about tomorrow, for each day has sufficient concerns of its own (see Matthew 6:34). Refusing to live in the past (or the future) in our thinking is one of the ways we can show that we trust God.

Today holds many amazing things that God wants us to enjoy, but we will miss them if we don't stay focused on today. Today matters, so be sure you don't miss it by drifting through it but not actually being in it! Give your mind to what you are doing and trust that God will indeed give you this day your daily bread, and that means He will give you *everything* you need for today!

Prayer: Father, thank You for today! Today is Your gift to me and I choose to live it fully.

✷ *Jesus Will Never Reject You* ✷

All whom My Father gives (entrusts) to Me will come to Me; and the one who comes to Me I will most certainly not cast out [I will never, no never, reject one of them who comes to Me]. JOHN 6:37

Rejection can be a very painful thing, and many who have experienced it are still suffering from it. Those who have been rejected often fear being rejected again and that fear controls their decisions. They may choose to isolate themselves, or avoid intimacy, rather than take a chance on being rejected again. The good news is that Jesus will never reject us. We can come to Him, be totally honest with Him, and have the assurance that He will always accept and love us. I have found that knowing that Jesus accepts me helps me survive any rejection I may get from other people.

In our relationship with God, He may correct us, but He will never reject us.

Speak this: God loves me unconditionally and He will never reject me.

November 3

✷ *Waiting for Healing* ✷

O Lord my God, I cried to You and You have healed me.

PSALM 30:2

After we pray for healing, we may have to wait patiently while God's healing power works in us. I have a head cold and sore throat right now, and I am very tired. I have prayed and I am trusting God not only for healing, but also to help me not to be grouchy with the people around me while I am recovering.

When we feel bad, it is very easy to be impatient and short-tempered, but we can lean on God, asking Him to help us display the fruit of His Spirit in the midst of our difficulty. Anytime we are suffering in any way but remain stable, we grow spiritually.

When we feel bad, it is not good to take it out on the people around us. If someone is dealing with a long-term illness, it is not only hard for them, but for the people who love them. We can pray not only for the healing of our friends and loved ones, but also for their caregivers and family members.

Prayer: Father, help me be kind and patient in all kinds of situations, not just when all of my circumstances are good. Thank You!

✷ Commitments ✷

For which of you, wishing to build a farm building, does not first sit down and calculate the cost [to see] whether he has sufficient means to finish it? LUKE 14:28

Do you ever say yes to things and then wish later with all of your heart that you had said no? Most of us do that until we learn to think through all we are already doing and what it will really require of us to take on another commitment.

None of us want to disappointment people who make requests of us, and that can be a good thing, but if it is carried too far, we end up frustrated, stressed, and unhappy ourselves.

I am doing an event in the near future that I said yes to but probably should have said no, because now I am not looking forward to it and I feel it is crowding my schedule. But it is my own fault. I will keep my word because that is very important, and I will have a good attitude, and hopefully, I will learn afresh the importance of saying no when I need to.

I encourage you to take the time to think through whether or not you have what it takes to finish something and maintain your peace before you begin it. Always keep your word, even if you have to suffer in order to do so.

Prayer: Father, help me discern when to say yes and when to say no. I want to finish what I start and keep my peace at all times.

✷ Chastisement ✷

. . . The Lord disciplines the one he loves, and he chastens everyone he accepts as his son. HEBREWS 12:6 (NIV)

God is our Father, and when He chastens or corrects us, we feel it in our spirit. It often simulates a mild grieving inside, or what the Bible calls a "godly sorrow" (see 2 Corinthians 7:10 [NIV]). I said something yesterday about another individual, and it wasn't done in love, but as soon as I realized it, I repented and received God's forgiveness. I do not feel condemned, but I do have a godly sorrow over it. I truly regret my actions, and to be honest, I am rather disappointed in myself.

The good news is this process is healthy for us spiritually! When this happens to you, don't waste your time feeling guilty, but do be sure that you take the correction seriously and then pray that you will learn from your mistake. God only chastens those whom He loves dearly.

The Holy Spirit uses the spiritual tool of chastisement in the inner man to help us stay on the right path in life. It is a blessed thing to be able to sense inwardly when our actions are not pleasing to God and to have the opportunity to turn and go in the right direction.

Prayer: Father, thank You for loving me enough not to leave me alone in my sin, but to always correct me and get me back on the right path in life.

✷ A Healthy Life ✷

Dear friend, I pray that you may enjoy good health and that all may go well with you, even as your soul is getting along well.

3 JOHN 2 (NIV)

It is God's desire that we enjoy a healthy life in every aspect of our being—in spirit, body, mind, and emotions. And He offers us wholeness to replace all of the brokenness in our lives.

It is vitally important to learn how to think properly, because our thoughts can affect all other areas of our life. We actually become as we think. Another way to say it is: "Where the mind goes, the man follows" (see Proverbs 23:7).

If any area of your life is broken, I urge you to take it to Jesus and ask for His healing! He cares about every part of you and everything that concerns you.

It is not possible to have a healthy life and an unhealthy mind.

Speak this: I am daily renewing my mind according to God's Word. I am learning to think like God thinks!

⁕ Character in an Age of Image ⁕

Rather, clothe yourselves with the Lord Jesus Christ, and do not think about how to gratify the desires of the flesh.

ROMANS 13:14 (NIV)

We would be wise to learn to be more concerned with what God thinks of us than what people think of us. We live in times when people are obsessed with their image, but God's Word tells us we are to be transformed into the image of Christ (see 2 Corinthians 3:18).

God sees our heart, but people merely see the outer man. No matter how attractive we try to make ourselves look, or what our level of success is in this world, the only thing that really matters is for us to develop godly character so we may glorify Him.

Prayer: Father, help me always know what is really important! Help me strive to develop good character more than I strive for an image that will impress people.

⁕ Guard Your Heart ⁕

Keep and guard your heart with all vigilance and above all that you guard, for out of it flow the springs of life. PROVERBS 4:23

I am often reminded of the importance of what I allow to remain in my heart (thoughts and attitudes). A guard keeps watch over an area in order to keep it safe, and that is what God wants us to do concerning our heart.

What is in our hearts will eventually be demonstrated in one way or another, so it is pointless to think that we can hide what is in our heart. Our thoughts and attitudes affect us in either a positive or a negative way. As God's Word teaches, the very springs of life flow out of the heart.

Are you carefully guarding your heart on a regular basis? If not, please begin doing so right away.

Prayer: Father, help me guard my heart and only allow things to dwell in me that are pleasing to You.

✷ Stillness and Silence ✷

But the Lord is in His holy temple; let all the earth hush and keep silence before Him. HABAKKUK 2:20

Most of us live a fast-paced, noisy life that is filled with continual activity, and because of that, we often miss something God is trying to show or tell us. We need to acquire the skill of waiting silently in God's presence and not feeling that we are only validated when we are constantly doing something. I encourage you to develop a love for silence. God won't shout over all the noisy activity in our lives. God speaks in a still, small, gentle voice, and I believe that He wants to speak to us on a regular basis. But in order to hear, we must be listening.

> Silence is one of the most beautiful sounds in the world.

Speak this: I enjoy being still and quiet.

✷ Be Filled with the Spirit ✷

And the disciples were continually filled [throughout their souls] with joy and the Holy Spirit. ACTS 13:52

Being continually filled with the Holy Spirit is very important to me, and we can feel the Holy Spirit filling us if we pay attention. His presence releases energy, ability, power, and might (see Acts 1:8).

Over the years I have discovered that there are things I can do on purpose that aid me in this goal:

1. Think good and godly thoughts because we feed on what we think (see Philippians 4:8).
2. Speak positive things that release hope and joy (see Proverbs 18:21).
3. Let the Word of God fill my mind. As I meditate on various Scriptures, I find the energy of the Holy Spirit being released in my soul (see Ephesians 5:18–19).
4. When I think about things I can do for other people to bless or help them, I always sense God's power and enthusiasm (see Acts 10:38).

I encourage you to try it, and I believe you will be amazed at the difference it makes.

Prayer: Father, I truly want to always be filled with the Holy Spirit. Help me form habits that will aid me in reaching this goal.

⁕ Run to God, Not Away from Him ⁕

But Jonah rose up to flee to Tarshish from being in the presence of the Lord... JONAH 1:3

This morning I was thinking about my brother. He was addicted to drugs and alcohol for most of his life, and I remember one time he said, "I have run so long and hard that I have run past myself. I don't even know what I am doing anymore."

Just as Jonah ran from God because he wanted to do his own will instead of God's, we often run from God, but it is unwise and useless. My brother wasted his life and died at a very early age, but it didn't have to be that way. He could have run toward God instead of away from Him.

Jonah ran and he ended up in deep trouble, but thankfully, he finally repented and ran back to God. You may be facing something that you either don't want to do or that is difficult to do, but I encourage you to face it head-on and don't run. God will help you and strengthen you.

Prayer: Father, help me face every challenge in life and never run from You or from anything I need to deal with. Thank You for giving me Your courage.

✷ Goodbye, Guilt ✷

But He was wounded for our transgressions, He was bruised for our guilt and iniquities; the chastisement [needful to obtain] peace and well-being for us was upon Him, and with the stripes [that wounded] Him we are healed and made whole. ISAIAH 53:5

A guilty conscience is one of the most miserable things in the world. I suffered with false guilt for many years before being set free from it. What is false guilt? It is guilty feelings that persist even after a person has sincerely repented of their sin. Of course, we will continue to feel guilty if we continue in sin, but we don't have to feel that way if we are sorry for our sins and have asked for and received God's forgiveness. Keep a clear conscience and you will enjoy life much more.

> A guilty conscience—no matter how faint the whisper is—causes stress.

Speak this: When I sin, I am quick to repent and receive God's complete forgiveness!

⁕ Remember ⁕

Do ye not yet perceive, neither remember the five loaves of the five thousand, and how many baskets ye took up?

MATTHEW 16:9 (ASV)

I had an absolutely awesome day yesterday, and this morning I have been remembering it. As I do, it seems I am enjoying it all over again. Each of our lives is a mixture of some good days and some that are not so good, but if we only focus on the ones that are difficult, we can easily become discouraged and downcast.

In the verse above, Jesus was encouraging His disciples to remember the miracles He had done in the past to keep them from worrying about a current need they had that they saw no answer to. We can do the same thing.

What can you think of right now that God has done for you in the past? If you remember it vividly and think it over, your faith will be stirred up and you will be able to press through any difficulty. Don't be discouraged—more good days are coming.

Prayer: Father, thank You for all the good things You have done in my life. Help me remember them often.

✷ Discipline Brings Reward ✷

For the time being no discipline brings joy, but seems grievous and painful; but afterwards it yields a peaceable fruit of righteousness to those who have been trained by it... HEBREWS 12:11

Last night I ate too much, and this morning I regretted it. The only way to live without regret is to discipline ourselves to do the right thing while we have the opportunity. I knew I was eating too much and I did it anyway, simply because I wanted more.

Do you ever do too much of anything and then regret it later? Do you grimace or groan when the word "discipline" is mentioned? We all seem to dislike the thought of discipline, but actually, it is our friend.

Had I followed my heart last night, I would have had peace this morning instead of regret. I was glad for the reminder God gave me that living a disciplined life is the way to peace and satisfaction.

Even though we know things, we often need reminders. So if you perhaps need to be reminded to discipline yourself in all things, then receive this and embrace discipline as your godly friend who is always trying to help you succeed.

Prayer: Father, thank You for giving me a spirit of discipline and self-control and help me to use it at all times.

✷ Getting Experience ✷

My son, be attentive to my Wisdom [godly Wisdom learned by actual and costly experience], and incline your ear to my understanding [of what is becoming and prudent for you].

PROVERBS 5:1

We learn a great deal as we go through life. Some of our experience is very costly and very valuable. Its value can extend beyond us to others, and the wisdom that others have gained can benefit us. When I was thirty, I thought I knew what was important in life, but after struggling for many years to obtain what I wanted, I realized that most of it wasn't really that important after all.

Let's learn to listen to those who have lived longer than we have, especially to those who have enjoyed a long life and are willing to share with us their mistakes and what they have learned from them. Always respect your elders and realize that *they really do know more than you do*!

If you think you know it all, that proves you know nothing at all!

Speak this: I am excited to learn, and I am willing to listen to those who know more than I do.

⁕ Soak Your Soul in the Word ⁕

Oh, how I love Your law! It is my meditation all the day.

PSALM 119:97

God has been showing me that if we soak or fill our souls with His Word on any given subject, we can see increase in that area of our life. For example, if we need healing, we should soak our souls in healing Scriptures, or if we need patience, we can soak our souls in Scriptures on patience.

God's Word has power inherent in it that will produce fruit. His Word is one of the tools the Holy Spirit uses to change and transform us (see 2 Corinthians 3:18). Just as we release the nutrition in our food when we chew it, we may also release the power of God's Word when we meditate on it. To meditate on something means you think about it and roll it over and over in your mind, or mutter softly about it.

God's Word will keep us from sin. The psalmist David said that he laid up God's Word in his heart that he might not sin against Him (see Psalm 119:11). I encourage you to trust the power in God's Word to help you. Take it as you would take medicine if you were ill.

Prayer: Father, help me grasp the amazing power in Your Word and meditate on it day and night.

✷ Aware of God's Presence ✷

I have set the Lord continually before me; because He is at my right hand, I shall not be moved. PSALM 16:8

An awareness of God's presence is very important to me, and I believe that all of us want to know without a doubt that He is with us. The good news is that God is never more than one thought away. We can bring God into our conscious awareness by simply thinking about Him or by acknowledging His presence. Stop for a moment right now and say, "Father, You are here with me right now." Rest for a while with that thought in mind and just enjoy His presence. Take the time to let God become real to you!

There are multitudes of things going on around us at all times, but they don't affect us unless we are aware of them, and awareness is based on what we put our minds on. If I think of my problems in life, they become larger than anything else, but if I think of my blessings, then they become larger, and this same principle holds true with all things.

God has promised to be with us always, and all we need to do is think about Him or meditate on one of His promises to bring Him into our awareness. Think of the Lord often and keep in mind that as long as He is with you, there is no need to fear anything.

Prayer: Father, thank You for Your presence and for helping me think of You often.

✷ The Ways of God ✷

For as the heavens are higher than the earth, so are My ways higher than your ways and My thoughts than your thoughts.

ISAIAH 55:9

We find it easy to be dissatisfied with God and our life because we do not understand His ways. We assume that because He is good, everything that happens to us should also seem good to us, but experience teaches us that is not the way things are. To make things even worse, God doesn't always seem to have much interest in explaining Himself. He wants us to trust Him, and not prolong what He is attempting to do in us by resisting everything that is unpleasant. If He allowed His own Son to suffer unjustly, can we expect anything less? Resurrection always comes, but it is on the other side of dying to self!

We often learn the most when life is the hardest!

Speak this: Even when I don't understand God's ways, I will trust Him!

✷ *Moderation* ✷

Let your moderation be known unto all men. The Lord is at hand.
PHILIPPIANS 4:5 (KJV)

God's Word teaches us to avoid excess or extremes. We have been given the fruit of self-control and we should use it at all times.

There are many things we do that end up making us miserable because we do them excessively. We are free to enjoy anything that is not sinful, but we can turn a good thing into a bad thing by simply doing too much of it. We can talk too much, work too much, eat too much, spend too much money, and thousands of other things, but thankfully, we can also use self-control. Let's make the right choice to always do things in moderation.

Prayer: Father, thank You for the fruit of self-control. I'm sorry for any excess I have allowed in my life, and I ask You to help me do all things in moderation.

⁕ Decisions ⁕

[For being as he is] a man of two minds (hesitating, dubious, irresolute), [he is] unstable and unreliable and uncertain about everything [he thinks, feels, decides]. JAMES 1:8

I was trying to make a decision this morning and I found myself vacillating between two opinions of what I would do. It was becoming very frustrating, but then the Lord reminded me that I really didn't need to make that decision for another thirty days. I felt instant relief!

Many things could happen during those thirty days that will influence my decision, and by waiting and trusting God to guide me in what to do when the time actually comes, I am giving Him an opportunity to work in the heart of the person that the decision involves, as well as in my own heart.

Most of us want to do the right thing, but deciding what that is can often be challenging, and it may be due to trying to make decisions before we have to make them. God gives us what we need when we need it, but not necessarily when we want it. Many things in life work themselves out if we will pray, give them to God, and wait for His perfect timing. God has promised to guide us, and He always keeps His promises!

Prayer: Father in Heaven, thank You for guiding me and showing me what to do at the exact right time. Help me not to make decisions rashly and possibly make a mistake.

November 21

✷ Trusting God When You Don't Understand ✷

Jesus said to him, You do not understand now what I am doing, but you will understand later on. JOHN 13:7

The thing that is the most difficult for me (and that I despise the most) may be the thing God uses to change me. Transformation rarely comes when we are continually joyful and all is perfect in our circumstances. God wants to make us strong spiritually, and that requires trusting Him when nothing makes sense to us.

I have found that those things I once thought were my worst enemy eventually became my friends because they pushed me deeper into my walk with God. When God is all we have, we usually tend to hold on to Him tightly and we get to know Him very well.

> Whatever makes you hold on tightly to God is valuable and should be embraced.

Speak this: When life hurts, I will let it drive me closer to God. Nothing can separate me from His love.

✷ Stand Strong ✷

Therefore put on God's complete armor, that you may be able to resist and stand your ground . . . and, having done all [the crisis demands], to stand [firmly in your place]. EPHESIANS 6:13

There are times when the devil is attacking my mind and I can resist him and experience freedom and relief right away, but at other times it seems that no matter what I do, his attack is relentless. I had one of those times this week, and for two days I felt as if my mind had been kidnapped. I kept trying to resist negative thoughts about a situation but felt that I was having no success at all.

I have learned that when that happens, we just need to stand strong in Christ, and the negative thoughts from the devil will finally go away. Life isn't much fun until they do go away, but we can stand and keep saying, "God, I trust You to take care of this. I cannot deliver myself, but I know that You are my Deliverer."

It is important for us to realize that we are not the only ones who go through things. Everyone has these types of attacks on their mind at times in their life; even Jesus was attacked relentlessly by the devil for forty days and nights (see Luke 4:1–13). The Scripture says that when Satan had ended the cycle of temptation, he went away.

The next time you find yourself in a "cycle" of temptation, remember that if you stand strong, it will come to an end and you will be stronger than you were before.

Prayer: Father, I love You and I always need Your help. Strengthen me in every battle and help me know that I am more than a conqueror through Christ.

November 23

⁕ Giving Too Much? ⁕

Receive instruction in wise dealing and the discipline of wise thoughtfulness, righteousness, justice, and integrity.

PROVERBS 1:3

We know it is possible to give too little, but is it possible to give too much? I think it is possible, and I believe we need to be discerning and Spirit-led in our giving. I have been blessed with the gift of giving (see Romans 12:6–8). I love to give, but recently I felt the Lord was showing me that in some instances, I was giving too much.

Although that sounds odd, I know from experience that we can prevent people from taking responsibility if we are excessive in what we do for them. True love can say no when it would be wiser to do so.

Many parents cripple their children and enable them to remain dysfunctional by rescuing them excessively. I watched my mother do this with my brother, and although she meant well, she ended up hurting him more than she helped him.

God loves us and He always gives when it is the best for us. He gives at the right time and in the right way. We can be generous givers and yet use wisdom in our giving by doing the same thing. Let's learn to say yes when we sense God is saying yes and to say no when we sense God is saying no. Whether you are giving time, money, or effort, it is important to be Spirit-led at all times.

Prayer: Father, I truly want to be a generous giver, but I want to be Spirit-led in all of my giving. Help me and grant me discernment in all my ways.

⁕ Self-Control ⁕

But I discipline my body and keep it under control, lest after preaching to others I myself should be disqualified.

1 CORINTHIANS 9:27 (ESV)

Most people groan when they hear the word "self-control," but the truth is that self-control is a huge blessing. I am grateful that God has given us the fruit of self-control. We develop it by using it, and although it may be challenging in certain areas in the beginning, self-control actually sets us free from being controlled by things that we don't want to control us.

Self-control helps us become the people we truly want to be, and do the things we know we should do. Start looking at it as your friend, rather than an enemy that causes you to groan at the thought of it.

Control yourself instead of trying to control other people!

Speak this: Self-control is my friend and it helps me be the person I want to be.

✷ Fully Satisfied ✷

As for me, I will continue beholding Your face in righteousness (rightness, justice, and right standing with You); I shall be fully satisfied, when I awake [to find myself] beholding Your form [and having sweet communion with You]. PSALM 17:15

When our dependence on and need for God grows to the place where He is the first thing we think about in the morning, we will also find that we have a satisfaction in life that nothing else could ever give us.

We seek many things in life, thinking they will make us happy and satisfy us, and when we find that they don't, we are soon seeking something else. Things alone cannot make us happy and content. They may excite us for a while, but they soon lose their luster and we begin seeking another thing.

Only God Himself can give us the complete satisfaction we seek. The fullness of life and depth of joy that we all desire is in Him. Let Him be your number one need and desire, and your life will be sweet and satisfying.

Prayer: O Lord, I am sorry for the time I have wasted seeking things that could never satisfy me. Teach me to seek You with my whole heart and then I will find the satisfaction I crave.

⁕ The Power of Generosity ⁕

There is a serious and severe evil which I have seen under the sun: riches were kept by their owner to his hurt. ECCLESIASTES 5:13

Although God wants us to enjoy the good things in life, He also wants us to be generous in giving to spread the Gospel message and to help the poor and needy. It is impossible to be selfish and happy at the same time, and God's Word says that it is more blessed to give than to receive (see Acts 20:35).

Solomon, the writer of Ecclesiastes, learned that to keep one's riches ends up hurting the one who owns them. Why? Our soul shrinks and becomes very small when we only have room in our life for ourselves and we live without any concern for others.

I don't for one moment believe that God tells us to give to Him and His purposes in the earth because He needs our money. He teaches us to give because we need to give! Giving always produces a harvest of greater blessings, with joy and many other wonderful breakthroughs for the generous person.

Prayer: Father, I repent for being selfish and stingy. Help me become generous and truly learn the joy of giving.

November 27

✷ Have a Conversation with God ✷

Then you will call upon me and come and pray to me, and I will hear you. JEREMIAH 29:12 (ESV)

God often reminds me that I can talk to Him about anything, and so can you. He already knows everything anyway, so why not discuss it with Him and let Him help us, or perhaps just listen?

This morning, something was bothering my conscience a little bit and I found myself trying to avoid even thinking about it, but trying to ignore it didn't help at all. So I had a conversation with God about it, and as soon as I did, I felt released from the burden of it. God is always listening, so tell Him everything and receive His wisdom and comfort.

> You cannot keep a secret from God, so don't bother trying to.

Speak this: I will talk to God about everything and never try to keep secrets from Him.

⁕ Rejecting Doubt ⁕

[For being as he is] a man of two minds (hesitating, dubious, irresolute), [he is] unstable and unreliable and uncertain about everything [he thinks, feels, decides]. JAMES 1:8

A few days ago, I sensed God showing me something really good that was going to happen soon, and of course that was good news. A few minutes after that, I realized I was already having doubts about what I believed God had shown me.

The apostle James wrote that we are to ask in faith with no doubting (see James 1:6). Just because doubt presents itself to our thoughts doesn't mean we have to receive it. We can be wise enough to realize the lies of Satan always come to try and take away the good seed God has planted in our heart.

I encourage you to remember all the good promises of God and do not doubt. Keep on believing and trusting God, because He is faithful and He loves you and wants to bless you more and more.

Prayer: Father, I'm sorry for doubting Your promises. Help me to be in faith at all times and not let the devil steal Your Word from my heart.

November 29

⁕ *Never Hidden from God* ⁕

Nothing in all creation is hidden from God's sight. Everything is uncovered and laid bare before the eyes of him to whom we must give account. HEBREWS 4:13 (NIV)

Sometimes when we are hurting and going through something very difficult, we may feel as if we are invisible and that nobody really understands what we are experiencing or how we are feeling. But you are never hidden from God! He knows exactly what is going on around you and in you, and He has your breakthrough planned. Remain hopeful, because hope is the anchor of our soul. It keeps us grounded while we are waiting for God to take care of our problems. Hope is an expectation that something good is going to happen, and that is something any of us can have if we choose to have it.

> Live your life as if you truly believe that God sees everything.

Speak this: God sees everything, He knows everything, and He can do anything that needs to be done in my life.

✵ Don't Give Up! ✵

Keep on asking and it will be given you; keep on seeking and you will find; keep on knocking [reverently] and [the door] will be opened to you. MATTHEW 7:7

You and I at times have prayers that we have said for a long time, and yet we still have seen no change or breakthrough. Today I was thinking about one of those prayers and for a moment I thought, *I am tired of praying about that, so I think I will just let it go.*

Immediately, the Scripture for today popped into my thinking, and I believe it was the Holy Spirit reminding me to not give up! Sometimes, when we are the most tempted to quit, that is when our breakthrough is very close.

If you are thinking about giving up on something, I want to encourage you to keep on asking, keep on seeking, and keep on knocking.

Prayer: Father, help me see the fulfillment and answer to my prayers. I trust You and I believe You will bring an answer right on time.

✷ Letting Go of Anger ✷

Make no friendships with a man given to anger, and with a wrathful man do not associate. PROVERBS 22:24

There are no good benefits to anger, so we should avoid it as much as possible. When we do get angry, we should pray that God helps us quickly get over it. Anger does not promote God's right way of living. Apparently the power of anger is so devastating that we are instructed not even to associate with angry people, let alone be one.

It is true that there are many unjust things in the world that we can become angry about, but it is also true that anger doesn't solve them. Trust God to be your Vindicator and get about the business of enjoying your life.

> Don't let someone else's bad behavior determine what yours will be.

Speak this: Being angry has no good benefits and it is a waste of time, so I will avoid it.

⁕ Our Helper ⁕

However, I am telling you nothing but the truth when I say it is profitable (good, expedient, advantageous) for you that I go away. Because if I do not go away, the Comforter (Counselor, Helper, Advocate, Intercessor, Strengthener, Standby) will not come to you... JOHN 16:7

Quite often, we feel that we are alone and have no one to help us, but Jesus promised that the Holy Spirit would be with us always and that He is our "Helper." One of the most powerful prayers we can pray is, "Help me, Lord," and we should pray it several times every day. It is a simple three-word prayer that declares that we are depending on the Holy Spirit and we know we cannot do anything without Him.

Don't struggle along in life, trying to do things by yourself, when you have the greatest Helper in the world available to you. James said that "you do not have, because you do not ask" (James 4:2), so I encourage you to start asking more often and expect to get more help than ever before.

Prayer: Father, through Your Holy Spirit, help me today and every day with everything I do. I am totally dependent on You!

⁕ Freedom ⁕

So if the Son liberates you [makes you free men], then you are really and unquestionably free. JOHN 8:36

Everyone wants to be free, but true freedom is a lot more than simply being free to do whatever one chooses to do. I think that true freedom is more internal than external. All of my circumstances may be happy ones, and yet I would still be in terrible bondage if my soul was tormented with guilt, shame, jealousy, resentment, and other things that make people miserable.

Jesus came to make us truly free. He came to do a great and wonderful work inside of us, one that can never be taken away from us. Ask yourself today if there is anything in your mind, will, or emotions that is keeping you in bondage, and if there is, I urge you to ask Jesus today to teach you how you can be free from it through His Word and Spirit.

Our inner life is much more important than our outer life.

Speak this: Through the death and resurrection of Jesus, I am truly free to be the person He wants me to be.

✵ Love Is Patient ✵

Love endures long and is patient and kind; love never is envious nor boils over with jealousy, is not boastful or vainglorious, does not display itself haughtily. 1 CORINTHIANS 13:4

This morning I was praying about walking in love and asking God to always help me do so, when suddenly He put two people on my heart who have personalities that make me impatient.

Love is displayed and can be seen through a variety of character traits, but the first one listed is patience. I am a bottom-line person, and these two individuals are extremely detailed. In order to tell me anything, they feel compelled to tell me many details that I don't need and don't want to hear.

The Lord reminded me that the first character trait listed that describes love is "patience," and if I want to walk in love, I need to be willing to listen to them a little more than I do. Ouch! That hurt, but I needed it! I am very certain that my personality can be frustrating to others at times, and since I want them to be patient with me, it is important for me to be patient with them. Let's always remember that we reap what we sow!

Prayer: Help me, Lord, to be the kind of person You want me to be at all times and to imitate Your behavior.

✷ Overlooking an Offense ✷

Good sense makes one slow to anger, and it is his glory to overlook an offense. PROVERBS 19:11 (ESV)

Yesterday someone hurt my feelings and offended me by something they said to me. We never know in life when something like this may happen, and it is wise to predetermine that as soon as offense comes, we won't take it, but instead we will overlook it. Is it easy to do? No, it is not easy, but it is certainly wise, and it is the will of God.

One of the things I have found helpful is to make every effort to believe the best of the person who hurt me, as God's Word instructs us to do (see 1 Corinthians 13:7). I don't just "try" to forgive them—I pray for God's help, asking Him to enable me to give the one who hurt me the same grace that He gives me when I do and say things that I shouldn't. Don't allow offense to hinder your spiritual growth or your relationship with the Lord.

> Anyone can take offense—only a strong person can overlook it!

Speak this: With God's help, I will not stay angry. When I am offended, I will overlook it!

⁕ Godly Sorrow ⁕

[As you draw near to God] be deeply penitent and grieve, even weep [over your disloyalty] . . . JAMES 4:9

Yesterday I encountered a person who was quite demanding that I do something she wanted me to do and would not take no for an answer. I ended up being rude to her and I feel a godly sorrow over my behavior. I always want to represent God well, and that means I often need to be long-suffering with someone who is irritating to me.

I don't feel guilty and condemned, because I have repented and know that I am forgiven, but I do feel a godly sorrow, and I think that feeling is healthy and right. We should take our sin seriously and be deeply penitent when we do something that we know is wrong.

Although this feeling is uncomfortable, I welcome it because it impresses on me the importance of my witness for Christ and reminds me of how easy it is to behave in a fleshly and carnal way. The Bible urges us repeatedly to be on our guard against the temptations we encounter in the world and to live carefully. Being rude to someone may seem a small thing, but it is the little foxes that spoil the vine (see Song of Solomon 2:15).

I believe we should appreciate any feeling of chastisement that we receive from the Holy Spirit, because it is God helping us be the kind of people who represent Jesus well.

Prayer: Lord, I appreciate Your conviction and chastisement and I am deeply sorry for my sins and grateful for Your forgiveness.

December 7

✷ *The Fire of God* ✷

For our God [is indeed] a consuming fire. HEBREWS 12:29

I believe that God often comes into our life as a fire, and to me that means He wants to burn up everything in our life that is not consistent with His nature and leave on fire what remains to be used for His glory. Fire can be a good thing or a bad thing, depending on whether or not it is controlled. A wildfire does a lot of damage, but a fire that is contained and controlled is used for very valuable purposes.

We can be assured when the fire of God comes into our life that it is a "controlled burn." God watches over it to make sure it purifies but does not destroy us. It is very important for each of us to ask God to do what He wants to do in us, so He can ultimately do what He wants to do through us.

> If you let God change you, then He can change the world through you!

Speak this: God is changing me, and I want to be everything He wants me to be.

✷ Faith Has No Expiration Date ✷

These trials will show that your faith is genuine. It is being tested as fire tests and purifies gold . . . 1 PETER 1:7 (NLT)

Faith is the evidence of the things that we do not see and the proof of their reality (see Hebrews 11:1). Faith is what we have while we are waiting for God to answer our prayer and provide what we need. But what if God takes a long, long time to answer? That is when waiting can become difficult, and that is also when our faith is tested.

I am currently waiting on at least seven things I have prayed about, and they are all things I have been waiting on for a long time, some of them for years. As I was feeling a little disappointed yesterday about having no answers yet, I was reminded that faith has no expiration date, and if it does, then it is not faith that can endure testing.

Faith means that we not only ask God for something, but also that we must trust Him to be the head of the "ways and means committee"! He chooses the way to answer us and the timing to do so. In the meantime, we get to be patient, or we can at least learn to be patient! I am still learning, and perhaps you are also.

Let me encourage you today to know that although God probably won't show up in your timing, He promises not to be late. Don't just trust God for *something*, but trust Him all the way through the process it takes to get it. Don't let your faith expire!

Prayer: Father, thank You that I have faith while I am waiting for a breakthrough in my situation. Help me remain faithful, even as You are faithful!

December 9

✷ It Is Never Too Late ✷

Jesus said, Take away the stone. Martha, the sister of the dead man, exclaimed, But Lord, by this time he [is decaying and] throws off an offensive odor, for he has been dead four days!

JOHN 11:39

Like Martha, we may think it is too late for God to help us with our problems because we have had them too long or they are too difficult to solve. But God reveals over and over in His Word that nothing is impossible for Him to do. If He can raise a man from the dead, surely He can raise up a lost son, or a dead marriage, or perhaps a dead dream for the future. I want to encourage you not to give up on anyone or anything. Talk to God about it and give Him a chance to work in your life and circumstances. Be patient and expect something good to happen!

> If you are going to ask God for anything, it might as well be something that seems impossible.

Speak this: God can do anything, so I am going to ask Him for everything!

✷ Making Mistakes ✷

For all have sinned and fall short of the glory of God.
ROMANS 3:23 (ESV)

Everyone sins. We all make mistakes and do wrong things, but Jesus has provided for our sins to be forgiven and for us not to be under the burden of condemnation. The Bible says there is no condemnation for those who are in Christ Jesus (see Romans 8:1). Recently I did something wrong, and as I talked with the Lord about it, I said, "I'm so sorry for my mistake, Father," and He spoke to my heart and said, "Remember, just because you make a mistake, that doesn't mean you are a mistake!"

Needless to say, that really ministered to me, and I want you to remember the same thing when you sin, fail, or make mistakes. Just because we fail at something, that doesn't make us a failure. We are still God's children, and He loves us just as much as He did before we failed. God meets us where we are and always helps us get to where we should be. The righteous man falls seven times and yet he rises again, according to God's Word (see Proverbs 24:16).

When we fall, the main thing we need to do is get up again. When we make mistakes, we can learn from them. When we sin, complete forgiveness for us has already been bought and paid for by the blood of Jesus. Celebrate the truth that God's mercy is always new and fresh every morning (see Lamentations 3:22–23).

Prayer: Father, I am sorry for all of my sins, and I am grateful for Your complete forgiveness. Thank You for teaching me that even though I make mistakes, I am not a mistake!

December 11

✷ Encourage One Another ✷

And let us consider how to stir up one another to love and good works, not neglecting to meet together, as is the habit of some, but encouraging one another, and all the more as you see the Day drawing near. HEBREWS 10:24–25 (ESV)

We are instructed in several places in God's Word to make sure we are generous in our encouragement of others. The worse things get in the world, the more encouragement we all need.

You need no special training to be an encourager. Just ask God to show you something good or kind that you can say to another person, and then do it! Make encouragement part of your daily lifestyle. No one ever gets too much encouragement! I am sure that you need encouragement also, and I believe that what you give to others, God will give back to you multiplied many times over.

What you do for someone else, God will do for you!

Speak this: I am an encourager, and I love to make others feel good about themselves.

✷ Get Away from It All ✷

But He Himself withdrew [in retirement] to the wilderness [desert] and prayed. LUKE 5:16

We all have times when we just want to get away from it all, and when that is the case, we need to know it is a very good choice to make. Jesus often walked away from everything and everyone and went somewhere alone to pray. He even walked away from valid needs at times so He could be refreshed in God's presence.

I walk every morning outside, if at all possible, and it is one of the times for me when I *get away from it all*. I like to walk alone and use the hour and a half that I am out to simply think, talk to God, and be out in nature. Although I'm exercising, it does a lot for me mentally and emotionally, too. You might think of a daily walk as a way of getting away from it all.

When my children were little, sometimes the bathroom was my place to *get away from it all*. This short break would help me collect my emotions and be ready to face the world again.

Your life may be very good and you may have no pressing problems right now, but you still need time to be alone and think prayerfully. If you do have difficulty in your life right now, you might need two walks a day! Don't hesitate to take the time you need in order to be the person you want to be.

Prayer: Father, thank You for helping me realize that I need time to get away from everything else and just be *with You.*

✷ Control Your Tongue ✷

For we all often stumble and fall and offend in many things. And if anyone does not offend in speech [never says the wrong things], he is a fully developed character and a perfect man, able to control his whole body and to curb his entire nature. JAMES 3:2

Jesus used great wisdom and restraint with His words because He fully realized the power they had. Proverbs teaches us that the power of life and death is in the tongue (see Proverbs 18:21). We need to be reminded very often of this truth, and we should pray regularly for God to help us control the tongue, because we certainly cannot do it without His help.

Let me simply encourage you today to say things that are positive and filled with life, rather than giving voice to negative comments that are filled with death. When our words agree with God's Word, we will see amazingly good things happen in our lives.

> If we ever truly understand the power of our words, we will be very careful about what we say.

Speak this: I will speak in agreement with God's Word, rather than according to how I feel or what I think.

✷ A Well-Balanced Day ✷

Be well balanced (temperate, sober of mind), be vigilant and cautious at all times... 1 PETER 5:8

People frequently ask me how I keep my priorities straight with all I do and all the responsibility I have as the head of a large ministry. I always say, "I keep them straight by continually straightening them out." In other words, I make adjustments as I see they are needed, and at times that happens daily.

When people say to me, "You must be very busy," I have learned to say, "I'm not just busy, but I am bearing good fruit." We can be very busy doing nothing, and if that is the case, then priorities need to be adjusted. God intends for us to live a well-rounded life in which we bear fruit from our labors, have rest, have fun, enjoy our life, do things for others, and take care of ourselves. In order to do those things, I've learned to take breaks from work and make sure that I do some things I enjoy. It may just be stopping for a good cup of coffee or taking a walk, but it adds pleasure to my day.

I believe the Holy Spirit will show us when we are out of balance. We may start to feel overwhelmed or bored or weary or taken advantage of. If I start to feel any of those things, I just change things up and it makes life fresh again. I urge you to work with God to have a well-balanced life, because that is the only way you can enjoy it.

Prayer: Father, help me to always live a well-balanced life and be willing to make any adjustments I need to make in order to see that happen.

✷ True Religion ✷

Religion that is pure and undefiled before God the Father is this: to visit orphans and widows in their affliction, and to keep oneself unstained from the world. JAMES 1:27 (ESV)

God wants us to help people who are hurting! It is important for us to show God's love to others, and one of the ways we can do that is through giving practical aid to those in need. Widows and orphans are two groups who find it difficult, or perhaps even impossible, to help themselves, and God seems to have a special place in His heart for them.

The way to serve God is through serving others. People need to know that God loves them, and it often requires more than mere words. Offering practical help and meeting needs is one of the best ways to show love to people. I encourage you to help as many people as you can, as often as you can!

> We may not be sure what we can do, but the one thing we must not do is nothing!

Speak this: I will always try to treat people the way I would like to be treated!

Distractions

Looking away [from all that will distract] to Jesus, Who is the Leader and the Source of our faith . . . HEBREWS 12:2

Our enemy, the devil, provides us with many things to distract us from what our purpose is—to glorify and serve Jesus with all of our hearts. Someone failed to communicate properly with me yesterday about an important matter, and his irresponsibility caused me extra work. I found myself being frustrated by it and continuing to think about it over and over this morning, but Jesus reminded me to deal with the things I need to deal with, and then swiftly move on to the higher things that are more important. Don't let yesterday's irritations steal any of your time today!

Don't let yesterday's sorrows steal today's joy!

Speak this: This day is a gift from God and I will not waste it living in the past!

✵ Finish a Project ✵

I have fought the good fight, I have finished the race, I have kept the faith. 2 TIMOTHY 4:7 (ESV)

I can hear the satisfaction in Paul's voice when he states that he has finished what he set out to do. In this case, Paul was talking about his life's goal of serving God faithfully, but we can and will experience a similar satisfaction in finishing any project. This is especially true when we finish something that a lot of hard work and time has gone into.

I just finished a book manuscript and sent it off to the editor, who will finish it up and send it to the publisher. I feel so satisfied and fulfilled! It took months of writing and creative planning, but now it is done and I feel like celebrating!

It is easy to quit on something, but when we do, it leaves us with an empty, dissatisfied feeling. We know that we have not done our best and it dampens our joy. Whatever you might need to finish, whether it is a small project or a big one, I encourage you to get back to it and get it done! Don't let unfinished projects hang around and annoy you, chipping away at your peace. There is no better time than now to finish what you've begun!

Prayer: Father, help me finish all my unfinished projects and do it with joy. Thank You!

⁕ Overcoming the Enemy ⁕

And they have overcome (conquered) him by means of the blood of the Lamb and by the utterance of their testimony...

REVELATION 12:11

We will never have a testimony without having a test. Our faith must be tested to see if it is truly genuine or merely talk. God never tempts us to sin, but He will test our faith by allowing us to go through difficulty. We can actually become stronger in our faith during these times if we maintain an attitude of trusting God all the way through the challenge. Trials are not fun for anyone, but we all have our share of them. Let's pass our tests so we can have an amazing testimony that will glorify God. Stay strong, and remember, "This too will pass."

We never have a testimony unless we have passed a test!

Speak this: I am strong in God, and I can endure whatever comes with a good attitude.

✵ A Busy Mind ✵

You keep him in perfect peace whose mind is stayed on you, because he trusts in you. ISAIAH 26:3 (ESV)

God never told us to have a busy mind, but a mind that is filled with peace. I recently experienced several days in which I was extremely tired. Actually, exhausted was more like it, and I couldn't understand why. I was getting good sleep, and, yes, I had a lot going on, but that is not unusual for me.

After putting up with it for a couple of days and complaining frequently, I finally asked God why I was so tired. I just didn't understand. He showed me that it wasn't physical tiredness that I felt, but mental tiredness. I had been thinking too much! I must say I was surprised, but as I took an honest look at all the things that were on my mind—while I was simultaneously doing a lot of things like recording for television, working on a book, and traveling—I understood what God was showing me.

In addition to all that, I was attempting to do a lot of creative thinking about upcoming teaching seminars, books, making changes in some ministry areas, finances, and other things. But I should have been giving my mind to what I was doing, instead of doing one thing and thinking about lots of other things. With God's help, I made a change and decided to give my mind a short vacation, and it helped a lot. Perhaps this example will help you too!

Prayer: Father, please help me keep my mind on what I am doing and remember that You want me to have peace of mind, not a busy mind!

✷ The Royal Law ✷

If indeed you [really] fulfill the royal Law in accordance with the Scripture, You shall love your neighbor as [you love] yourself, you do well. JAMES 2:8

God loves everyone, and He has called us to do the same thing. He does not show prejudice, nor does He show favoritism to certain people, and we should follow His example. Let's make a commitment to treat everyone with respect, and to make them feel valuable. I think we should make an effort to reach out to those who look lonely or rejected, because we may change a person's life by simply noticing and including them. The world is filled with people who feel invisible, so let's make sure they know that they are important to God and to us.

You can change a life with a smile.

Speak this: I will value people where they are, not just where I would like them to be.

⁕ God Will Make a Way ⁕

And I will make all My mountains a way, and My highways will be raised up. ISAIAH 49:11

The prophet Isaiah told the people that their mountains would be made low, the crooked places would be made straight, and the rough places a smooth, flat area (see Isaiah 40:4). Do you have any mountains that you are facing right now? I have had many in my life, and I am sure you have also.

Through trusting God and watching Him work in your life, you can expect those mountains to be flattened and actually become a road for you to travel on in your journey of life. The problems I had, and conquered with God's help, actually became the basis for a lot of the messages I share with people now. Once you defeat a problem, you have experience that can be a benefit to others who might be going through what you once struggled with.

I want to encourage you to declare God's Word to the mountains in your life and expect them to become highways for you to safely travel on.

Prayer: Father, thank You for granting me grace to never back down from any mountain because You are with me, and with Your help I can conquer mountains and see them become highways.

✷ Love Your Life ✷

And He died for all, so that all those who live might live no longer to and for themselves, but to and for Him Who died and was raised again for their sake. 2 CORINTHIANS 5:15

It is not possible to live a life that you truly love and also be selfish and self-centered. Being selfish may help us get things that we want, but it won't give us joy. Joy is found in being a blessing. When we love others, our lives have true meaning and purpose. If you are not content with your life, I suggest focusing more on how you can bless other people, and God will reward you.

We cannot be selfish and truly happy at the same time.

Speak this: I love to do things for other people.

✷ Knowledge Can Be a Hindrance ✷

For I resolved to know nothing (to be acquainted with nothing, to make a display of the knowledge of nothing, and to be conscious of nothing) among you except Jesus Christ (the Messiah) and Him crucified.
1 CORINTHIANS 2:2

Education is a good thing, but we always need to depend on God and not merely on what we think we know. The quest for knowledge should not outweigh the quest for the knowledge of God. In the Garden of Eden, Eve had an opportunity to know God intimately, but she craved knowledge she was not supposed to have and it caused big problems for her and all of mankind.

Paul was highly educated, but as he followed Jesus, he quickly realized that knowing God was more important than all the education he could ever have (see Philippians 3:8–10). Sometimes highly educated people have difficulty with the simple, childlike faith that we are encouraged to approach God with. Get all the education you desire, but don't let your brain become bigger than your spirit!

All of man's knowledge cannot save him from sin—only Jesus can do that! Thank God for what you know, but don't ever let it stop you from leaning entirely on God in every situation.

Prayer: Father, I am grateful for my education and what I know, but I want to know You more than I know anything else. Teach me about You and Your ways! Amen.

⁕ Gifts ⁕

And on going into the house, they saw the Child with Mary His mother, and they fell down and worshiped Him. Then opening their treasure bags, they presented to Him gifts—gold and frankincense and myrrh. MATTHEW 2:11

Today is Christmas Eve, and in four hours my entire family (twenty-two in all) will descend on our home with great enthusiasm. Today we give gifts to the people we love. Why do we celebrate Jesus' birth with gifts? We do it because He is the greatest gift that has ever been given to mankind. When the wise men heard of Jesus' birth, they went to worship Him with gifts, and it is our privilege to do the same.

I urge you not to lose sight today and tomorrow of what the holiday is truly about as you celebrate this blessed season. Don't get so busy cooking, preparing, shopping, and giving gifts to others that you forget the reason for the season.

Thank God for the gift of Jesus and take time to thank Him for all He has done and continues to do in your life. As you give gifts to others, keep in mind that you are celebrating the greatest gift of all—Jesus!

Prayer: Father, thank You for the gift of Jesus. We celebrate today as a way of saying "Thank You" for giving us the greatest gift ever given.

⁕ The Most Amazing Gift ⁕

For God so loved the world that He gave His only begotten Son, that whoever believes in Him should not perish but have everlasting life. JOHN 3:16 (NKJV)

As we celebrate the birth of Jesus, let us remember what an amazing gift God has given to us and what a sacrifice it must have been for Him. Then let us be willing to also give sacrificially to help others not only find Christ, but also learn to live the large, free, and full life that He has provided.

There are many ways in which we can give. We can pray, serve, give time, money, encouragement, and help. Our tradition is to give at Christmastime on a broader scale than we do at other times of the year, but I don't believe it should be that way. I believe we should make every day an opportunity to give to others. Someone said, "We make a living by getting, but we make a life by giving."

I wasted many years living selfishly, and all it did was bring me unhappiness and a narrow life filled only with myself. I have learned to love giving and I find that it enlarges my life in ways that are amazing. I am happier, healthier, more energetic, and have the satisfaction of personal fulfillment. I don't feel that I am wasting my life on things that don't matter, but instead I believe that I am investing in eternity.

If you feel you need a change, this just might be the change you are searching for. Jesus said to forget yourself and take up your cross and follow Him (see Mark 8:34). I know it sounds like a frightening thing to do, but if you take the leap of faith, it will be the most rewarding thing you have ever done.

Prayer: Father, thank You for the gift of Jesus and for the sacrifice You made in giving Him to me. Help me not to be afraid to live a life of sacrifice in order to help others as You have helped me.

✳ Guided by God ✳

But if you are guided (led) by the [Holy] Spirit, you are not subject to the Law. GALATIANS 5:18

We have the privilege as children of God to be guided daily by Him. If we invite Him into everything we do, He will help us and show us if we are going in the right or wrong direction. Being led by the Spirit sets us free to be adventurous and to follow His promptings rather than lifeless rules and regulations. He is with us always and we can rejoice that we are never alone or without help.

> The most frequent prayer that we offer should be, "Jesus, help me!"

Speak this: I will listen for God's guidance daily.

⁕ When You Don't Know What to Do ⁕

. . . I know that [the determination of] the way of a man is not in himself; it is not in man [even in a strong man or in a man at his best] to direct his [own] steps. JEREMIAH 10:23

I have found that there are many times in life when I have a situation that I simply don't know how to handle. I feel that I need to do something, but I don't know what to do. Does that feeling resonate with you also? When we don't know what direction to take in a situation that arises, thankfully we have relationship with God, and He knows everything!

When I don't know, I trust God to reveal His direction at the precise right time, and my experience has been that He is never late. As humans, we do not like the feeling of not knowing. It makes us feel out of control, but perhaps that is exactly the way God wants us to feel at times.

If you are facing a situation today that requires an answer but you don't know what to do, I recommend that you keep doing what you know to do—like praying, worshipping, being thankful, being a blessing to others, studying the Bible, going to church, etcetera. As you continue being faithful, God will give you an answer concerning the direction you need to take, but don't be shocked if it comes from a surprising source. God has ways of doing things that we would never think of!

Prayer: Father, I trust You to guide me in all of my decisions and to always show me what to do at the exact right time.

✱ All Things Work for Our Good ✱

And we know that in all things God works for the good of those who love him, who have been called according to his purpose.

ROMANS 8:28 (NIV)

No matter what you might be going through right now, if you simply continue loving God and wanting His will in your life, He promises to turn your difficulties into something good. I encourage you to remain steadfast and to never give up on believing you will see God's goodness in your life. Even if things don't turn out the way you wanted them to, they can turn out better than you ever believed they would.

Bad things can become good things when we put God in charge of all things!

Speak this: I am expecting my problems to turn into blessings!

✷ How Close Is God? ✷

Do you not know that you are God's temple and that God's Spirit dwells in you? 1 CORINTHIANS 3:16 (ESV)

God is not only *with* us, but He is *in* us. We are the home of God, according to His Word. Paul says that this truth is a great mystery (see Colossians 1:27). It truly is difficult to understand why a perfect and holy God would choose to dwell in imperfect and flawed humans, but that is the privilege of those who receive Christ as their Savior. And God cannot be any closer to us than He is by residing in us! In Christ, we are never alone or without the power we need to do His will.

Does God feel comfortable and at home in you?

Speak this: I am the home of God, and I am never alone.

✷ *You Can Have a Good Life If You Want One* ✷

...According to your faith and trust and reliance [on the power invested in Me] be it done to you. MATTHEW 9:29

The promises of God found in His Word are abundant, and they offer each of us an opportunity to have a wonderful and amazing life. All we need to do is believe and keep believing, even when it seems we are going to be left out. Remember: God does not have favorites. His promises are for all who will believe them!

No matter how bad of a start someone may have had in life, they can have a good finish if they learn to trust and obey God. That means you can have a great life if you want one. Just hold on to the promises of God and refuse to let them go. If God can do anything good for anyone, He can do good things for you. His goodness is not based on our good record or works, but on His. Let today be the beginning of the best life you can possibly have. Stretch your faith into new areas and believe that every promise in God's Word is for you!

Prayer: Father, I am sorry I have believed for so little when You have offered so much. By faith, I ask for the best life I can possibly have and the grace to do all You want me to do.

⁕ Looking Ahead ⁕

...But one thing I do [it is my one aspiration]: forgetting what lies behind and straining forward to what lies ahead. PHILIPPIANS 3:13

Perhaps you have enjoyed a great year, or perhaps it has been a difficult one, but either way, it is ending, and a new year is in front of you. I am sure we can all look back at this past year and find things we regret, but mere regret can be self-defeating. The better thing to do is learn from the past. Let it educate you for the future.

At the end of a year, I enjoy going over my calendar for the year and remembering the things I did. Some of the memories are pleasant, but I also find things I now see were a waste of time or things that I wish I had not done. I enjoy the good memories and try to learn from the bad ones. It is important that we don't take this past year into the new one. Your future has no room for your past. If you did something good, look forward to doing something better, and if you did something bad, determine to never do it again.

Be sure to enter the new year with a positive, expectant attitude. I believe God has good plans for all of us and we can be excited about finding out what they are!

Prayer: Father, thank You for this year. Thank You for guiding me through it and giving me the grace to enter the new year with enthusiasm and expectation.

Do you have a real relationship with Jesus?

God loves you! He created you to be a special, unique, one-of-a-kind individual, and He has a specific purpose and plan for your life. And through a personal relationship with your Creator—God—you can discover a way of life that will truly satisfy your soul.

No matter who you are, what you've done, or where you are in your life right now, God's love and grace are greater than your sin—your mistakes. Jesus willingly gave His life so you can receive forgiveness from God and have new life in Him. He's just waiting for you to invite Him to be your Savior and Lord.

If you are ready to commit your life to Jesus and follow Him, all you have to do is ask Him to forgive your sins and give you a fresh start in the life you are meant to live. Begin by praying this prayer...

Lord Jesus, thank You for giving Your life for me and forgiving me of my sins so I can have a personal relationship with You. I am sincerely sorry for the mistakes I've made, and I know I need You to help me live right.

Your Word says in Romans 10:9, "If you declare with your mouth, 'Jesus is Lord,' and believe in your heart that God raised him from the dead, you will be saved" (NIV). *I believe You are the Son of God and confess You as my Savior and Lord. Take me just as I am, and work in my heart, making me the person You want me to be. I want to live for You, Jesus, and I am so grateful that You are giving me a fresh start in my new life with You today.*

I love You, Jesus!

It's so amazing to know that God loves us so much! He wants to have a deep, intimate relationship with us that grows every day as we spend time with Him in prayer and Bible study. And we want to encourage you in your new life in Christ.

Please visit joycemeyer.org/salvation to request Joyce's book *A New Way of Living*, which is our gift to you. We also have other free resources online to help you make progress in pursuing everything God has for you.

Congratulations on your fresh start in your life in Christ! We hope to hear from you soon.

About the Author

JOYCE MEYER is one of the world's leading practical Bible teachers. Her daily broadcast, *Enjoying Everyday Life*, airs on hundreds of television networks and radio stations worldwide.

Joyce has written more than 100 inspirational books. Her best-sellers include *Power Thoughts*; *The Confident Woman*; *Look Great, Feel Great*; *Starting Your Day Right*; *Ending Your Day Right*; *Approval Addiction*; *How to Hear from God*; *Beauty for Ashes*; and *Battlefield of the Mind*.

Joyce travels extensively, holding conferences throughout the year and speaking to thousands around the world.

Joyce Meyer Ministries

ADDRESSES

Joyce Meyer Ministries

P.O. Box 655
Fenton, MO 63026
USA
(636) 349-0303

Joyce Meyer Ministries—Canada

P.O. Box 7700
Vancouver, BC V6B 4E2
Canada
(800) 868-1002

Joyce Meyer Ministries—Australia

Locked Bag 77
Mansfield Delivery Centre
Queensland 4122
Australia
(07) 3349 1200

Joyce Meyer Ministries—England

P.O. Box 1549
Windsor SL4 1GT
United Kingdom
01753 831102

Joyce Meyer Ministries—South Africa

P.O. Box 5
Cape Town 8000
South Africa
(27) 21-701-1056

Other Books by Joyce Meyer

100 Ways to Simplify Your Life
21 Ways to Finding Peace and Happiness
Any Minute
Approval Addiction
The Approval Fix
The Battle Belongs to the Lord
*Battlefield of the Mind**
Battlefield of the Mind for Kids
Battlefield of the Mind for Teens
Battlefield of the Mind Devotional
*Be Anxious for Nothing**
Being the Person God Made You to Be
Beauty for Ashes
Change Your Words, Change Your Life
The Confident Mom
The Confident Woman
The Confident Woman Devotional
Do Yourself a Favor . . . Forgive
Eat the Cookie . . . Buy the Shoes
Eight Ways to Keep the Devil Under Your Feet
Ending Your Day Right
Enjoying Where You Are on the Way to Where You Are Going
The Everyday Life Bible
Filled with the Spirit
Good Health, Good Life
Hearing from God Each Morning
*How to Hear from God**

How to Succeed at Being Yourself

I Dare You

*If Not for the Grace of God**

In Pursuit of Peace

The Joy of Believing Prayer

Knowing God Intimately

A Leader in the Making

Life in the Word

Living Beyond Your Feelings

Living Courageously

Look Great, Feel Great

Love Out Loud

The Love Revolution

Making Good Habits, Breaking Bad Habits

Making Marriage Work (previously published as *Help Me—I'm Married!*)

*Me and My Big Mouth!**

*The Mind Connection**

Never Give Up!

Never Lose Heart

New Day, New You

Overload

The Penny

Perfect Love (previously published as *God Is Not Mad at You*)*

The Power of Being Positive

The Power of Being Thankful

The Power of Determination

The Power of Forgiveness

The Power of Simple Prayer

Power Thoughts

Power Thoughts Devotional

Reduce Me to Love
The Secret Power of Speaking God's Word
The Secrets of Spiritual Power
The Secret to True Happiness
Seven Things That Steal Your Joy
Start Your New Life Today
Starting Your Day Right
Straight Talk
Teenagers Are People Too!
Trusting God Day by Day
The Word, the Name, the Blood
Woman to Woman
You Can Begin Again

Joyce Meyer Spanish Titles

Belleza en Lugar de Cenizas (Beauty for Ashes)
Buena Salud, Buena Vida (Good Health, Good Life)
Cambia Tus Palabras, Cambia Tu Vida (Change Your Words, Change Your Life)
El Campo de Batalla de la Mente (Battlefield of the Mind)
Como Formar Buenos Habitos y Romper Malos Habitos (Making Good Habits, Breaking Bad Habits)
La Conexión de la Mente (The Mind Connection)
Dios No Está Enojado Contigo (God Is Not Mad at You)
La Dosis de Aprobación (The Approval Fix)
Empezando Tu Día Bien (Starting Your Day Right)
Hazte un Favor a Ti Mismo... Perdona (Do Yourself a Favor... Forgive)
Madre Segura de Sí Misma (The Confident Mom)
Pensamientos de Poder (Power Thoughts)
*Sobrecarga (Overload)**

Termina Bien Tu Día (Ending Your Day Right)
Usted Puede Comenzar de Nuevo (You Can Begin Again)
Viva Valientemente (Living Courageously)
*Study Guide available for this title

Books by Dave Meyer

Life Lines